The
Family Circle

Book of
CAREERS AT HOME

The Family Circle

Book of

CAREERS AT HOME

MARY BASS GIBSON

COWLES BOOK COMPANY, INC.
A Subsidiary of Henry Regnery Company

331.702
G

Dedicated to my husband
GEORGE ROLLINGS GIBSON
whose enthusiasm for my careers-at-home
project helped to make it a reality

Contents

Contents

PREFACE

The women you will meet in this book have discovered a new world of creativity in their homes. Like their grandmothers and their great-grandmothers, by means of their modern interpretations of traditional crafts many are making and selling the heirlooms of tomorrow.

Some of the most successful at-home money making projects include hooking rugs, sewing, cooking, painting, making jewelry, and other crafts—many of which were learned at classes after marriage. Having worked as typists, bookkeepers, or laboratory technicians in offices before becoming housewives, many women never suspect they have such aptitude.

Profits of from $1,000 to $60,000 have gone into family bank accounts as a result of the home careers of the women featured in Part II of this book. These women demonstrate the range, variety, and practicality of occupations that can be pursued successfully in the home.

My travels over the past three years have taken me thousands of miles. I have visited careerists at home over the length and breadth of the United States. I have chosen to talk about typical rather than exceptional careers in order to show housewives who consider themselves "average" that they too can convert their skills into profitable careers.

Identifying with the women who have succeeded and learning by reading about the problems that beset the beginner can be helpful to those who plan to embark on the same adventure.

The National Home Study Council reports that over one million women are successfully operating their own small businesses at home. Of this number fewer than half have had any formal training. Thus, the need for instructions in conducting business procedures and in making their skills marketable is acute.

Until the boutique boom came along to provide a market for crafts and superior needlework, the Woman's Exchanges were the only year 'round showcases and salesrooms in which women could take their handmade goods to be sold. A small fee is charged by this nonprofit organization. State and local fairs and church bazaars have always featured such items, but these are usually annual events lasting only a few days.

Then Mrs. Vanderbilt Webb founded the Museum of Contemporary Crafts in New York City, which has brought recognition to the field of crafts as a creative form of distinction.

Through its extension services and cooperatives, the Department of Agriculture has likewise helped to keep traditional crafts alive. And the Office of Economic Opportunity has given its support to such movements as "The Mountain Artisans" of West Virginia and Kentucky, prominent in the renewed popularization of patchwork as a fashion as well as a household quilt.

To overemphasize the craft aspect of careers at home, however, would be to underestimate the enormous importance of all sorts of profitable services that housewives are rendering from their homes to their communities. The Small Business Administration has created a division to help women and men start small businesses and specialized services. SCORE (Service Corps of Retired Executives) offers free to the novice the kind of experience and knowledge money cannot buy and only experience provides.

In researching this book I have drawn upon all these organizations, and I thank them for their help.

My appreciation goes also to Arthur Hettich, the editor of *Family Circle*, who introduced the careers-at-home series to the reading public; to Adelaide Fine, who researched and organized the Guide in Part III; and to Clara Claasen, who read the manuscript and gave me the benefit of her editorial knowledge and experience.

Lastly, I extend my own fondest gratitude to the talented and intelligent housewives of this country who are making my own life so exciting. I hope that this book puts to rest forever the self-deprecatory phrase, "I'm just a housewife" and that it will be a source of guidance and encouragement to many housewives with hidden talents who need the confidence and courage to go ahead on their own.

MARY BASS GIBSON

The
Family Circle
Book of
CAREERS AT HOME

ADD DIMENSION TO YOUR LIFE

"And what are we dreaming up today?"

My husband stuck his head in the door of my careers-at-home office as I sat reading the day's mail. For many months we had been fascinated, amused, amazed, impressed, and at times incredulous as housewives wrote to me about the things they were doing at home to add to the family income. These letters poured in from every corner of America in response to a series of articles I had been writing for *Family Circle* magazine. My assignments had taken me by plane, by car, by bus, and by train across the nation from coast to coast into homes in small towns and farms, into apartments in large cities, and even into a trailer temporarily parked in a north woods lumber camp. The range and variety of what women were doing and making—their ingenuity and creativity—seemed infinite; their energies, inexhaustible; and their enthusiasm, irrepressible.

The new dimension that had been added to their lives and to the lives of their families brought excitement for the whole family, especially their husbands, who often seemed to get into the act. No one was bored, no one felt trapped, and no one bemoaned an empty nest.

Down the cellar stairs we would sometimes be taken to see Mom's "workshop," a combination laundry room and work area where, like an assembly line worker, she would shift from washer to sewing machine, pottery kiln, cutting table, or whatever equipment she might be using to "do her own thing." A telephone extension usually rested on a dilapidated desk where bills and papers were stuffed into drawers.

Pilgrimages to attics or to upstairs rooms over garages were almost as frequent as to workshops in the cellars. A nursery often doubled as a workroom.

The average annual earnings of the woman were from $1,000 to $5,000. This money had helped to ease financial strain in many families, and in others it had made possible extra dividends they would not otherwise have enjoyed, such as vacation trips for one family, building an extra room on the house for another, and paying room and board for a college daughter and recapping a mouthful of crooked teeth for one mother of five.

Most housewives have more talent and skills than they think they have. When a woman says to me, "But I have no talent," I tell her to sit down and make a list of the things she does in her own home that are special. Invariably the list includes such items as cake decorating, flower arranging, needlework, dressmaking, crocheting and knitting, all of which sound routine to a housewife until she finds out how much money people will pay for these skills. Discovery of her own worth is the first and most important reward to a housewife who launches a career at home.

Many housewives whose husbands and children are away from home all day suffer from loneliness unless they can afford to do volunteer work in their communities. These are the women who find ways to bring the world to them in their own homes by caring for children or the elderly, by organizing home cooking or needlework classes, or by performing some service that will bring customers calling.

"My teenage children say I'm doing my own thing refinishing antiques," said one isolated housewife in a rural area. "Collectors who want me to restore the treasures they've picked up at second-hand stores are a continuous delight. Now I not only refinish old pieces, I'm also teaching a class in my basement twice a week."

Another who lives in Havelock, Iowa, says:

"The nearest good restaurant here is fifty miles away. Lots of farmers would like to eat out, especially on Sunday after church, so I invite paying guests. I set up a smorgasbord buffet, and use my best china and glassware. We always have more calls for reservations than we can take."

The most irrepressible of all home careerists are women with creative and artistic urges that are expressed in the things they make—jewelry, pottery, hooked rugs, candles, toys, fashion accessories, decorative objects—so many it would be impossible to catalog them. Imagination runs rampant, and even the cast-offs of nature, such as watermelon and grape seeds and bleached chicken bones end up as costume jewelry, fashioned into star-fish, tiny duck pins, and dangling earrings. "We now can buy extras for our home and two children and spend winter vacations in Bermuda and Florida," says the Connecticut housewife who dreamed up this fantasy world of costume jewelry.

The story of careers at home has many facets. The home is a research center for family living and family needs. Once stimulated to think, the resourceful and inventive housewife will begin to read, to observe, and to experiment.

But this doesn't happen overnight. Sensible and practical women know it takes more than an initial spurt of enthusiasm to get a worthwhile project going. They start in a small way and learn to be realistic and practical about what they can and cannot do. They learn how to find out whether the things they make or the services they perform are needed and wanted. The coming chapters tell you step by step what it takes to launch yourself on this journey into self-discovery.

Here are the wisest and most moving words I have heard as an endorsement for a career at home:

"There are only two bequests that you can give to your family—roots and wings. Roots are deeper with a home-centered life, and the mother who takes flight imaginatively in a career within the home has given her children wings."

Part I
Choosing Your Dimension

1 How to Get Started

Be it ever so humble, there's no place like home for making money. Every little bit helps in these days of galloping inflation, and often profits from a home career add up to more than just a "little bit." Besides, when you have a home career, you are your own boss; you work when you want to and quit when you want to. You can always be home to ride herd on your children when they return from school in the afternoon.

But a home career takes energy, and you should have a skill or hobby in which you have enough confidence to "go professional." If you have an idea for a service, you must know that it is needed.

In the years I've traveled through the country interviewing housewives who have successfully managed careers at home, I've gained many general impressions—and hard facts—that might be helpful to those planning to embark on similar ventures. The most encouraging and unexpected revelation has been that three-quarters of the homemakers I interviewed discovered hidden talents within themselves. In most cases their home businesses turned out to be completely different from the kind of work they'd done before they married. Homemaking apparently released creative abilities they never suspected they had.

For examples: an airline hostess became a gourmet cook and eventually earned $5,000 a year by conducting cooking classes in her home; a former accountant, one housewife discovered and developed her talent for making decorative window shades; a course in hairdressing after her marriage opened a profitable new world of home earning power for a housewife who had been brought up on a farm.

Many women have gone on to improve their talents by taking additional courses in cooking, needlework, fashion design, office skills, crafts, and other moneymaking endeavors.

The First Step—Know Yourself

At the very beginning you have to ask yourself: What do I do well? What do I like to do? Do I need to make money more than I need to express my creative urge?

Be honest and realistic. After you have explored the possible areas of your potential, you should proceed to ask yourself how your family will feel about your undertaking. It's a good idea to talk over your ideas with your husband and children before you decide to go ahead. You'll have to communicate your enthusiasm and confidence to them and stimulate their interest because their instinct may well be not to want to share you with your career.

Behind every successful career housewife are a cooperative husband and helpful children.

If the children are old enough, they should be required to pitch in and help with the housework. "If your husband doesn't go along with your home career and is going to use it as an excuse to criticize your housework, you might as well skip the whole idea," is the way one housewife put it.

Does It Cost Money?

For the majority of women it costs very little to start a home career. Many women feel that they need extra training, and for them a small investment in a local adult education class would be well worth the cost.

Many who are especially imaginative save money because they see opportunities and materials in their natural environment and use things that grow or exist in a natural form. A woman in Concord, New Hampshire, creates what she calls "Little People" made of things that grow—pods, seeds, and rose hips, which she converts into doll faces. She mounts these on stones and sells them through the League of New Hampshire Craftsmen in their nine shops throughout the state.

"I have sold hundreds, and I can't keep up with the demand," she says.

A housewife in Peru, Massachusetts, who worked as an IBM key punch operator before her children were born, lined up advance work from business firms in her community and rented an IBM key punch machine for $36 a month. With the money she earned on jobs during that month she paid for the machine and had such an encouraging surplus that she has gone on to establish a profitable independent business.

The high cost of working outside the home adds to the appeal and profits of substituting lucrative projects in the home for a weekly pay check. The cost of clothing, hair care, cosmetics, transportation, and child care so diminish an office weekly pay check that many secretaries, laboratory technicians, and clerical workers discover that they cannot afford to work away from home.

Love Thy Neighbor

Are you well known in your community? Do you belong to church organizations or other clubs? Usually your first sales will be made right in your own living room, and the word-of-mouth publicity will attract other customers who have seen your work or have heard about the service you are performing. If you are new to a community and want to make friends, a career at home can help you to make new friends if you join various local groups. And if you have hidden your light under a bushel, with talents no one knows about, your talent can be the bridge to your popularity if you take the opportunity to exhibit your creations at bazaars and fairs and if you join groups with similar interests.

Test Your Market

Many women overlook the vital steps in market testing to find out whether their envisioned career at home is needed and in current fashion.

A woman with a high degree of skill and taste, who had lived a sheltered life on a plantation in Georgia, could not sell the exquisite handmade garments she made for babies and small children. They looked like christening robes out of Queen Victoria's reign. This woman was still living in the past and was out of touch with today's needs and standards. She had not observed the precaution of comparison shopping as a market test before investing her time in making up samples.

All big department stores have comparison shoppers, people who spend their days going from store to store to find out whether the merchandise in their employer's store compares favorably in price, quality, and style with their competitors. Before you start to sell your creations or services, stop at the shops and stores in your area to find out what is being sold, how much it costs, and whether the quality of what you have to offer is as good or better than what is available in the retail stores. It is especially important to discover whether the product you have in mind will fill a public need.

A child's "training apron" with zippers to zip, laces to lace, buttons to button, all ingeniously attached to the apron in a way that makes it possible for little people to "learn by doing," was invented by a young mother of four children. The aprons are made in one piece, of machine washable fabric. The inventive housewife took her gay and durable little garment to the buyer of children's clothing in the department store nearest to where she lived and came away with an order for a dozen. The aprons sold well at $3.95 apiece. They were reordered and subsequently sold to stores in other parts of the country.

Between direct sale to a customer, which returns you the full retail price of what you offer, and wholesale selling, which puts distribution into expert hands and frees you to produce, there is an intermediary step. This step is selling through cooperative outlets: exchanges, guild stores, fairs, and bazaars. At a fair or bazaar the producer pays the sponsor either a fee or a percentage of sales. At an exchange or guild store the goods are usually taken on consignment, and the producer is paid, less the handling percentage of the store, when her goods are sold. Wholesalers must be paid, so the percentage of profit is lower; but the increased volume of sales makes up for the lower markup and the time saved, to increase production.

Watch a Pro at Work

One of the most practical preludes to a career at home is getting to know other women who are successfully doing what you think you would like to do.

Let's suppose you are interested in party catering from your home. Locate one or more professional caterers—not necessarily those working from their homes but any who do high-level catering. If you don't know any, look in the yellow pages of your classified telephone directory, or ask an organization for the name of their caterer for conventions, wedding receptions, anniversaries, and other such events. Stop in to see one or several caterers to offer your part-time services or to offer to make things for them at home when there's a rush of business. Seeing a price list is a good beginning. You can get an idea of the professional know-how and acquire leads for customers of your own.

Assisting in the alterations department of a dress store will serve a similar purpose, as will acting as a helper in a nursery school, if those are services that will fill a need in your neighborhood.

Where You Live

An important consideration in organizing your home career is whether your house will be open to the public or remain private to you and your family. In a later chapter I will discuss the various legal and community regulations concerned, but here we are concerned with the decision you make about the type of home career you undertake and how the location and size of your home and the arrangements for family living coordinate with your ambitions.

If your house is to be used only for producing what you make and you will offer delivery service to your customers, the space you will need will depend entirely on what you make, storage space necessary for materials, and the kinds of equipment your work requires. For many women no major change in daily living is involved until their business grows to the point at which they find their workrooms bursting at the seams.

If your house is to be used to exhibit crafts, to care for children, to arrange fittings, to hold classes, or to style customers' hair, you may have to think about such things as a separate entrance so that your customers won't collide with your husband and children as they come and go. The part of your house through which the public enters must be kept attractive and orderly, which can be a strain on the rest of the family. Set up business hours during the time when most of the family is out of the house and put a sign on your door stating what your hours are. If other members of the family are home during those work hours, have them come and go through the back door.

The location of a home business becomes important when customers must *come to you*. Therefore, if you are going into dressmaking or starting a nursery school or a showroom of any kind, you should be situated where it will be convenient for customers to reach you. Your clientele will be built gradually, based on the reputation you acquire as your work pleases and satisfies your patrons. Being located in the shopping area of your neighborhood is not an advantage because you don't want to attract "traffic"—women who are just looking. But being accessible, within fifteen minutes to a half hour of traveling time of those you are serving in a residential area, will induce your customers to come back.

Take the Time Test

Make a list, including activities outside the home, of just how you spend your time from morning until night. Can you free yourself for enough hours of the day or week to have a home career? It is useful to include the hours your husband is at home and the hours your children especially need your attention. If you can never catch up with the ironing, if you get uptight every time something unexpected comes along to interfere with your daily routine, or if your energy runs out before the dinner dishes are out of the dishwasher, you have not passed the careers-at-home "readiness" test. However, most women have more time than they think they have, judging by surveys made of how housewives schedule their housework. Ninety percent of the women surveyed are finished before noon and are free in the afternoons and often in the evenings. Such women would welcome the diversion of a hobby or home career.

Booby Traps

Impatience is one booby trap of the inexperienced. Taking an ad in an out-of-town metropolitan newspaper, lured by the large circulation and dreaming of big orders pouring in by the gross, is an example of impatience that doesn't pay off unless a product has been thoroughly market tested in advance. Such an ad may bring mail and telephone orders, which will require packaging, labeling, and postage. To fill such orders merchandise has to be made up in quantity in advance, thus creating a costly inventory and taking up storage space. Your profit can be eaten up by the cost of packaging and postage, which both require expert calculation.

A Christmas wreath operation described in a later chapter was introduced in a Chicago Sunday newspaper advertisement.

The wreaths sold for $40 each. They were very beautiful but very expensive, and one hundred of them were never sold. ("Ours was the most decorated house in Lake Geneva that Christmas!" said the creator of the wreaths.) Avoid mail order experiments until your business is well underway and you are sure of what you're doing.

Another booby trap of the inexperienced is innocence and gullibility, especially when dealing with agents. One innocent young housewife, selling her goods through an agent she knew nothing about, shipped a dozen gross of paper flowers to a gift shop five hundred miles away only to discover that the gift shop had declared bankruptcy the week she shipped the order.

"Look before you leap," is the advice of Mrs. David A. Doyle of Milwaukee, Wisconsin, who undertook to make housecoats at home for a Milwaukee novelty dress and accessory shop.

"The minute I saw the inside of the shop I should have known the owner was unstable. It had a black ceiling and floor, and the walls were covered with silver aluminum foil, the background for the exotic accessories and housecoats the shop featured. I invested in the fabric, made up a dozen housecoats, and delivered them on consignment. When I returned to cash in on my investment, the shop had totally disappeared!"

A fashion designer who invented a beguiling patio hostess apron was dizzy with success when one of New York's finest Fifth Avenue stores, after seeing the samples she took in, placed an order for six dozen. Anticipating that she would have to line up outside pieceworkers, she hired six local dressmakers to make up the hostess aprons as the orders came in. As a result of the speedy and occasionally careless methods of production, the workmanship she produced was uneven. Much of it was unprofessional. Nearly half the aprons were not even acceptable to the New York store.

While ignorance can be chalked up to painful experience when it involves only an individual producer, it is not excusable in the eyes of the law. Every home producer must be familiar with tax laws, postal regulations, labor regulations, and any other business details appropriate to his or her venture. Such regulations will be discussed in later chapters. Ignorance of regulations can cause untold problems in a career at home. For example, one woman started a nursery school and assumed that the parents of the children for whom she was caring had observed the health laws of the Department of Health. This assumption did not excuse her, however, when she was unable to produce health certificates for four children in her school.

Make a Name for Yourself

Naming your business early is a good idea, and it can be an asset. The name you choose should serve as your introduction to the public, and it can carry an advertising message as well. When you have business cards printed, your own name should appear on your cards. You may choose to use your own name as the name of your business, but a name descriptive of what you do is recommended by experts.

To many people naming a business is like naming a child; they like to romanticize. Sometimes this leads to good publicity. Examples of names with intriguing sounds are: "Personal Touch" for a party service; "Choice Pieces" for an antiques dealer; "The Unexpected" for a costume jewelry maker; and "The Fabric Surgeon" for a dressmaker. Start dreaming up your own name and prepare to embark on a new adventure in living—a career at home!

2 Organizing Your Life for a Home Career

"The idea hit me when my husband and I were on a camping trip in the High Sierras searching for a better fishing hole. I decided to start making driftwood lamp bases with finials [ornaments] to match and sell them to gift shops."

Most careers at home sneak up on you, as this one did on Pauline Lehman of Culver City, California. The ideas surface because you are a person who dreams a little, likes to be busy, and enjoys hobbies. Often you find yourself volunteering to do things for other people.

Once you begin getting paid for your work, a whole new set of responsibilities enters your life. You have to plan and schedule how you are going to do the housework and the marketing, supervise your children, keep the clutter of the things you make out of the way, and keep track of the time and money that goes into the business part of your life.

You may become a much better housewife because you have taken on a home career. You'll learn the reality of the old saying, "If you want to get a job done, get the busiest person you know to do it." You'll become that busiest person, and you'll find yourself able to get more done in a short time than ever before.

How to Plan for Your Family and Home Career

As your dream for a home career becomes a reality, your ball point pen, the classified telephone directory, and your public library will become your best friends. Chain several ball point pens in various locations (near the telephone is a must) and place a memo pad nearby. Lists will dominate your life. You'll begin to write yourself notes about everything. You'll keep a running list of supplies on which you are running low, of social engagements, of coming events, of checkup times at dentists and doctors for your children. There will be peak periods of activity when you may have to do what I do: tape important reminders to the bathroom mirror. One home career woman I know became so absorbed in her work that she lost track of time. So she set her alarm clock for four in the afternoon and put a printed sign over her work table that read, STOP WORK. GET DRESSED UP FOR JIM AND DON'T FORGET TO KISS HIM! Another put an egg timer by her telephone to cut down what she called "telephonitis," the great American time waster. An overly preoccupied housewife who was running beauty classes in her home was humorously reprimanded by a hungry husband when he mailed her a cartoon showing a woman creaming her face while her husband watches. The caption read, "Your complexion *should* be flawless; it gets better fed than I do."

Because your children and husband should come first, you must plan and organize your life *around them*. When they realize that you have a real job that pays you money, they will help and cooperate. Most of those errands and nasty little jobs that were always allotted to you because you were home all day and had "nothing important to do" should be divided up, with each member of the family attending to his own "nitty gritty."

Enjoy Being Your Own Boss

When you are your own boss—and it's a glorious feeling—you'll have no one to blame but yourself if things don't go smoothly. You'll be turning the tables on the wife you may have envied as she went off to an outside job every morning. You can make your own schedule. Your time is your own, but you'll soon learn that time is money and that today's procrastination is tomorrow's headache.

The family situation will vary according to the husband's job, hobbies, and sports and the ages of the children. The standard pattern is for a husband to be out of the house by eight o'clock in the morning and home by six at night. The aforementioned survey made in preparation for this book revealed that ninety percent of all housewives have finished their routine housekeeping by eleven or twelve every morning. They have three to five free hours in the afternoon and one or two free hours in the evening to be devoted to social and other activities. Shopping trips once a week took care of the marketing, and the daily routine usually involved morning preparation of a main dish or dessert for dinner. Many of the career-at-home housewives like to get started as early in the day as possible and do the minimal tidying up for an orderly house by nine or nine-thirty. The once-a-week major jobs such as ironing they do in the evening while watching television or talking with their husbands. Most of the husbands pitch in and help to get these jobs done in half the usual time. When children are old enough, they take on a share of the housework.

One woman said, "My seven-year-old Andy's toys are stored in bins rather than open shelves so that it's easier to keep them looking neat. His bed is covered with a comforter rather than a bedspread so that he can make it up himself. All of his clothes are knits or no-iron fabrics."

Every career-at-home housewife must be well organized. She must follow a schedule and use her ingenuity to discover every kind of labor-saving expedient available, such as no-iron dresses, no-iron bedding, and large quantity cooking for freezer-stored meals. These principles apply to all good home management, but they become priorities in home career households.

"I feel that to be a careerist at home you must enjoy it and have a certain sense of humor about it because at times you will not be able to control the confusion that can occur. Never give up until you are sure you have exhausted every means of trying to set up your own business. One last important point is to be very careful of your accounting and always keep your books up to date. Also you must know what is going on in your line of work by reading or doing research *all the time.*" These words of advice were sent by the operator of a very successful at-home beauty and charm school for teenagers and their mothers.

The creative stitchery that one housewife sells in kits by mail order has tripled in business in three years even with the advent of twins. She sums up her double life by saying:

"The whole thing is totally impossible without a husband who wants it to work. If he helps occasionally with baby-sitting or vacuuming, that's nice but not enough. He has to really care, to be proud enough of your efforts to brag about you to people, to give you confidence, and to boost you back up when you get discouraged and feel as if you're too small a frog in too large a pond. He must really understand that you can't be happy without your own creative work, and he must be good-natured even when supper is late and consists of pancakes.

"I don't want to give the impression that things always run smoothly. Three of us had the mumps, and two of us had the German measles this summer. Things pile up on me, and the mountains of dishes and diapers can get horribly depressing. But when we're all well and I'm functioning in as highly organized a way as my scheduling indicates, things run smoothly and everything gets done."

There are three immutable laws to be observed in combining a happy household with a sucessful business at home:

(1) Get the beds made and the breakfast dishes out of the way before you turn your back on your housework.

(2) Involve your children, whatever their ages, in some interesting participation. One dressmaker with two children—ages three and four—set up a miniature sewing and cutting center for them. Thus a modified two-child nursery school equivalent was accomplished. For out-of-doors supervision she placed her sewing next to a window overlooking the backyard so that she could keep an eye on the children during their playtime in the fresh air.

For older children home is never boring when there's something interesting going on that they can be a part of. If they can help with deliveries, packaging, and labeling, they can share in your success. The children can be paid for the specific jobs they do instead of receiving handouts in the form of allowances.

(3) Don't take on more than you can do well. You are building a reputation and starting a new way of life. Your success depends on keeping everybody happy. It's hard to resist a big order when you are new to the business and big orders are scarce, but unless you can get help to take over the family for the days you will be involved in production, turn the order down. Later in your career you'll be prepared to handle such situations. Don't let your home become a madhouse overflowing with bows, decorations, fabric, or whatever.

So far we've stayed on familiar ground in our discussion of how you should organize your life at home to cope with your new business. We must move to unfamiliar ground now, the professional part of business management: everything from the desk you must have that's all your own to the new equipment and physical arrangements necessary for running your business.

Your "Think Center" and Workshop

Running a business, like running a home or a government, is basically a question of good housekeeping; and good housekeeping takes good headwork. Your desk will be your "think center," the place where you will list and place the orders for materials you need, pay bills, keep records, and keep file card indexes of your customers' names and addresses and those of the wholesalers who provide your materials. Before your business has reached the point at which you can allocate a special room to do your clerical work, you will need a desk with enough drawers to keep your unpaid bills and checkbook separated from your paid bills, which you will file at the end of the month. It is essential that the desk be yours alone—private, untouchable, sacrosanct. Curious little hands and nosy relatives must be banished. The old-fashioned roll-top desk that can be closed and locked would be ideal, but that kind of desk has become a collector's item, and unless you can find a modern version, you'll have to depend on the standard flat-top type (the kind that efficient businessmen are supposed to keep "clear as the deck of a battleship ready for action"—a myth that belongs to the movies). Your desk top will seldom be clear, so it is advisable to place it away from the living room, where you receive and entertain visitors. If the kitchen is big enough, it is the ideal place. Or you can use your bedroom or a roomy hall.

If you don't own a flat-top desk with drawers banked on one or two sides, you can pick one up in a second-hand store or in the unpainted furniture section of a department store. The second-hand variety would be the least expensive, and you can be sure that the drawers won't stick because they have been loosened by years of use.

Your telephone will probably be the lifeline of your business, so place it on your desk if possible. Get an extension phone to be used by the rest of the family. The monthly added charge for an extension is only about $1.

Writing of business letters should be kept to the minimum. A rubber stamp imprinted with your name and address can

be used to head bills and orders, blank envelopes, and letter-
heads. Using the stamp will save you the expense of printing.
It is very important to keep duplicates of bills, orders, and
letters.

A sturdy armless desk chair that can be pushed in and out
from under your desk is also a good investment. Check second-
hand stores for this sort of chair. A kitchen chair will do, but
you'll find that it interferes with traffic because you can't just
push it under your desk counter with a flick of your wrist.

A homemade desk can combine the advantages of a desk, a
work table, and a file. A standard door bought at a local lumber
company costs under $10. Two two-drawer steel filing cabinets
about $28\frac{1}{2}$ inches high should be picked up at a second-hand
office supply store as the new ones run to $50 each or more.
Placed under the waxed or painted door at each end, the area
allows more room than a standard desk. This type of arrangement is very good for workers in crafts or for designers whose
filing system involves more than bills and letters. This is particularly practical if located in a basement, attic, or garage workroom. If your desk will not involve drawing, tracing, or cutting,
the standard size desk with a deep file drawer on one side would
provide enough desk filing space and take up little room, no
more than $3\frac{1}{2}$ feet x 2 feet. The fiberboard shelf files that look
like oversized dictionaries when standing on a shelf will provide
all the filing space you will need for correspondence and bills
for a year or two. They cost only a fraction of the cost of steel
filing cabinets. There are alphabetized sections inside to make
your sorting convenient and efficient. An accordion folder that
can be inserted in your desk file drawer and alphabetized can
serve the same purpose. You can file away your papers from
day to day after you do your desk work.

An office equipment catalog (usually free of charge) would
be worth your time and the postage to order. Goldsmith Brothers, 77 Nassau Street, New York, New York 10038, is one of the
suppliers with national distribution. If you decide to order
supplies through the catalog, you will be entitled to the wholesale price. It is always worthwhile to compare a home carpentry
job for shelves and other storage items to the cost of mass-
produced equipment designed specifically for office use. Ingenuity and mobility apply more to at-home work than to the usual
office setup. Many handmade things, especially needlework, can

Movable Office Deluxe. If your dream of a desk could include all the shelves, compartments, record-keeping facilities, and storage space you need and could also be movable on castors, you might wind up with something like the unit on this page. There is handy space available for a typewriter, telephone, and most other equipment you may need for your home career.

The Home Office closed.

The Home Office by Greatwood Products, Inc.

The ingenious inventor of this unit makes it disappear behind closed doors so that nobody can invade your privacy. Homemade versions of this model can be achieved by skilled carpenters, but the cost might exceed the cost of the unit shown above, which is less than $300. The measurements of this unit are 64½″ high by 45″ wide by 30″ deep. Be sure to investigate the quality and cost of various products available in your area before investing in a movable office.

be taken from room to room, and a portable work table can be very convenient. If you have a rolling cart with two tiers for supplies, you can keep your materials within easy reach and get the clutter out of sight quickly when you're entertaining. An office version of this in metal, two tiers on castors, can be bought for less than $25.

You will need a loose-leaf or spiral-bound desk calendar with pages big enough to record appointments, due dates for your customers, and "to do" items to keep track of your own schedule. Calendars that show the week, with roomy spaces for each day, will help you keep everything you are doing right in front of you. An address book, a card file, and a supply of ball point pens, pencils, and memo pads will complete your desk essentials.

Your desk does not have to be in your workshop, especially if you work in the basement, the attic, or the garage. Most of your paper work and your telephoning will be fitted into evenings or weekends, when you're not involved in creating your product or rendering your service. If your desk is away from your workshop, a second telephone extension is advisable. For the small additional charge of $1 a month (now you would have two extensions for $2) you would be spared the wear and tear of racing up and down stairs.

If you work in a part of the house that is remote from the front or back doors, such as the basement, the attic, or the garage, you had better get your husband to hook up a bell-ringing system that will ring where you work as well as in the living quarters of your house. An intercom system with a speaker for announcing your visitors might be well worth considering. Maybe you don't mind running up and down stairs a dozen times a day to answer the doorbell (it's a form of jogging that might be good for you) , but it can be very tiring and distracting. Intercoms aren't all that fancy or expensive. For about $145 you can have a speaker installed at your front door with a little talk box in your workshop. Visitors, delivery men, and other callers can identify themselves, state their business, and receive your instructions.

When you make the really big time in your business, you may want to look into a telephone answering service. You may wish to install a message recorder that you can turn on during the hours you must be away from home; a recorder costs about $250 to install. When you return home, you play back the tape and answer any messages. You can be assured that no business has been lost due to possible inefficiency by an answering service. Once the message recorder has been installed and paid for by means of monthly installments, you own it.

Storage to Banish Forage

Get off to a good start by providing special storage space from the very beginning. Try to clear out one closet, cupboard, or a set of bureau drawers to store supplies and protect your finished products. Shelf space and bins are usually more important than hanging space unless you're in the dress or costume business, in which case you will need both. Since a home career is experimental in many ways, it is better at first not to make installations such as wall shelves that can't be transferred without expense to other parts of your house. That is why bookshelf units that can be used as room dividers are so practical. They can also be made to look very attractive. These shelf room dividers are sold ready-made and can be put on tracks to divide space and slide back and forth. Corrugated cardboard and fiberboard file cabinets are inexpensive and attractive for storage, and they cost much less than standard metal cupboards or cabinets. (A free catalog of storage supplies will be mailed to you by Mr. Michael Plitman of the Safco Products Co., 7425 Laurel Avenue, South, Golden Valley, Minnesota 55427.) Cardboard cartons from your own supermarket can be made to look attractive with decorative coverings and used for storing all kinds of supplies. Do-it-yourself sets of storage walls can be ordered in sections. The kit includes directions for putting the units together to suit your own requirements. Your husband might be delighted to help—a nostalgic throwback to the days of erector sets under the Christmas tree.

A cork bulletin board for thumb-tacked memos (preferable to the magnetic variety) is invaluable. The most important item on it should be your running inventory and location chart. By having the list available at a glance you don't have to rummage through bins, closets, drawers, or shelves in search of materials. Securely attached, such a location chart can cut your storage housekeeping time in half. The bulletin board can serve in other ways, such as a place to keep samples, designs, clippings, and many other items.

"Idea Center"—Picture, Magazine, Catalog, Booklet Storage

One of the most fascinating aspects of your home career will be attempting to become an expert in your field. You will take out subscriptions to special magazines, and send for catalogs and booklets containing information about new materials, ideas, and designs. You will keep a file of clippings. Protect this source material from finding its way into the wastebasket by providing a special storage area—an "Idea Center," where you can refer to the information when you need it. Catalogs and magazines related to your business will be a constant source of stimulation and reference, and any cost for them is a tax deductible business expense.

Prevent Operation Headache

Letting bills pile up and never being quite sure of where you stand financially can take the joy out of anything—especially running your own business. Even if you decide to employ the services of an accountant, the performance of such services will be limited to about four times a year until your business begins to produce real volume, at which time you may need accounting services once a month. The next chapter will tell you how to minimize the headaches of money management.

3 Money Management

"I only want to know enough about money not to be stupid!" someone told me.

"Is that *all?*" I answered. I couldn't resist a laugh because if you know enough about money not to be stupid, you know, in practical terms, everything that is important in your working life. I like to stick to the eternal verities and let the economists argue about the gold standard, the inflationary spiral, and the Keynesian theory of spending yourself into prosperity. Our concern is what you must do from day to day to meet your financial obligations and to make a profit in your career at home.

What you're going to learn in this chapter will involve buying materials and equipment you need; pricing your goods or services so that you will make a profit; keeping records to comply with the requirements of the Bureau of Internal Revenue; knowing what tax deductions you can claim at the end of the year as a self-employed person; understanding your Social Security status; and learning what legal requirements you must look into about appropriate licensing, zoning, sales taxes, fire regulations, and health regulations.

Keep Your Own Records

Your husband may be brilliant when it comes to making out your joint income tax return, but don't hand your day-to-day, week-to-week, month-to-month business records over to him. Avoid arguments and interference in your business by *keeping these records yourself* and setting up a separate checking account as soon as possible.

If you don't have the extra cash at the outset to maintain the bank's minimum balance on a regular account, you can start a special checking account that does not require a minimum balance. A service charge of about $2 a month is customary, but some banks charge by the check. At a small extra expense, check books will be printed for you with the name of your business and with spaces for itemizing the materials or services paid for by the check drawn. Such checks will be your most valuable record for income tax computation and records.

Since your records can make or break you, your desk should be equipped with a hard-cover simple columnar cash book, in which you can keep a daily record of money paid out for your business expenses and the money that comes in as you receive payments. The bookkeeping term for this is "double entry." In addition to this you should have an alphabetized fiber board desk file for bills, correspondence, insurance policies, tax records, etc. It's a good idea to have your insurance policies, deeds to property, inventory of your possessions, will, contracts, and other documents duplicated. (Duplicating machines are everywhere, so the cost of this amounts to from 10¢ a page to no more than 25¢.) The originals of these papers should be kept in a safe or in your safe deposit box at the bank in order to be protected from fire, theft, or loss of the copies of the records you keep at home. Even if you update your household and business inventory only once a year, this record would be of major value in collecting insurance. Your "accounts payable and receivable" ledger and your fiber board file can be purchased at stationery stores or business supply houses. The costs for these materials and for your safe-deposit facilities can be deducted from your income tax as business expenses. Even the housekeeping money that most home career women use to make up samples and test their market is considered a tax deduction.

When Are You Legally in Business at Home?

The Small Business Administration says:

> When you open your doors to customers you are in business, *if* you have complied with licenses, permits, unemployment insurance coverage, social security coverage, sales and income as well as personal property taxes—all of which depend upon state and county regulations. These differ in accordance with the locality and the nature of the business.

In Maryland, for instance, a trader's license is required if a person buys something to resell. But if a person makes an item in her own home, such as in a dressmaking business, she does not need a license. The information offices in the office of the secretary of state in your state capital will tell you whether you require a license for the type of business you will conduct at home. Licenses are usually inexpensive and easy to obtain for business ventures in which only the resale of merchandise is involved. In services that require inspection by the health and fire departments, such as dog kennels, foster homes, beauty parlors, and food preparation service, a license may cost $25 or more. For many home businesses no licensing at all is required.

The Small Business Administration may have a branch near you (see Part III for address). Your local Chamber of Commerce can also supply much information about these regulations. After you have found out which licenses you need to start your business, you should write for the appropriate application forms to your state capital and local authorities.

How to Buy Materials Wholesale

All states require sales taxes of one kind or another; in most states there are some additional county, city, and, of course, federal taxes. You are required to register your business if you make things for sale or if you buy things for resale. This entitles you to a resale number, which authorizes you to buy goods in the wholesale market without paying a sales tax. You will, however, be required to add a sales tax to the items you sell. Wholesale prices are usually forty percent less than the retail price of the merchandise. There are wholesale price privileges for equipment in the services categories as well as in the materials purchased for making gifts, toys, and other items of merchandise for sale.

What to Charge in Your Home Business

Items manufactured in the home for resale represent such a wide diversity that only the most rudimentary rule of thumb can be your guide. First, you must know what prices are being charged by your competition for similar items. Your products must compete in price, but if you incorporate a special feature or unique appeal into your merchandise, you may be entitled to charge more than your competition. The inherent charm of even a pot-holder or an apron, its originality of design or imaginative color combination, will encourage a buyer to spend a few cents more for individuality.

Since the manager of even the smallest business should keep a detailed record of costs, she can figure the time her effort represents and the amount of materials used. Then she should compute her overhead, even though the work is done at home, electricity, heat, phone, and rent payments must be included as part of the cost. Consider roughly one-fourth of the overall household utility charges as expenses. Packaging, delivery, and publicity costs will vary widely too, and they must be regarded as basic expenses. The investment of time in the early stages of setting up a business should be evaluated at about half of the standard $5-an-hour rate. At first you will work at a much slower rate than you will later, as your speed and skills increase with experience. Adding a sixty percent markup to the combined cost of your materials and your overhead should give you a fair profit. If you are selling through a middleman—a store, an agent, or a distributor—you will most likely cut your margin of profit per item in half. Such middlemen usually charge a commission of from five to fifty percent.

A quality craft item or an item that is unique in artistic appeal is usually sold directly. Such a product has the "one-of-a-kind" prestige that justifies a price set at what the market will bring for your special talents.

The Bureau of Standards, in Washington, D.C., can give you expert information on everything from the sizing of ready-to-wear clothes to the regulations controlling the manufacture of food and cosmetic items. Federal food and drug laws require labels on packaged foods. The producer must itemize the contents of every package, and the product must pass government specifications and inspection. Packaged food and cosmetic items are rarely produced in the home because they require a volume of sales and specialized packaging that usually exceeds facilities that the home base can afford or accommodate. Laws are strict about the listing of ingredients, but the pricing of such items bears little relation to the price of ingredients. The cost is determined more by many outside factors, such as advertising, publicity, and distribution.

Many of the same principles that apply to pricing merchandise apply to fees charged for services provided within the home; but in computing the cost of a service the overhead will take precedence and be proportionately higher, and equipment and materials will represent what is known as capital investment, which can be deducted on your income tax return. For example, if you run a secretarial service that has required you to invest in an electric typewriter, the Internal Revenue Service permits you to charge off the cost of that machine or any other business equipment over a ten-year period. If a new typewriter or adding machine costs $300 and is expected to last ten years, you are allowed a deduction of $30 a year for ten years.

If you must invest in equipment for the care of elderly people or if you have to equip a nursery school, this cost too can be charged off. The charge for your own time, exclusive of your overhead, will be high from the beginning since many services require specialized training, which becomes much more costly when provided in the usual commercial establishment. The home base gives the price advantage to the career housewife. Her hourly rate can range from $3 to $10 an hour, depending on the amount of responsibility and the technical proficiency her service requires. Foster care of the ambulatory elderly (not handicapped or senile) who are receiving Social Security benefits provides an income of about $225 a month per person. Thus, if four patients are accommodated, the annual income before overhead is deducted is $10,800. A home with two extra double bedrooms can be adapted to the requirements with a modest investment. The approval of the Department of Health, Education, and Welfare must be obtained before the care of the elderly may be undertaken.

A home secretarial service on a part-time basis can bring in $5,000 a year in a business area with a low overhead and a high rate of profit.

Services demand longer hours, more responsibility, and more training than many of the home merchandising operations; hence they do not give the career housewife the advantage of being able to say her time is her own. But many services pay better than the sale of products. Home incomes from services rendered can average $8,000 to $10,000 a year, but they usually entail around-the-clock responsibilities.

Checking Customer Credit

As in any business venture, in a home career operation it is important to determine the reliability of your clients—cus-

SCHEDULE C (Form 1040)
H&R BLOCK **Profit (or Loss) From Business or Profession** (Sole Proprietorship) **1970**

Social security number

Name as shown on Form 1040

product
(For example: retail—hardware; wholesale—tobacco; services—legal; manufacturing—furniture; etc.)

C Employer Identification Number   (ZIP code)

A Principal business activity (See separate instructions)

B Business name

D Business address

E Indicate method of accounting: (1) ☐ cash; (2) ☐ accrual; (3) ☐ other.

F Was there any substantial change in the manner of determining quantities, costs, or valuations between the opening and closing inventories?
☐ YES ☐ NO. If "Yes," attach explanation.

G Were you required to file Form 1087 for the calendar year 1970? (See "Item G" in separate instructions for Schedule C.)
☐ YES ☐ NO.

1 Gross receipts or ...
2 Inventory at beg... attach explana...
3 Merchandise pur... withdrawn fr...
4 Cost of labor (...
5 Material and s...
6 Other costs (a...
7   Total ...
8 Inventory at ...
9 Cost of goo...
10 Gross profi...

OTHER BU...
11 Depreciati...
12 Taxes on ...
13 Rent on ...
14 Repairs ...
15 Salaries ...
16 Insuran...
17 Legal ...
18 Comm...
19 Amor...
20 Reti... in...
21 Int...
22 Ba...
23 D...
24 O...
25 ...
26 ...

SCHEDULE SE (Form 1040)
Department of the Treasury
Internal Revenue Service

Computation of Social Security Self-Employment Tax
► Each self-employed person must file a separate Schedule SE
► Attach to Form 1040.

1970

► If you had wages, including tips, of $7,800 or more that were subject to social security taxes, do not fill in this page.
► If you had more than one business, combine profits (or losses) from all of your businesses and farms on this Schedule SE.

Important.—The self-employment income reported below will be credited to your social security record and used in figuring social security benefits.

Name of self-employed person (as shown on social security card)   Social security number   Check applicable block 1 ☐ Male 2 ☐ Female

Business activities subject to self-employment tax (grocery store, restaurant, farm, etc.) ►

Part I   Computation of Net Earnings from BUSINESS Self-Employment (other than farming)

1 Net profit (or loss) shown in Schedule C (Form 1040), line 26. (Enter combined amount if more than one business.) .
2 Net income (or loss) from excluded services or sources included on line 1 . . . .
  Specify excluded services or sources . . . .
3 Net earnings (or loss) from business self-employment (Subtract line 2 from line 1, and enter here and on line 1(a), Part III, below.) . . . .

Part II   Computation of Net Earnings from FARM Self-Employment   **SE**

A farmer may elect to compute net farm earnings using the OPTIONAL METHOD (line 3, below) INSTEAD OF THE REGULAR METHOD (line 2, below) if his gross profits from farming are: (1) $2,400 or less, or (2) more than $2,400 and net profits are less than $1,600. If your gross profits from farming are not more than $2,400 and you elect to use the optional method, you need not complete lines 1 and 2.

Computation under Regular Method

1 Net farm profit (or loss) from:
  (a) Schedule F, line 52 (cash method), or line 69 (accrual method) . . . .
  (b) Farm partnerships . . . .
2 Net earnings from self-employment from farming. Add lines 1(a) and (b) . . . .

Computation under Optional Method

3 If gross profits from farming are:*
  (a) Not more than $2,400, enter two-thirds of the gross profits . . . . . . }
  (b) More than $2,400 and the net farm profit is less than $1,600, enter $1,600 }
*Note.—Gross profits from farming are the total of the gross profits from Schedule F, line 28 (cash method), or line 67 (accrual method), plus the distributive share of gross profit from farm partnerships as explained in instructions for Schedule SE.
4 Enter here and on line 1(b), Part III, below, the amount on line 2 (or line 3, if you use the optional method) . .

Part III   Computation of Social Security Self-Employment Tax

1 Net earnings (or loss) from self-employment—
  (a) From business (other than farming—from line 3, Part I, above) . . . .
  (b) From farming (from line 4, Part II, above) . . . .
  (c) From partnerships, joint ventures, etc. (other than farming) . . . .
  (d) From service as a minister, member of a religious order, or a Christian Science practitioner. If you filed Form 4361, check here ☐ and enter zero on this line . . . .
  (e) From service with a foreign government or international organization . . . .
  (f) Other (director's fees, etc.). Specify . . . .
2 Total net earnings (or loss) from self-employment reported on line 1 . . . .
  (If line 2 is less than $400, you are not subject to self-employment tax. Do not fill in rest of page.)
3 The largest amount of combined wages and self-employment earnings subject to social . .

Form **1040-ES**
Department of the Treasury
Internal Revenue Service

Estimated Tax Declaration—Voucher for Individuals—1971

Voucher 1
(Calendar Year—Due April 15, 1971)

To be used for making declaration and payment

See instruction 8 for information on overpayment elected for credit to 1971 estimated tax.   Fiscal year taxpayers—See instructions.

Your social security number   Spouse's social security number

First name and initial (if joint declaration, use first names and middle initials of both)   Last name

Address (Number and street)

City, State, and ZIP code

Please type or print

1. Estimated tax for the year ending . . . . . . $. . . . .
   (month and year)

2. Amount of this payment . . . $. . . . .
   (also enter in your Record of Payments on page 2)

Sign here ► Your signature

Spouse's signature (if joint declaration)

Return this voucher with check or money order payable to "Internal Revenue Service."

15

Form 1040-C. Even if you and your husband file a joint Federal Income Tax Report, you will need to attach two supplementary schedules, which you can find at most post offices or at your local Internal Revenue Service. Form 1040-C is a profit and loss statement from your business. This form is a summary of your business income and the expenses incurred in the production of your income. Most deductible expenses are listed on this schedule, but blank spaces are provided so that you may specify unlisted deductions to which you are entitled. It is important to become familiar with the deductions particular to your field of business.

Keeping records of expenses is the most convincing evidence you can produce should your expenses be questioned. A diary or an expense book accompanied by canceled checks, bills, and receipts are invaluable documents and will usually satisfy the authorities if you are called in for an audit.

Form 1040-SE. The *SE* in this form stands for *self-employment,* and the form is filed for the purpose of paying your Social Security tax. If your net earnings from self-employment are less than $400, you are not required to pay a self-employment tax, but you still must complete the 1040-SE form. If your earnings exceed $400, you are subject to a Social Security tax of 6.9 percent.

Form 1040-ES. The third form to be filed by a self-employed person is Form 1040-ES, Declaration of Estimated Income. This form provides for paying currently any income tax, including the self-employment tax, that is due. You are required to estimate your earnings for the forthcoming year and pay the tax you will owe in quarterly installments. This form is filed on January 15, April 15, June 15, and September 15. A penalty can be imposed for failing to file this form, but the penalty does not apply if at least 80 percent of your final tax is paid through withholding and quarterly installments.

tomers or middlemen. In checking the credit of an individual, that person's local bank is a good place to start. If you are dealing with a company new to you, the Better Business Bureau, the Board of Trade, the Chamber of Commerce, and Dun and Bradstreet are reliable sources of information. When dealing with out-of-town stores that place quantity orders, agents who represent you, and distributors of food products, it is vital to know that they are financially responsible and have good business reputations. An exchange of references is an accepted business practice. Taking the precaution of getting a signed order for merchandise will nearly always protect you because it is a legal document. If the order blank contains "fine print," however, be sure to read it carefully for loopholes or have your lawyer look it over before you go overboard.

Insuring a Home Office Business

The portion of your home that is set aside for commercial purposes—a rumpus room to be used as a nursery school, a sun porch converted into a gift shop, a family room designed as a beauty parlor—is not covered by a standard homeowner's insurance policy. Arrangements can be made for coverage by means of a special paragraph or a rider attached to the homeowner's policy. This is something that should be handled with your insurance agent. However, if you are doing typing at home, the homeowner's policy covers the theft of or damage to the typewriter since that is part of the homeowner's property, not classified as a part of the house set aside for commercial purposes. The Insurance Information Institute, 110 William Street, New York, New York, has numerous publications free of charge that are helpful in determining your insurance status. But each situation is different and must be discussed with your own insurance agent.

Income Tax Deductions for a Home Business

In the operation of a home business you will be entitled to tax deductions for rent, utilities, telephone, supplies, business travel, business entertaining, equipment, repairs, and other maintenance, but only in direct proportion to their use in conducting your business. If you have a workshop devoted exclusively to your business, your deduction will be greater than if you use the family kitchen, for example, to produce the casseroles or tea sandwiches you make to sell as a catering service. The same is true of the telephone and utilities, business entertaining, and travel. Your Internal Revenue Service office can advise you about your specific situation. The address of your local office will be listed in your telephone directory.

Social Security Benefits for Careers at Home

When your net earnings are $400 or more in a year, you receive Social Security credit for all of your net earnings up to $7,800. If you receive other wages in addition to your home career income, you will receive credit only for a sufficient amount of your net earnings from self-employment up to $7,800.

The following kinds of income do not count for Social Security credit:

(1) dividends from stocks and bonds;

(2) interest from loans unless your home business is to lend money;

(3) rentals from real estate unless you are a real estate dealer.

After the end of any year in which you have net earnings of $400 or more from your home business, the following tax forms must be completed: Form 1040–ES, the U.S. Individual Income Tax Return; Schedule 1040–C, which is the profit and loss form; and 1040–SE, which is the computation of Social Security self-employment tax.

These forms are available from the Internal Revenue Service and at many banks and post offices.

Send the income tax return and schedules along with your self-employment contribution to the Internal Revenue Service. If you do not already have a Social Security number, you may apply for one at any Social Security office. The amount of Social Security tax you will be contributing for your retirement income will be computed according to your earnings. Your Social Security office will assist you with any computation or you can communicate with any office of the Internal Revenue Service. Both are listed in the telephone directory.

Rules for Money Management

In managing the finances for your home business, there are several *dos* and *don'ts* you should know:

Do set up a separate checking account for your business finances.

Don't spend money on materials, equipment, or home alterations until you have tested your market.

Do keep a duplicate set of records—business expenditures, orders, contracts, insurance policies, deeds to property, and an inventory of the contents of your house and business. Store the originals in a safe or safe-deposit box. Keep all copies in a safe place in your home.

Don't go overboard on inventory. Quantity buying is cheaper than are small orders, but new materials come on the market constantly, and your business itself may fluctuate.

Do get help to meet a big order promptly. The extra expense will be tax deductible.

Don't let financial obligations pile up. Keep your paper work up to date.

4 Getting Customers

There's a story attributed to Benjamin Franklin about telling secrets. He said that as soon as three people were in on a secret, it became known to one hundred and eleven. This is the kind of gossip that any career housewife would love because she doesn't want to keep her home business a secret. Being talked about is very important to her success and very good for her reputation.

Unless she is a born extrovert and self-promoter, the housewife, usually inexperienced in the techniques of public relations, is often baffled about how to advertise herself and her home career. She may be unfamiliar with such promotional aids as printed announcements, business cards, classified advertising, store and window displays, fashion shows, exhibits, and demonstrations, and she usually has an exaggerated idea about how much they cost.

Your Printed Announcement and Business Card

Printed announcements or business cards can be ordered in quantities of 250 for as little as $10. Each should feature the name of your business, your address and telephone number, and a line or two of "come-on" copy. Let yourself go with originality but never obscure or overshadow the main thrust of your message—what your business is and where you can be reached. Sample business cards are reproduced here to give you an idea of the variety of possible style and wording. Even a small business card can reflect your personality and the character of your business. For instance, a wedding advisory service would use different gimmicks and catch-phrases than those used for adver-

29

Business Cards on this page demonstrate the range of possibilities and printing costs in different parts of the country. For instance, in Rockville, Indiana, 1,000 printed cards without art work can be printed for about $9.50. The same card printed in Southampton, New York, was estimated at three times that amount. A touch of color, a complementary sketch, a photograph, or an appropriate decoration may add to the cost of a business card, but the additional money is usually well spent.

RICHARD PEARL
VE 7-6549

Fern Pearl Studio
Boutique Unique

10470 DUNLEER DR.
LOS ANGELES
CALIF. 90064

Decorative Candle Making

CANDLE MAKING
for
FUN AND PROFIT
Instructed by:
"Mrs. New Jersey" 1966-67
EILEEN BURKAN
335-0060

(Bring home a completed candle at conclusion of every lesson)

PHONE 794-7647

The Red Door
ON ROUTE 202, SPRING VALLEY
BUCKS COUNTY, PA.

ANTIQUE LAMPS and CUSTOM SHADES
BY HELEN H. NAUL

MAIL ADDRESS
RD 2, DOYLESTOWN, PA. 18901
10 TO 5 TUESDAY THROUGH SATURDAY

Little Miss Muffet
Story Book Catering

LET US ARRANGE YOUR CHILDREN'S PARTIES
YOUR SITE OR OURS
CLOWNS - GAMES - FUN - FAVORS
CAKE AND DECORATIONS
CALL 288-6154   FREE ESTIMATES

tising toys or novelties. The free lessons offered on the card of the floral craft shop called The Pink Lollipop is an excellent example of how a business card can work for you. The free lessons will pull in the customers, and the profits will be derived from the sale of the materials required for learning.

"Little Miss Muffet Story Book Catering" includes all necessary information on a small card and includes an appealing little drawing. Printed on a gay bright yellow background, the card explains that all food, decorations, games, favors, and live clowns are available through the party service. It's the kind of card women tuck in their purses or tack to kitchen bulletin boards. Distributed through a neighborhood nursery school and in the waiting room of the local pediatrician's office, the service was off to a great beginning in less than a month with only an additional eight-line classified ad in the newspaper.

In the early stages of your home career business cards will be especially useful to take with you on visits to store buyers to whom you show your samples.

Packaging, Labels, and Invoices

The professionalism with which you present the things you make to sell will exert a powerful influence over your initial success. Efficient, orderly work will encourage customers to reorder. You will be concerned with two types of packaging—the packaging that protects your wares in transit and the packaging that attracts attention and helps to sell what you make.

The packaging required for shipment will usually be a carton. The classified section of your telephone directory lists dealers and jobbers for container manufacturers. The magazine *Modern Packaging*, with a separate directory called "The Packaging Encyclopedia," contains valuable information about ordering labels, tags, and cartons.

If you are producing kits for sale, packaging for the kits will be important to any distributor or mail order catalog house offering your kit for sale. Otherwise, when you are making your original customer contact, your samples do not have to be specially packaged unless materials are perishable or colors will fade. This type of merchandise may have to be slipped into a cellophane envelope or sack.

When you ship or deliver, attach or enclose an invoice. Use a printed form and include: your name and address, the store's name and address, the delivery point, the store's order number and date, the number of items, the name of the product, the price per item, and the total amount of your billing. Sellers often allow a two percent discount for payment by the tenth of the month; if you choose to adopt this practice, it should be so stated on your invoice.

How to Make a Date with a Store Buyer

Most store buyers set aside one or two days a week to see new merchandise in their offices. The best days are usually Tuesdays through Thursdays. Busy periods in the working day should be avoided. Make a telephone call to the store and speak to the buyer or store owner (if it's a boutique or specialty store) to arrange an appointment. If you are contacting a department store, talk to the buyer in the appropriate department. Be patient but be persistent. Drop into the store if communicating by telephone is difficult. You will have to take your samples around yourself in making your first sales. These will be the hours or days your career will take you away from home, and you may have to make special arrangements for sitters or houseworkers on those days.

Your first visit will be to local shops, where the atmosphere is more informal than it is in department stores or buying offices. By the time you are ready to take big orders you may want to investigate agents who will be making the rounds of buyers' offices for you.

Orders and Deliveries

If what you make is seasonal, show it six to eight months in advance of its special season; for example, Christmas items should be shown in April or May. Guarantee the buyer exclusive rights to the item in an area. Do not accept an order too large to fill on time. Find out when, where, and how the merchandise should be delivered. Ship by the route and method the store prefers. If your shipments are to be prepaid, allow for shipping charges in your price.

When you make a sale, get a written order on the buyer's form or use order forms that you will have with you. Be sure that all transactions are recorded in duplicate. There is a free catalog of modern business forms entitled The Drawing Board, Inc., available at 256 Regal Row, Dallas, Texas 75221. Study the forms in this catalog even if you want to order your own from a local stationery store.

In introducing your items in gift shops, boutiques, art needlework stores, and other specialty shops you may be asked for merchandise on consignment. Your samples will be put on display and sold from special orders in return for a forty to one hundred percent markup on your wholesale price. Your price will be anywhere from twenty percent to fifty percent over what it cost you to furnish the materials and pay yourself $5 an hour for your time. Even prestige craft retail stores often accept merchandise on consignment. You will benefit by the established following of such stores, and you will have an invaluable market-testing opportunity, which will tell you a lot about the appeal of what you are producing. You will find out whether the price is right, which colors and sizes are most popular, and how you can alter or improve your design to increase its sales appeal. The very fact that your item is accepted for consignment is a vote of confidence in you.

Don't overlook gift shops in hospitals and in hotels, especially if you live in a resort area. And if you are lucky enough to have a Woman's Exchange in your area, this nonprofit organization will take what you make on consignment and give you a much higher percentage of profit than most commercial establishments because these shops seek only to cover their expenses. A listing of the locations of Woman's Exchanges appears in Part III of this book, where the branches of the Small Business Administration (SBA) are also listed.

Selling a Service Means Selling Yourself

Your personality, competence, responsibility, and judgment, and the convenience, comfort, and adequacy of the facilities you offer will make your service successful. You must build a reputation, earn the confidence and good will that endears you to your customers and keeps them coming back. Your neighbors must love you too. Zoning laws may give you the legal right to do business in your home, but it may antagonize your neighbors. If you must have a sign, it should be one in keeping with the spirit of the community. The privacy and comfort of your neighbors must be considered. Whether you run a day care nursery school, a beauty parlor, a dog kennel, a telephone answering service, an employment agency, a secretarial office, or a cooking school—to mention a few of the most popular services —you have to cultivate the disposition of a saint and the diplomacy of an ambassador. These traits must be inherent in your personality to succeed in a service enterprise. Your cheerfulness and common sense must make people like you as well as trust and respect you.

The Personal Touch

Although business cards will be as helpful and inexpensive a means of advertising a "service" as they are in selling merchandise, the personal touch in carefully written and planned mailings will be much more important. These should be written to sound like *you,* and you must invite new customers as you would friends to let you help and serve them. Quality, not quantity, should govern the compilation of the list of people who will receive your letters. Twenty-five, fifty, or a hundred letters directed to the right people can bring worthwhile results. The two letters that follow are examples of letters that attracted the right people at the right time.

Dear

On Tuesday afternoon, April the fifteenth, I hope you will join me and a few of our other neighbors for cake and coffee at three-thirty at a little preview party to celebrate the opening of my Sun Porch Gift Shop, which I hope will turn out to be a blessed event in the lives of all of you when you need to pick up a birthday gift, a bridge prize, an anniversary present, or a "new baby" gift. My shop will be open from ten o'clock in the morning to three o'clock every afternoon.

I will look forward to hearing that you can come on Tuesday.

Sincerely,

RSVP by Phone El 5-0220

The following letter was sent to a list of one hundred members of a community high school PTA to attract a two-generation enrollment in a charm and beauty school.

Dear

The week of June 1st will be good neighbor week at my Community Charm School, which opens officially on Monday, June 18th. You are cordially invited to attend the daily demonstration, which will be held in my studio over the garage every day at three o'clock, and to make an appointment for your free consultation on hair styling and complexion care any day during the following two weeks between four and six o'clock. Kindly phone Mo 7-5550 to let me know what afternoon you will attend the demonstration.

Cordially,

A visit by a housewife interested in starting a day care center in her home to the personnel director connected with a university research center resulted in a hand-picked list of working mothers of preschool children. The typewritten letter was sent to thirty secretaries and laboratory technicians.

Dear

As one of the working mothers in our community who has felt the need for a day care center for your preschool youngster, you will be interested to know that within a ten-minute drive of your office, in my own home, I am undertaking to care for ten two-to-five-year-old children every day from eight in the morning to five-thirty in the afternoon. My nursery school room and play yard are ready to be seen, and I will be happy to meet you any day during the next two weeks after your office hours if you care to phone me in advance for an appointment. My phone number is Ch 7-0302.

Sincerely,

Here is an example of a classified ad for a catering service.

Casserole Kitchen—Main dish and dessert party specialties, including beef stroganoff, deep dish chicken pie, sea food Jambalaya, lemon meringue pie, pistachio ice cream cake, tutti-frutti Bavarian cream pudding. For details and prices phone 267-3685.

Needlework was advertised in a Junior League benefit program as follows:

Decorated Sweaters — Handmade crewel-embroidered or beaded evening sweaters from me to you—no specialty shop markup. Bring me your cashmere or handknit sweaters, and I'll convert them to Paris creations, silk-lined and luxurious. Prices from $25 up, depending on design and lining.

A classified ad for Cheese Cake Supreme was placed in a society weekly.

Cheese Cake Supreme—the best you ever ate, garnished with fresh strawberries or cherries, 9-inch pie serves six for $3. Recipe for this famous cheese cake will be included with each order for $1 extra. Place order 24 hours in advance. Phone Po 8-1954.

Let the Yellow Pages Bring You Customers

A listing in your classified telephone directory, the most obvious and effective selling device known to the public, is often overlooked by the career housewife. It has the advantage of listings by categories of services and products. Be sure you are placed in the right category. If you run a nursery school at home see that you are listed under *Schools, Nursery;* if you cater food from your home, list yourself under *Catering,* not under *Food; Antiques* would be a better category listing than *Furniture* if your specialty is antique furniture. Two listings should sometimes be used so that you might attract two different kinds of customers in closely related categories such as *Dressmaking* and *Tailoring.* The classified telephone directory method has been found so effective by many small businesses that the extra expense in taking display space—five to ten lines instead of one— has paid off.

Dramatizing Your Career

You can't hide your light under a bushel and be a success in a career at home. Even if you're a sensitive, creative genius, there has to be something of P. T. Barnum in you to see that what you make gets into exhibitions, competitions, feature newspaper stories, and on radio and television interviews.

A woman who starts and succeeds in business at home has a big advantage when it comes to free publicity. She has a special spark—initiative and imagination—that makes her interesting. Often there are circumstances in her personal life leading to her career at home that make her story inspiring to others. The way that she combines raising a family with running her business at home attracts women newspaper readers. There is human interest there and a local feature aspect that editors welcome.

If yours is a craft career, your opportunities for attracting customers through publicity are more diverse than in almost any other field. Your objects will be photogenic. A supply of glossy black-and-white prints will be useful in case of requests for reproductions in programs, crafts magazines, or newspapers. Eight by ten-inch glossy photos can be made up from enlarge-ments of photographs you yourself have taken, or a local photographer can help you with your composition and do the photographing for you. Keep all the negatives and reorder as you need pictures. Six are enough to keep on hand at the start. These can also be used as posters when you have an opportunity to be represented in a local store window, at a club, library, or hotel.

State fairs, crafts exhibits, museum shows—any opportunity to display the things you make—are of major importance to your progress. You will have to write for an application and in most cases submit what you would like to place on exhibition if it's your first try. Booths can usually be rented at state and trade fairs.

The Fabulous World of Fashion

Fashion shows are always a popular means of attracting attention if you are a dressmaker, designer, milliner, or fashion accessory specialist.

One young mother of five children had always enjoyed sewing and making her own clothes. She launched a home career as a "designer-seamstress" and decided to do in her own home just what the fashion designers in New York and Paris do about fashion openings. She showed her new designs six weeks in advance of the season, to small groups in her living room, and took orders. The same clothes were booked for fashion shows at banquets and women's clubs. On Friday evenings twice a month her fashions were featured at the town's most glamorous restaurant. In the course of these developments her best friend had joined her to become her manager and to share the burden of detail work that swamped her. Within a year and a half she had become a "couturière" in the most exclusive sense of the word, no longer doing alterations or using commercial patterns.

If your home career provides a service rather than home-manufactured items, this can be dramatized in many ways in the community. For instance, one home beauty shop owner's contribution to a fashion show benefit was setting the fashion models' hair and giving the money to the benefits. Since the models were the town's most attractive women, her work was brought to the attention of excellent prospective customers. Offering permanent waves as door prizes also made her popular.

An imaginative housewife whose home career was decorating

cakes presented the governor of her state with a birthday cake in the shape of the state capitol at a dinner in his honor. This same baker lived in a college town and had a list of the birth dates of each member of the freshman class every year, along with the names and addresses of the parents. A letter two weeks in advance of the birthday offered to deliver a birthday cake to the dormitory and turn over two dollars of the cost to the college baseball team, which raised money to replace uniforms and finance out-of-town games.

At the beginning of each season, an open house for young parents in the community was the way the director of a nursery school brought her project to their attention.

A career-at-home typist just getting started volunteered to help the Junior Chamber of Commerce send out invitations to a convention rally.

These good will gestures not only contribute to worthy causes and dramatize the home career, but they can frequently lead to free newspaper and radio publicity.

Free Publicity—How to Get It

An anniversary celebrating a successful venture is usually newsworthy. Your success story may find a particularly responsive newspaper or magazine editor. A woman who has the enterprise and ability to conduct a business at home successfully while bringing up a family is a very special person, and people want to know more about her.

If you have competed for an award and won, such news is always worthy of publication in your local newspaper.

Knowing how to prepare publicity statements to submit to editors and program directors is helpful. Your name, address, and telephone number should always appear at the top of the story. Your copy (text) should be typed and no longer than one page, presenting essential facts.

The newspaper will rewrite or send a reporter for an interview. If you live in a city with a metropolitan newspaper that is departmentalized, any home career stories should be addressed to the woman's page editor. If you can make an appointment to drop in to see this editor personally, taking your story with you, all the better. The first paragraph of your story should answer the who, what, when, where, and how of what you are doing. Some biographical background about yourself and your family can follow. If you have had some support and encouragement from local leaders or organizations, it will add interest to your story to include that information.

Sample News Releases

The following news release to the society editor of a local paper announces a new home career:

From: Mrs. Erwin Whitney
      125 Jane Street   *For immediate release*
      Woodside, California
      Phone: 722-7346

"Weddings Unlimited," a service that manages all of the details of running a wedding, was announced by Mrs. Erwin Whitney of 125 Jane Street. She will set up her office in her home and see prospective brides by appointment. Mrs. Whitney's service will arrange the entire wedding—including the photography that will accompany the announcement of the engagement, the bridal pictures to be sent to the local press, the ordering and addressing of the wedding invitations, the decorations for the church and reception, the catering of the food, and the travel arrangements for the bridal couple—or she will undertake to supervise the arrangements for any part of the wedding that her clients request. Her fee will depend upon the extent of the services required.

Mrs. Whitney, a past president of the Women's Club and active in the Junior Chamber of Commerce Women's Auxiliary, will provide the only wedding service of its kind in our city. She already has five spring brides in consultation on the arrangements for their weddings. They are: Miss Sally Newton, Miss Marguerite Hinson, Miss Ida Strong, Miss Sandra Shaw, and Miss Helen Jenkins.

Keeping your name before the public through newspaper publicity when your career-at-home activity can supply news or feature interest will continue to be important long after your first announcement. The following is the release for a story that was sent to newspapers in the state of Washington when Mrs. Ann Mesdag, owner and operator of a dog kennel that specializes in raising German shepherds, was chosen as a career-at-home housewife for the series featured in *Family Circle.*

From: Ann Mesdag
      Van Nassau Kennels
      22131 31st Avenue   *For immediate release*
      Bothell, Washington
      Hunter 6-0211

When Ann Mesdag, her husband Matthias, and their eight children moved from Seattle to a country home in Bothell two years ago, the whole family pitched in to construct a real kennel—complete with nine runs, a fiberglass shed, and twenty rooms that sleep two dogs each. Labor has never been a problem as the Mesdag children clean up the kennel and feed the dogs every day.

"Before a kennel can succeed in making a profit," Ann says in an article in the current issue of *Family Circle* magazine, "years have to be invested in establishing top bloodlines. In the early days any money I made went into acquiring and producing fine dogs. During the first seven years of operation, my kennel produced twelve American and Canadian champions—and I didn't make a dime."

Now, ten years later, Ann has owned or bred close to 100 champions, and she nets between $10,000 and $12,000 a year.

Ann and Matthias Mesdag were both Dutch prisoners of war in Indonesia during World War II. After the war Ann and Matthias met, married, and decided to come to America, originally settling in Seattle. Their early days in America were a struggle, and both worked while Matthias learned English and attended night classes at the University of Washington. Matthias is now a sales supervisor for the Boeing Aircraft Company.

Ann and her family are grateful for the good fortune they have enjoyed since coming to this country seventeen years ago. "America to us is the symbol of everything that's good in life," Ann says in the magazine article. "We love the air we breathe and the space and the freedom—where we can raise children and dogs to our hearts' content."

5 Methods of Selling

"One for the money, two for the show, three to get ready and four to go." We all grew up with those words ringing in our ears as we set off to win a race. Making a success of a career at home is very much like running a race. You mustn't use up all your steam and reserves in the initial sprint.

What you make or the service you perform will determine your selling techniques. You may have to experiment with a number of methods before you find the one—or the combination of methods—that produces the best results.

Your Home as Your Showroom

You can make an asset of having your business at home if the things you make or sell can be dramatized by your home background. For instance, if you make decorative window shades, demonstrating them on your own windows will help to show your customers a variety of styles before they place their orders. Or if you make hooked rugs, needlepoint covers, picture and mirror frames—anything pertaining to the decoration of a home —your displays against a home background will be to your advantage. A letter from a customer who bought gift aprons from an at-home career housewife says:

"She inspires and amazes everyone who sees her aprons. Her display room is in a front bedroom, where aprons from tiny bibs to men's barbecue aprons are hanging. The racks and closet are bulging. She has open house around the middle of November to show her aprons and sells them sometimes by the dozen to a single customer. She serves refreshments and welcomes those who are just looking as well as those who come to buy."

Selling from Your Workshop

For those of you dealing in arts and crafts with workshops in basements, garages, or attics, the workshop can be an added attraction. Shelves can be installed to display your handiwork; needlework can be hung on the walls; and stencilled or hand-painted furniture can be attractively arranged. The setting of a workshop is perfect for two or three special events a year to which you can invite the public to an exhibition of your work. And if you are a dressmaker or have a franchise to sell ready-to-wear fashions or items for interior decoration, such as wall papers and fabrics, your workshop will serve to dramatize your activity.

Classes Bring in Customers

Many women have made their start by giving classes in their homes. Frequently, if they sell the materials used in the craft, no charge is made for the instruction. This is particularly effective when the materials can be packaged as learning kits. You will have an opportunity to display the range and variety of your work, which will also be on sale. As a skilled worker in a particular craft, you can also take orders on your own creations, and this exposure will help to spread the word about you.

The Shop within the Home

The shop within the home is frequently a gift shop, a crafts shop, a flower shop, or an accessory boutique. These are similar in money management and financing to other types of home career procedures except for the possible need of a cash register or sales slips for individual cash transactions. You will have to keep a certain amount of cash on hand to make change, and you will have to balance your accounts at the end of each day instead of by the week or the month, which is customary when you make items in quantity to fill orders for outside stores.

The licensing and zoning requirements you have already read about may be a significant factor, depending on your community. Outside signs, the use of windows for display in a residential area, and facilities for parking that won't inconvenience your neighbors must be worked out with tact and taste. Your neighbors' good will can be a big help in bringing patronage to your shop. Many home gift shops begin by receiving customers by appointment during two or three hours of the day. Initially their business is built on selling prizes and favors for benefits, gifts for bridal showers and baby showers, and favors for parties. Arrangements can often be made with manufacturers to stock small amounts of merchandise on consignment. This eliminates the need for immediate outside financing. The record of your weekly sales will be your guide to the amount of stock you will need to keep on hand and what storage facilities you will have to provide. As one earns, one learns which price lines sell, which items have special appeal, and the quantities that should be stocked.

The equipment needed for a shop within the home will depend upon the merchandise sold. With small items such as jewelry, a display counter with a transparent glass top is a necessity. For small antiques and china, second-hand cupboards with glass doors can be converted into attractive display cabinets. Many at-home shops acquire a special appeal by not looking too commercial, retaining the hospitality of a home by providing chairs for customers to sit down while making their selections. A paintbrush, some pieces of second-hand furniture, and a flair for color can convert a room into a "personality shop" on a shoestring budget. One woman in a small town in Pennsylvania created The Sun Porch Gift Shop, which specializes in jewelry and wedding gifts. She has acquired a reputation for miles around for always having the gift that is needed on the spur of the moment or for being available as a personal shopping service for wedding presents.

The manufacturer's representative and franchise type of home selling operations are based upon demonstrations and sample selling. Kitchenware party selling is familiar in many communities throughout the country. Ready-to-wear clothing sold on this basis is becoming more widespread. The only special requirements for this type of selling are storage facilities for the samples and a home background spacious and attractive enough to accommodate the public who come to view the merchandise or attend a demonstration party. The woman taking the orders is paid a commission on the sales she makes. Acquiring a franchise for selling nationally advertised products or services involves a substantial initial investment. This is discussed in detail later in the chapter entitled "Professional Know-How."

How Agents Give You Distribution

"I used to get tongue-tied when I had to make a sales pitch,

and I was all thumbs when I had to dangle my jeweled ornaments in front of a busy buyer's eyes. My boxes and wrappings
messed up his office. He was so distracted by his phone and by
people rushing in and out that I couldn't make a getaway fast
enough—and without an order!"

In spite of her timidity this career housewife has been selling
her Christmas tree ornaments by the gross without having a face-
to-face selling session with anyone. The key to her success is an
agent who took her line of Christmas tree ornaments on the
road in July, saw department store buyers from New York to
California, and received a commission of eight percent on every
order delivered.

The ornaments had novelty: they were prism-like, paved with
tiny plastic mirrors on hanging balls, unique in the market. And
the price was right. In addition to the personal calls on buyers,
her agent also had displays at the major gift shows in New York,
Dallas, and San Francisco, which are attended by regional buyers in search of "exclusives" on novelty Christmas items.

An agent represents a number of clients who produce closely
related items within an established territory that he covers regularly. He normally expects exclusive rights to the sale of your
product in this area. Such a representative may give you better
access to the trade through his connections with customers of
his other lines or through his special standing with particular
customers because of long-established relationships. He is able
to carry on the personal selling that you would otherwise have
to do yourself.

An agent solicits orders for you on a commission basis; you
ship and bill the purchaser directly, thus retaining control over
prices, terms, credit, and other conditions of sale. However, an
agent will give you the benefit of advice and assistance on these
matters.

According to the Small Business Administration, the average
commission for manufacturers' agents from all kinds of businesses
is approximately six percent of net sales, after shipping costs and
all returns and allowances have been deducted. The commission
might be higher if your product is new and unknown and requires extra effort by the agent to build up demand.

In selecting your agent, you should acquire as much knowledge as you can about his background and the sales outlets in
which he specializes. Get a list of the other products he repre-

sents and find out whether he sells to wholesalers or retailers. An agent is in business to make money, and unless you can produce in sufficient volume to bring him a profit, he will not be interested in taking you on as a client. If you can produce ornaments, gift items, or toys by the gross, or more expensive items such as aprons, dresses, or jewelry by the dozens, with a prospect of increasing production as orders come in, an agent is for you. What he is looking for is a continuing relationship with you over a period of years, and he must believe in the growth potential of your business.

The first step is to find an agent who handles your type of product. The trade associations listed in Part III will guide you.

After establishing that one or more agents you have investigated handle your type of item and deal with the wholesale or retail markets to which you hope to sell, arrange a personal interview and exchange references. There must be confidence and trust between you. You should have a comprehensive written contract with your agent. The major benefit of such a contract is not primarily to bind you irrevocably together. Such contracts normally have termination clauses, and many techniques can be applied to free either party from such an agreement. The major benefit is that it will create agreement about numerous policies and procedures. A model agent contract to serve as a guide is available to you through Manufacturers Agents National Association, 626 North Garfield Avenue, Alhambra, California 91802, care of A. X. Schilling, Executive Secretary. This organization can also direct you to the trade association that can give you a list of agents in your area.

Mail Order Selling on Your Own

The biggest market for careers-at-home items is mail order selling. This applies to craft items, do-it-yourself kits, novelty and hobby articles, and convenience manufactured goods bought at wholesale and resold through catalogs.

The whole operation can be handled personally from your home, beginning with the original design of a needlework pattern, for instance, through the step-by-step process of assembling and packaging a kit, writing the catalog and having it printed, and writing the advertising copy that will appear in specialized crafts publications. Later in this book you will read about Jan Carter and Joan Moshimer, both of whom have found their largest outlet through the sale of kits by mail order. Each had perfected her skill through class work in museum and YWCA workshops, and each had subsequently taught in these workshops. Early in their projects both had set goals to develop mail order businesses, which they had analyzed during the period in which they were learning their trades. Their studies included collecting every mail order catalog and crafts magazine they could find that dealt with their fields, filling in coupons, and receiving similar merchandise in order to see how their competition was packaging and delivering kits.

Jan Carter is the originator of "Stitchendipity," the patterns that are "Quick to Stitch." The name and trademark were copyrighted by Mrs. Carter and went on every label attached to a kit. A twenty-four-page catalog was prepared to sell her designs and kits. The five- by eight-inch catalog had an order blank on the back cover. Photographs and captions described the designs—printed on linen to become embroidered pictures for framing or as ornaments for bags, belts, bed headboards, dirndl skirts, and aprons. These designs were priced from $1 to $50, including the materials. Some were assembled in kits, and others only included the printed linen, with wool to be purchased separately. Getting these catalogs into the hands of women who did crewel embroidery meant widening her market far beyond Austin, Texas, where she lived. She had to have a national market, so she decided to advertise in a national needlework magazine, taking a fifty-line, two-column advertisement, which at that time cost her several hundred dollars. "Always plan to use more than one ad," says Jan, "because women needleworkers are constant readers of these magazines, and they get used to seeing your name. Coupon orders for my catalogs came in twice as fast on the second and third ads as they did on the first." Her catalog was offered for sale at $1, a price that paid only the cost of its production since it was designed to bring in the orders for her kits and designs.

To finance the printing of the catalog Jan had to find credit. She did not go to a bank. She went to a photographer and a printer who believed in her and were reassured by the advertisement that she was prepared to place in the magazine. The art and printing costs were taken care of by the sale of the catalog, and the resulting sale of her designs has brought her business that's making a good profit now, two years later.

IT'S WHAT'S NEW IN NEEDLEWORK FROM

Stitchendipity ™·
Contemporary Creative Stitchery Kits

Stitchendipity ™
P. O. Box 3113
Austin, Texas 78704

NAME ———————————————————————— ZIP ——

ADDRESS ————————————— STATE ——————

CITY ————————————————————————————

CATALOG NO.	HOW MANY	NAME OF ITEM — DESCRIPTION	PRICE EACH	TOTAL PRICE
			SHIPPING	
			TOTAL	

Add the following for
shipping, insurance,
and postage:

Up to $4.99—add 45¢
$5.00 to $9.99—add 75¢
$10.00 to $14.99—add $1.00
$15.00 to $24.99—add $1.25
Over $25.00—add $1.50

Texas residents please add
3% sales tax.
Austin residents add 4% tax.
Satisfaction guaranteed or
your money back.

Add 50¢ and we'll send a friend a catalog.

NAME ———————————— CITY ——————— STATE ——— ZIP ——

ADDRESS ——————————————————

Mail Order Selling on Your Own. Stitchendipity sells a 24-page catalog for fifty cents, with illustrations of needlework patterns and kits, to support a mail order business. Included in the catalog is a full-page order form. Above is shown the cover of the catalog, by Jan Carter. At left is the order blank included on the back inside cover.

No profit is made on the sale of the Stitchendipity catalog, but the advertisement in a national needlework magazine brings in enough coupon orders to pay for the catalog and build a customer following. Merryland Acres *(below)* uses a four-page leaflet and a mailing list to attract mail orders.

Joan Moshimer's mail order catalog had a similar history except that Joan made all the drawings and wrote the descriptions for the 196-page spiral-bound catalog in India ink script herself. It took her six months of concentrated work every evening, but when she finished, she had an impressive and beautiful book that sold for $2, also a nonprofit price. The money she had been saving from teaching and making individual custom designs paid for the first printing.

Outside Mail Order Selling

Individual items can be presented for sale to mail order houses on an exclusive basis, volume quantity being guaranteed and shipped to the mail order warehouse where such orders are filled. The market for quality crafts is limited in this type of selling, but novelty items that can be supplied in quantity, toys in particular, often sell profitably with this kind of promotion.

The Mail Order Association of America, 612 North Michigan Avenue, Chicago, Illinois 60611, will direct you to the catalogs that feature items in your field and price lines.

The Mail Order Shopping Guide, by Elizabeth Squire, published by William Morrow & Co., Inc., 6 Henderson Drive, West Caldwell, New Jersey 07006, lists mail order catalogs and sources of merchandise designed for mail order sale. The guide sells for $1.95.

Time Out to Sell Yourself on the Road

If you can get away from home three or four times a year for a week or two, selling on your own would be profitable and invaluably educational. These breaks in domestic routine can also be welcome refreshers in the excitement and stimulation of meeting new people and being exposed to new ideas. The rounds of old customers must be made also to keep enthusiasm for your product alive. The time for these expeditions into the marketplace should coordinate with trade fairs, state fairs, and exhibitions. Arrangements for exhibits and demonstrations must be made in advance.

Though not all items made in the home will be seasonal, it is important to arrange appointments with store buyers for those that are—at least six to eight months ahead of the season. If you can arrange a trip to a trade fair once a year (this applies especially to makers of gifts, toys, food, home furnishings, and fashion accessories) , you should attend to see what is going on and to meet store buyers and manufacturers. A listing of trade fairs related to careers at home appears in Part III. A letter of inquiry to the publicity department of the trade association handling the fair will supply the exact dates. Three of the most famous are:

The Chicago Merchandise Mart, a year-round colossus of thousands of trade exhibits. Special events are scheduled every month of the year.

The New York Toy Fair draws store buyers from all over the country in March, when Christmas business is booked. A whole building is devoted to toys at 200 Fifth Avenue. The publicity director of the Toy Information Bureau at that address will provide dates and other information about the toy industry.

The gift industry has an entire building with manufacturers' showrooms at 225 Fifth Avenue, New York City. Twice-a-year gift trade events bring out-of-town buyers to New York. (See Part III for trade show listings.)

6 Ideas and Inventions

Two words transformed a soda fountain drink into a financial empire. The two words were not a slogan that could be trademarked, such as "It's smart to be thrifty"; they did not include a patentable device, and they had nothing to do with the product—its taste, its ingredients, its benefits. The two words were "bottle it."

The idea and the timing produced the results. Being first and being fast with an idea so that you can outdistance your competition is the secret of success whether or not you own a patent, a copyright, or a trademark.

Ideas are like germs—they get around and are communicated simultaneously in ways that are often telepathic, often mysterious, but much more often obvious. Like all creative people, idea people fall in love with their own ideas, and the inexperienced likewise become enchanted with the sound of their own voices talking about their ideas. The "brain pickers" often cash in. The great majority of ideas and inventions can be neither copyrighted nor patented. Those that can be protected by copyrights, trademarks, or patents should be, and those that cannot be protected legally can be protected only by promises and good faith.

C. Howard Mann, an invention management consultant with the Institute of American Inventors, maintains, "One of the most important factors in successful business competition is originality in meeting customers' needs and wants. A new application, a new approach, or a whole new concept very often is necessary. Fortunately for the businessman, new ideas are circulating around the business world all the time. Both businessmen and idea men have certain rights, and both should have certain kinds of protection."

To paraphrase two copybook maxims that say what these wise and experienced men have said: "Discretion is the better part of invention; don't bandy your ideas around; an ounce of protection is worth a ton of pirating." Get your applications for patents, trademarks, and copyrights started, use the "Pat. Pend." and "TM Pend." when you set out to market your idea. But even before clearing your applications, move quickly so that someone else does not beat you to the punch.

What Is a Patentable Invention or Device?

Here is the definition of a patentable device, according to the U. S. Department of Commerce Patent Office:

> The discovery of any new and useful process, machine, or composition of matter, or any new and useful improvement thereof, or any distinct and new variety of plant other than tuber-propagated plant, which is asexually reproduced or any new, original, and ornamental design for an article of manufacture.

This wording is more than a bit baffling to the average career housewife, which is why the services of a patent attorney are recommended to establish whether your invention is a "thing," an object, a process, or a "new variety of plant" that introduces something unique—the product of your own inventive mind.

Some years ago a woman named Merry Hull produced an invention in the construction of gloves that revolutionized the industry. She called it "the finger-free glove" because her glove was constructed to give a third dimension to the way in which gloves fit the fingers by inserting a separate panel on either side of the fingers. After obtaining the patent, she had the right to license one or more manufacturers to use her method of glove construction and to receive a royalty fee on every pair of gloves sold that featured that construction for the next seventeen years. When the patent ran out, she was able to improve the design and to extend the patent for another few years. In this case a patent was essential to her success and resulted in long-range profits and protection.

However, this same designer conceived an idea that seemed to her equally patentable, but it turned out to be so easily altered and copied that she was the victim of almost overnight pirating by her competition. Her second idea was for a line of "Merry Mite Clothes" for children, which incorporated an expandable feature that would enlarge the clothes to double their usability. Her substantial investment in launching these clothes did not prevent competing manufacturers from horning in and profiting from her invention.

A very recent invention by a woman who had previously been on the welfare rolls is in the Horatio Alger tradition and demonstrates that the old precepts of faith, determination, and fortitude can pay off if you stay with your idea.

The woman who invented the "M. D. Inflatable Bedpan" went to the Small Business Administration branch office on the West Coast to make a last ditch appeal for financial and business know-how in getting her invention on the market. It was designed for orthopedic cases, burn victims, surgery patients, and the obese. After the management assistance officer talked with her, she was counseled by two experienced businessmen, retired from their executive duties and serving the Small Business Administration (SBA) on a voluntary basis through its subsidiary organization known as SCORE (Service Corps of Retired Executives). Together they worked long and hard with an SBA officer to secure a $5,500 loan to produce the first fifty-five units. During this period she was able to apply for a patent, which she now holds. The filing fee for the patent was $65 plus the additional charges for drawings and specifications and the final issue fee of $100, all of which came out of the SBA loan.

When the manufacturer and the distributor saw the fine product she had invented, a substantial sum was advanced to her for the rights to manufacture and sell her invention. The SBA loan was paid off, and a new contract was drawn up to pay royalties on each unit sold. The surgeon general's office also accepted the product for use in some military hospitals.

More typical is the case of the woman who invented a children's toy with a patentable feature and a trademark name. The item was a stuffed animal with a zipper on its underside, which opened to produce a baby replica. This was to be one of a line of stuffed animals identified by the trademark Zip Zoo. The locking device of the zipper made it eligible for patenting. The procedure she followed, described below, will serve as a step-by-step description for all patent applicants.

The First Step After an Idea Is Born

Before consulting a patent attorney Mrs. Zip Zoo made up a model of her toy, kept a paper pattern, and described the idea and the construction in detail. The physical model is not a requirement of the patent office, but eventually mechanical drawings and specifications have to be made. A model is inevitably a part of the procedure and can clarify the concept for the attorney who will make the patent search prior to filing the application. The written description is made in duplicate so that one copy can be registered and mailed back to the inventor with the postmarked date, to keep on file. This does not constitute legal protection, but it might support a claim whether or not a patent is granted. Another type of contract instead of a patent might be made with a manufacturer, for instance, and then not honored. Such a description is also valuable to the patent attorney. If the patent is to be made for a cosmetic or food product or for a process, formulas and descriptions have to be similarly prepared.

How to Find a Patent Attorney

The Zip Zoo lady inventor did not have the slightest idea of how to locate a patent attorney, and she was going to file an application form without one. However, the Patent Office in Washington, D.C., advised her to employ an attorney or agent who was registered in the Patent Office. A government pamphlet entitled *Roster of Attorneys and Agents Registered to Practice before the U.S. Patent Office* was sent to her for $1, along with two other pamphlets she had ordered from the Superintendent of Documents, Washington, D.C. 20402 entitled *General Information Concerning Patents* (cost 30 cents) and *Patents and Inventions, an Information Aid for Inventors* (cost 15 cents).

The Patent Search

Before filing her application her attorney had to make a patent search in the Search Room of the Patent Office in Arlington, Virginia, to determine whether Zip Zoo was indeed a patentable toy and its name eligible for trademark.

Legal work on Zip Zoo started in October, and the patent and trademark were issued in June of the following year. However, the Patent Office says two and a half years must ordinarily be allowed. In a very few special circumstances a small business owner requiring a patent before starting a manufacturing program can ask for special consideration if he is willing to swear under oath that sufficient capital and facilities are available for the manufacturer to begin production in quantity. Zip Zoo was a comparatively simple patent to search, and the legal costs amounted to $358.99, low in comparison to patents for complicated machinery. Whether simple or complicated, the law stipulates that a period of six months must elapse between the time a patent application is made and issued.

While the Zip Zoo inventor was waiting for the patent, she began to search for manufacturers who might be able to make her toy in time for the Christmas trade the following year. A "Pat. Pending" was put on her models, and she showed it to two manufacturers, who turned her down. A third manufacturer asked to borrow her models to have his factory designer examine them for a mass production assessment. The report revealed that the baby stuffed animal was too skinny to have the cuddly appeal that such toys must have to sell, but the idea had sufficient appeal to warrant experimentation with different materials. A new material that did not require stuffing but was soft and cuddly on the outside, leaving room in the middle for a plump little baby animal was to have been substituted. But as of this writing the toy has yet to go into production.

How Long Does a Patent Provide Protection?

Seventeen years from the date of issue is the time limit for patents except for those on ornamental designs, which are granted for terms of three and a half, seven, and fourteen years. These periods can be extended only by a special act of Congress, which occurs only in the most exceptional circumstances. After a patent has expired, the invention is in the public domain and may be used and sold by anyone.

The Difference Between a Trademark and a Copyright

Trademarks are registered by the Commissioner of Patents, Department of Commerce. Copyrights are registered by the Copyright Office, Library of Congress. Both offices are located in Washington, D.C. The trademark application is made by companies that distinguish by name or symbol a product used in commerce subject to regulation by Congress. They can be registered for a period of twenty years and renewed for additional periods of twenty years. Copyrights protect authors, composers, and artists from the pirating of their literary and artistic work. Copyrights are effective for twenty-eight years and may be renewed for the same period of time. Applications for either will be sent to you by writing to the Department of Commerce or the Library of Congress, depending on whether you are applying for a trademark or a copyright. Legal advice is not necessary in making such an application.

When There Is No Legal Protection

The lack of legal protection is the dilemma that confronts everyone with an exciting idea. Some large companies have specialists whose main job is dealing with new ideas. Research and development firms have sprung up independently around the country in order to scout ideas that are marketable. If these companies believe in your idea, they will act as your financial backers to the extent that they will market test your product, make up models, recommend improvements, apply for patents or trademarks, and find a manufacturer to launch your product. Finding the right research and development company is like finding a needle in a haystack. Trade associations can be helpful, and your local Chamber of Commerce can give you guidance. Before you reveal the invention or idea that you *have not* patented or that cannot be patented, there are precautions you can take that will be the equivalent of a contract in case your idea is ultimately sold to a manufacturer. In collaboration with the Small Business Administration in Washington, this is the procedure that we recommend.

When the businessman agrees to review your invention or idea he will sign the following *Agreement to Review Idea,* which constitutes a contract.

John Doe Co.
112 Fourth Street
Anytown, U.S.A.

Gentlemen:

I have developed a new idea for the packaging of your product, which I believe would greatly increase your sales and profits. The new method of packaging would not raise production costs.

If you are interested in details of the idea, I shall be glad to forward you complete information if you will kindly sign the enclosed agreement form. Promptly upon receipt of the signed form, I shall forward to you all the information I have regarding the idea.

Sincerely,
Robert Roe

Agreement to Review Idea

We, the undersigned, agree to receive in confidence full details about an idea for product packaging to be submitted for our consideration by Robert Roe.

It is further understood that we assume no responsibility whatever with respect to features that can be demonstrated to be already known to us. We also agree not to divulge any details of the idea submitted without permission of Robert Roe or to make use of any feature or information of which the said Robert Roe is the originator, without payment of compensation to be fixed by negotiation with the said Robert Roe or his lawful representative.

It is specifically understood that, in receiving the idea of Robert Roe, the idea is being received and will be reviewed in confidence and that, within a period of 30 days, we will report to said Robert Roe the results of our findings and will advise whether or not we are interested in negotiating for the purchase of the right to use said idea.

Company _____

Street and Number _____

City _____ State _____ Zip Code _____

Official to receive disclosures (please type)

_____ Title _____

Date _____ Signature _____

Accepted: _____
Robert Roe, Inventor

The above agreement should be prepared in duplicate so that when both copies have been signed, the businessman will have one and the inventor, the other. The acceptance of these conditions by the signing of the agreement constitutes a "meeting of minds," and once that has been accomplished, a contract has been established. The businessman is bound not to divulge any features without proper compensation to the inventor. Likewise, the businessman is protected against any unwarranted claim.

Trust and Lady Luck

It is only common sense to say that hard and fast protection rules cannot be made and that confronting a business executive with a contract in hand will be a "thanks but no thanks" gambit unless you soften him up a little first in order to get him to sign the agreement. Even patents and copyrights are challenged, and the patent owner frequently must file suit of an infringement in a federal court. You have to use judgment, make an intelligent appraisal of the integrity of the company you are approaching, and demonstrate that you are amenable to suggestions and changes with some written assurance that you will be protected. Some businessmen protect themselves by setting up special methods of handling ideas. Frequently they are channeled to one individual, making it impossible for the information contained in that idea to become accessible to employees at large. By doing this it can be proved more easily in court that the ideas have not been used or permitted to escape.

Do Your Own Thing

If you can manage it financially, it would be to your advantage first to produce your own product and to market it locally or regionally. This is particularly true of food products, which can attract the interest of large companies or distributors, who may then want to buy into your business, as was the case of a product known as "Dilly Beans." Dilly Beans were originated by two school teachers who started by making them in the bathtub of the apartment they shared. The process involved pickling raw snap beans in dill brine, and bottling, labeling, and selling them through local gourmet food shops at first. Clever young women, they knew the value of publicity and brought their product to national attention through feature stories in newspapers and national women's magazines. The popularity of their product on a small production scale plus the attention the publicity attracted brought about their partnership with big business, which put their product on a basis of national distribution. However, before big business bought them out, they had long since transferred from the bathtub of the first few months to factory-type production.

The story of the woman who started the Butternut Farm products detailed in Part II provides a good example of a food product that could not be patented but was protected by having the field to itself for several years before competition rushed in. The process that put Butternut Farm on its feet was a bottled hollandaise sauce that would stay fresh. An effort to patent the process had failed because the recipe for hollandaise sauce is basic—using butter, yolks of eggs, and lemon juice—and the special ingredient that preserved theirs wasn't original enough to warrant a patent. Protection depended upon being first and making a product superior enough in flavor to keep customers reordering. The same company developed a name for another sauce that could be trademarked "Broccalaise," a combination of Hollandaise and a mustard flavoring with a special affinity for vegetables in the broccoli family. Name identity becomes very important in the success of a food product.

The Race with Time

"Housewife Hits the Jackpot," recorded later in this book, tells the story of Harriet Nelson, who did not try to patent or trademark an invention that earned her $25,000 in the second year it was on the market. Luck was on her side. Being a mother, she had worked with an item familiar in every American home where there are growing boys—the sleeping bag. She had adapted the sleeping bag to the shape of an alligator and named it "Slumberchum." Harriet Nelson took her invention personally to the president of a toy company. The president saw possibilities in the item, made an agreement similar to the one we've already described, market tested the item, sold it to department stores, and found mail order acceptance for it in the catalog of America's largest mail order company.

Less than a week after the acceptance of the Slumberchum another idea person, a man with a much more professional approach, presented an idea almost identical to Harriet Nelson's. He had been working on his model for two years. He had not found it patentable, but he knew it was marketable. He lost the race with that particular company. It was impossible for these two idea people to have copied each other; it was a clear case of the simultaneous idea with the advantage of time on the side of the product that went on the assembly line first. There was nothing to prevent him from taking his model to other manufacturers, which he probably did.

If the inventor of a product can collaborate with a manufacturer on a royalty basis, this is often a short cut to success if the product "clicks." It's worth trying. It's also worth trying to make it on your own if you can't find a manufacturer. The branch offices of the Small Business Administration are always there to help with counseling and sometimes with financing.

Ideas and inventions, like babies, are easier to conceive than to deliver.

7 Professional "Know-How"

If you were asked to name the ten most popular home study courses taken by women to prepare themselves to supplement the family income, what would you answer? The results of a survey made for this book by the National Home Study Council included some surprises along with some of the expected answers.

The Ten Most Popular Home Study Courses

A course on "Interviewing," for instance, has made interviewing a full-fledged career at home. Interviewers are needed by market research firms to gather information from housewives concerning products that are used in the home. Manufacturers are constantly trying to improve their products, to create new products, and to test how existing products are satisfying needs and competing with similar products in price, efficiency, and sales appeal. This type of research is also widely used by newspapers, magazines, radio, and television to get the reaction of the public to editorial features, advertising messages, programs, and commercials. Public opinion polls and the U.S. Census regional offices also make extensive use of the personal interviewer. Such interviews are conducted over the telephone or by personal door-to-door visits.

In order to get an accurate cross section of public reaction, market researching has become a science of measurement that must take into consideration different income and occupational groups, geographical areas, and levels of educational background. Some interviewers are instructed by the companies, and

others have taken short courses of preliminary training in how
to approach a subject, how to ask questions, and how to record
the answers specifically enough to give the analyst the information required. The courses are short, consisting of about
twenty lessons, and the cost is reasonable, usually under $100.
A guide to opportunities in professional interviewing, which
lists the companies using interviewers, is provided as a part of
the course. (Most of the major users of market research interviewers for commercial products are in the New York City and
Chicago areas.) Public opinion polls, newspapers, magazines,
radio, and television involve all areas of the country. Interviewers are paid by the hour plus their expenses, the hourly
rates ranging from $1.60 to $2.50. Many companies take new
interviewers to their headquarters for special briefing on the
company's policies before sending their new employees out to
begin interviewing schedules.

Another comparatively new home career for women, second
on the list, involves accounting and income tax work, for which
the National Tax Training School supplies home study instruction. A housewife in Pedro, Ohio, reported that she earned over
$1,000 by working at home a few hours a day during the first
year of income tax work. The pay for this work averages a much
higher rate than interviewing—between $7 and $8 an hour—
since the training and educational background necessary are so
much more demanding. There are many sources of training
other than home study courses available to women who can get
away from home to attend business schools or adult education
courses. Home study courses at moderate expense are available
and give certification for various types of accounting.

The training for income tax work offers year-round home
employment to women as bookkeepers for small businesses. If
this skill is combined with a proficiency in typing, a steady flow
of part-time work can usually be counted on in urban and
manufacturing centers.

Third on the list of most popular home study courses among
women was the study of dollmaking and repair, but it cannot
compare to the others as an income producer. Doll collecting is
the third most popular hobby in the country. There is even a
National Institute of American Doll Artists, so it is not surpris-
ing that so many women want to extend the hobby of doll
collecting to dollmaking and repair.

Fourth and fifth on the list of most popular home study

courses are interior decoration and combined dressmaking and millinery instruction. Art instruction, jewelrymaking, real estate sales, and writing are almost equal in popularity to those previously mentioned. Courses that are not as convenient for home study but are generally available outside of the home in all communities for more professional instruction include the crafts workshops and classes in cooking, cake decorating, and hair dressing. An extensive guide to training in the arts and crafts in each state appears in Part III of this book. The National Home Study Council, 1601 18th Street, N.W., Washington, D. C. 20009, will provide a free list of home study courses available. This Council was founded some years ago by a group of educators after the report of the Carnegie Foundation and the National Better Business Bureau recommended a review of all instructional materials offered to determine whether they meet the standards for accreditation.

Training, Training Everywhere

Like diamonds in Africa, opportunities for professional training in dozens of skills that can be made to pay off at home are scattered all over the country. But unlike diamonds, which are restricted to the minority, instruction is available to every woman with aptitude, initiative, and time. Some of the training is available free of charge through government programs or at nominal cost through organizations such as the YWCA, art associations and alliances, university extension courses, and museums. The YWCAs located throughout the country have inexpensive courses in sewing, cooking, cake decorating, needlework, and crafts. For example, an eight-weeks course in advanced tailoring can be studied for as little as $12.

A woman from Sudbury, Massachusetts, learned the stained glass craft at her local art alliance and said, "This is indeed a commercial product that I now produce. From one year's earnings of $4,800 only $390 went for the material required. I personally have had no formal artistic training, but I have always been interested in arts and crafts as hobbies. I took this course through the local art association and soon tried selling on a consignment basis. It proved a popular item, and soon I found it easier to sell wholesale with cash on delivery than on consignment to small shops. Equipment is not costly. The tools I needed for class lessons cost about $10 or less."

Museum and university courses offer credits toward college degrees in the arts and often work in cooperation with each other in providing the art or craft training necessary. Many have evening courses, but full-term registration is required. The cost of such courses varies, for example, from $65 in one museum for fifteen sessions to $250 for a five-classes-a-week schedule. The college degree earned gives the student the additional advantage of being qualified to teach professionally.

Our Government as Talent Scout

Opportunities for more professional know-how are available through four departments of the U. S. Government: the Small Business Administration, the Department of Agriculture, the Department of Commerce, and the Department of Labor. Much of the training and many of the workshops are directed to women who have the necessary skills but need guidance in selling. Craft marketing cooperatives through the Farmer Cooperative Service of the Department of Agriculture have brought a rich cultural heritage in the crafts to other parts of the country.

The Cumberland Mountain Craft Association, located at Holiday Hills, Tennessee, is an example of how hundreds of Cumberland residents have gained a better living by selling their home-produced crafts. Until the women workers joined together in a cooperative, they were not able to make money. Now the cooperative handles over a thousand items and attracts buyers from stores and shopping centers all over the country.

The Freedom Quilting Bee, a group of eighty-five rural women in Wilcox County, Alabama, became a part of the Southern Cooperative Development Program. With the help of an industrial consultant provided by the government, they were able to sell $20,000 worth of quilted items to department stores and shops in other parts of the country.

The Mountain Artisans in West Virginia had a similar grant from the Office of Economic Opportunity to help market the craft products in stitchery in West Virginia. This government agency provides loans and grants throughout the country and occasionally helps in providing specialists who will advise on the most saleable items. The best place for crafts workers in rural areas to find out about cooperative programs is to start with the county, regional, or state extension specialists of the Department of Agriculture.

How to Make a Craft Marketable

The following list of suggestions for attracting attention to and promoting the sale of a product was prepared in cooperation with Mr. Sydney Selengut, marketing consultant to the government and industry in the crafts field.

(1) Personalize what you make by signing it or attaching a tag with your name and the words "Original by" in order to classify it as a unique work of art.

(2) Contrast the colors and textures of fabrics used rather than just using up leftovers at home. Remnants of fabrics can be bought inexpensively, and the use of velvet, satin, and woven designs brings a much higher price.

(3) Variety in size and shape give a design increased sales appeal. A doll can be executed as a pillow, a pin cushion, or a hanging ornament for a Christmas tree, for example. The same doll can be miniature or life-size and can be made as part of a family.

(4) Adapt patchwork designs, for instance, to a variety of items such as table covers, clothing, and toys, using standard commercial patterns for the seamstress part of the project.

(5) Clip pictures from magazines, catalogs, and advertisements for ideas and subscribe to trade magazines.

(6) Show your work to store buyers and suggest creating ensembles of accessory items for kitchens, bathrooms, and closets. Or try grouping related fashions such as bags and belts.

(7) Shopping columns in specialty magazines and newspapers like to receive samples of crafts with price information and often give free publicity, which can result in orders.

(8) Packaging distinctiveness helps, giving the flavor of the region or the craft to your product.

(9) When orders start to come in and you need help to fill them, create a group or cooperative so that you can increase your production to a volume that will increase your profits and allow others who share your skill to make some money too.

Business Management Workshops

Many housewives with talent in making things that sell or in performing services that are in demand are lost when it comes to knowing how to manage their money so that they can make a profit. They need help in knowing how to keep a system of records after they have grown from a "pin money" business to a more profitable business operation. Many don't know what is meant by the "break even" point in their sales or how to price their services.

The Small Business Administration offers help to such women at its more than two hundred counseling chapters. (See list in Part III.) Learning workshops for newcomers to individually owned businesses are conducted by a corps of retired executives who contribute their services in an advisory capacity (SCORE). These counselors include retired retailers, production analysts, office managers, lawyers, engineers, accountants, economists, bankers, advertising and public relations men, sales managers, wholesalers, comptrollers, plant managers, scientists, and former owners of small businesses of every description. There are counselors especially qualified to give advice on fashion, beauty, food, and other related fields. Counseling and workshop participation can be arranged through the Small Business Administration regional office in your area, listed in the "Where to Learn" guide in Part III of this book.

Department of Labor Apprenticeship Program

The mothers of teenagers in school all day might find it worthwhile to consider preparing themselves for a future career at home in a skilled trade by joining the apprenticeship program created by the Department of Labor in cooperation with employers in many skilled trades. This is "earn as you learn" on-the-job training, which requires participants to sign an agreement with an employer for a given length of time. On the completion of the agreement, workers would be certified journeymen or skilled craftswomen recognized throughout the industry and eligible for top pay when ready to go out on their own as upholsterers, photographers, caterers, cosmetologists, jewelers, or as repairwomen. The Labor Department's apprenticeship information centers are located in approximately thirty-five cities. They conduct interviews, counsel applicants, and refer prospects to apprenticeship openings. The nearest State Training and Employment Service office will also assist. (See Apprenticeship Center List in Part III.)

Franchising—A New Home Career Field

Franchising sets you up in your own business by providing national advertising for a trade name of established reputation, promotional materials to bring customers to you wherever you set up shop, and training.

Many men and women acquire franchises that can be run from their own homes. A cash investment of several thousand dollars or more is usually required in return for the expert knowledge of specialists who have built up a market and a reputation. The learning period of about eighteen months gives the buyer of the franchise a chance to get the business going. Women are beginning to discover the opportunities in this type of home business, especially in services such as interior decoration, wedding management, selling of cosmetics, employment agencies, and child care services. One woman's franchise involves the sale of window shades. She made an initial investment of $400 for training, samples, and decorating ideas. An employment agency franchise in the Pittsburgh area earned another woman $12,000 the first year she owned the business.

A franchise is not always easy to get. The franchise licenser is not going to risk the money and reputation already invested unless he feels the prospective buyer is well qualified to make the business a success in his area. According to David Seltz, author of seven books on franchising and a leading authority on the subject for seventeen years, the business failures in franchised businesses are only ten percent as opposed to fifty percent among independently launched businesses. This is because the risks of experimenting with a totally new business are considerably lessened in a franchise operation.

Franchises are granted on an exclusive basis in a particular area and must produce a certain quota of business within a period of six months to a year to become firmly established. If within a specified time the business does not produce, the franchise licenser has the right to withdraw the franchise. A word of warning before taking on a franchised business: be sure that the product or service has the stability, the reputation, and the financial foundation to back up its claims and be sure to call upon the services of an accountant-lawyer team to investigate the company before any commitment is made. A nonprofit organization with services designed to give the investor the information and assistance he needs in making an informed decision has been set up in Washington. Write The National Association of Franchised Businessmen, Inc., 1404 North York Avenue, Suite 608, Washington, D. C.

8 Outside Financing

The type of outside financing with which this chapter deals, concerns cash required to make your home career more successful, not money you need to prop up a failing business. Your business is ready to expand when you can't meet the demand for what you sell, when you need more space, when you need more equipment, when you need more help in producing and selling, when you are ready to take the giant step from a one-woman business to a payroll operation. You may be losing money in spite of your popularity because you are trying to meet your commitments singlehandedly.

So what do you do? What you *don't* do is go to your family and friends to ask for handouts unless you are prepared to form a partnership or a corporation deal, the details of which are spelled out later in this chapter.

Whether you need only a few hundred dollars or a loan in the thousands, the bank where you have an account should hear your story first, even if you know in advance the collateral you have to offer is not sufficient. You shouldn't go to personal finance companies because their loans carry exorbitant interest rates.

Who Will Lend You Money?

There are about eighty field offices of the Small Business Administration throughout the country, the primary goal of which is the stimulation of small businesses in every area of the United States. In addition to these SBA field offices, loan officers visit many small cities on a regularly scheduled basis to arrange guaranteed loans to small businesses that cannot satisfy the collateral requirements of private commercial banks. Collateral consists of one or more of the following: a mortgage on land, a building, or business equipment. The SBA can guarantee up to ninety percent of the loan, but the applicant must have applied to a commercial bank first and have been turned down before making application for a guaranteed loan from the SBA.

The following examples will serve to illustrate how these loans have helped women of noteworthy character and ability to increase their businesses and put them on a firm financial foundation.

How Two Women Qualified for an SBA Loan

Miss Luella Schroeder, the founder of The Craft Shop at Molly's Pond in Cabot, Vermont, moved to that state from Cranbrook Institute of Science in Michigan. An artist in creating jewelry, she began to specialize in original designs from nature, utilizing much of the flora and fauna of her Vermont surroundings as models.

During the next few years, while creating and producing her own jewelry, she and her partner became acquainted with a great many Vermont craftsmen who were producing handmade items of high quality, which their craft shop began to display and sell along with Miss Schroeder's own jewelry. Her work and the other items gained national recognition, and soon an enlarged shop was necessary. The Small Business Administration and a Vermont bank, the Howard National Bank, offered a joint loan for the construction of a large addition to The Craft Shop. More than a thousand persons from all over the state and from outside attended the formal opening when it was completed.

A dressmaker in a rural area, assisted by the SBA, reports: "After my husband died, our eight-acre farm and dairy was too much for me to handle because of my health and the shortage of competent labor. I decided to sell my dairy herd, pay off the debt on it, and take the balance to open a fabric shop in the nearest town, three miles away.

"At the time, my three daughters were in college, one a premedical student, one a language major, and the third a piano major. My son was still in high school.

"For years I had had to supplement our income as a dressmaker at home, so I applied for and was granted a $10,000 SBA loan to finish buying stock for my fabric shop. This is being paid back at the rate of $200 a month plus interest over a five-year period. I have been able to cover my home and family expenses and some of the college expenses, the balance being underwritten by National Defense loans. Had I not been granted the SBA loan I would not have been able to get my new business off the ground."

Seven Steps to Outside Loan Financing

If it becomes necessary for you to seek financial aid for the expansion of your business, observe the following steps.

(1) Prepare a current financial statement, also called a balance sheet, listing all assets and liabilities of your home business. Do not include personal items. The following example should serve as a guide.

SAMPLE FINANCIAL STATEMENT TO SUBMIT TO BANK*

Balance Sheet

ASSETS

Cash on Hand	$ 75.00	
Cash in Bank	420.00	
Inventory	2000.00	
Furniture and Equipment	400.00	
Less Depreciation	40.00	$2855.00

LIABILITIES

Bills Payable	300.00	
NET WORTH (assets minus liabilities plus capital and profit)		
Operating Capital	1000.00	
Surplus or Profit	975.00	$4530.00

*Your bank book and your inventory listing, including furniture and equipment, should accompany your typed balance sheet.

Your operating capital is the sum you keep in a separate account to pay fixed charges such as insurance, utilities, and taxes. If you have mortgageable property against which you can borrow, the bank will require the deed or certificate of ownership. If your business is still so small you do not have a separate account for operating capital, your net worth will be figured by subtracting your liabilities from your assets and adding whatever profit your business has made. If your business has not been operating at a profit but you can show advance orders that can establish the acceptance of your product or service, the bank will consider your application for a loan.

(2) Prepare a current financial statement of your personal assets.

(3) List collateral to be offered as security for the loan, with your estimate of the present market value of each item—your house, land, investments, personal bank account, equipment, etc.

(4) State amount of loan requested and explain exact purposes for which the money will be used.

(5) Take this material with you when you go to see your banker. Ask for a direct bank loan. If the loan is declined, *ask the bank to make the loan* under SBA's Loan Guaranty Plan or to participate with SBA in issuing a loan. If the bank is interested in this arrangement, ask the banker to contact the SBA for discussion of your application. In most cases of guaranty, SBA will deal directly with the bank.

(6) If a guaranty or a participation loan is not available, write or visit the nearest SBA office. If you are not near a main branch, ask to see a loan officer on his next scheduled visit to your area. To speed matters along, make your financial information available when you first write or visit the SBA. By all means, write to the Small Business Administration for a free list of publications, invaluable to you in dealing with your technical problems.

What Is SCORE?

As mentioned earlier, SCORE is the Service Corps of Retired Executives—men and women who have successfully completed their own active business careers and now offer their free services to help small businessmen and businesswomen with operating problems.

In the nearly two hundred SCORE chapters throughout the nation, there are more than 3,300 counselors, including former retailers, wholesalers, service managers, jobbers, plant managers, lawyers, accountants, engineers, economists, bankers—experts in almost every phase of private enterprise. Before you apply for an SBA guaranteed loan, you may want to talk over your situation and your plans with one of these counselors. The SBA office branch nearest you will put you in touch with a counselor.

Ineligible Loan Applications

Because it is a public agency using taxpayers' funds, SBA has an unusual responsibility as a lender. The pamphlet issued on this subject by the Office of Public Information, Washington, D.C., from which all Small Business Administration publications are ordered, states the following reasons for not making loans:

- If funds are otherwise available on reasonable terms.
- If the loan is intended to (a) pay off a loan to a creditor of the applicant who is in a position to sustain the loss, (b) provide funds for distribution or as salaries to the owner or partners, or (c) replenish funds previously used for such purposes.
- If the loan allows speculation in any kind of property.
- If the applicant is involved in a nonprofit enterprise.
- If the loan finances recreational or amusement facilities, unless the facilities contribute to the health or general welfare of the public.
- If the applicant is a newspaper, magazine, or book publishing company, radio broadcasting company, or similar enterprise.
- If any of the gross income of the applicant (or of any of its principal owners) is derived from gambling activities.
- If the loan provides funds to an enterprise engaged primarily in lending or investing.
- If the loan finances real property that is, or will be, held for sale or investment.
- If the loan encourages monopoly or is inconsistent with the accepted standards of the American system of free competitive enterprise.
- If the loan is used to relocate a business for other than sound business purposes.
- If the purpose in applying for a loan is to effect a change in ownership of the business. However, loans may be authorized for this purpose if the result would be to: (a) aid the sound development of a small business or to keep it in

operation or (b) contribute to a well balanced national economy by facilitating ownership of small business concerns by persons whose participation in the free enterprise system has been hampered or prevented because of economic, physical, or social disadvantages or disadvantages in business or residence locations.

Outside Financing Can Be Credit

The companies from which you buy equipment or merchandise may also furnish capital in the form of credit. Manufacturers of equipment such as store fixtures, cash registers, and industrial machinery frequently have financing plans under which you may buy on the installment basis and subsequently pay for the equipment out of income. If goods are intended for resale, no security other than repossession rights of the unsold goods is involved.

A firm order from a customer or store for manufactured goods of your design will often result in credit to you from the manufacturer, who can foresee his financial investment being paid off with a profit within a short period.

Credit financing may prove expensive as cash discounts are quoted if a bill is paid within ten, thirty, or sixty days. For example, a term of sale quoted as "2-10 net, 30 days" means that a cash discount of two percent will be granted if the bill is paid within ten days. If not paid in ten days, the entire amount is due in thirty days. If you do not take advantage of the cash discount, you are paying two percent to use money for twenty days.

Growing Pains to Bigger Business

Decisions, decisions, decisions! Should you remain sole owner of your business? Should you take in one or more partners? Should you become a corporation?

With the help of the Small Business Administration, the following advantages to each form of organization have been formulated. Each has important financial bearing on the expansion of your business, the extent to which you can raise capital, and the risks involved.

So far, your application for outside financing has applied only to you, as the single proprietor of your business. On the one hand, you are in full charge, you avoid the problems of opposing factions and divided responsibilities, and you have complete control of the profits. On the other hand, you are personally liable for all debts of your business to the extent of your entire property. In getting started all you had to do was to find out whether you needed a license and whether you had to pay a state tax or a license fee.

A general partnership can be formed very simply, without even a written agreement. The general partner need not invest capital; she shares financial liability equally with you to the limit of her assets, as well as management responsibilities and the right to inspect the books and to obtain full and complete information regarding your business. If your business makes money, she shares likewise in the profits.

Limited partnerships are somewhat more difficult to set up. To form one you file, with the proper state official, a written contract drawn according to certain legal requirements. This contract permits you to limit the liability of one or more of the partners to just the amount that they invest. But you must designate at least one general partner in addition to the limited partners. All of the limited partners must have actually invested in the partnership. According to the Uniform Limited Partnership Act, those investments may be either cash or tangible property, not services. Lastly, you must conform strictly to the laws of the particular state in which you organize; otherwise your business will be considered a general partnership in which all partners are totally liable.

Corporations are more complicated to form than any of the other types of business contracts. You can create one only by following the legal procedures of the particular state in which the corporation is being established. You must file with the designated state official a special document called the Articles of Incorporation. Then you must pay an initial tax and certain filing fees. Finally, in order to do the business for which the corporation was formed, various official meetings attended by certain responsible people who have become officers in the new corporation must be conducted to deal with the details of organization and operation.

As far as risk goes, corporations have a real advantage over other legal business structures. Creditors can force payment on their claims only to the limit of the company's assets. Certificates of stock, which represent investments and ownership in

the business, are issued. Stockholders do not necessarily participate either in operations or in policy formulation, but they may.
Administrative functions are centralized, usually in a small
group of executives or one—you—who does not necessarily own
the controlling financial interest in your company.

Tax advantages are a great incentive to incorporation. As sole
proprietor you have to pay personal income tax on the entire
profit of your business. When you become a corporation, you
pay a personal income tax only on the salary the corporation
pays you. However, until a home career has reached the point
of a five-figure profit, incorporation should not be a major consideration.

9 The Human Equation

The career at home that comes naturally to many women and that can be the most rewarding in human terms is the foster care of children and the elderly. This kind of work is often a continuation and an expansion of a woman's life as a homemaker and a mother.

"Money doesn't come first with these women. Recognition and public acclaim don't exist for them. Creative self-expression to do crafts or artistic things is not their driving need. These are the women whose gifts and whose emotional lives are served by helping other human beings—children, the aged, and the handicapped. They open the doors of their homes and their hearts to the lonely, the bereft, and the homeless. The monthly board of approximately $135 for children and $200 for the elderly would not come near to equaling the minimum wage if all the hours of care and responsibility were counted."

This statement comes from John J. Keppler, member of the Federation of Protestant Welfare Agencies, which, in cooperation with Catholic Charities and the Federation of Jewish Philanthropies, seeks homes for children who are the victims of family breakdowns due to sickness, unemployment, homelessness, or illegitimacy.

How To Become a Foster Parent

There are a number of ways to arrange for the foster care of children. Local child welfare agencies are connected with community social service groups, with churches, and with the Department of Health, Education, and Welfare, a part of the Social Security Division of the federal government. Notify one of these agencies by phone or letter or by a personal visit that you are interested in becoming a foster parent, and they will inform you about the needs and requirements.

A social worker with one of the agencies will make an appointment to interview you. The interview will be followed by a visit to your home if you qualify. Since a child is a big responsibility, the worker may need several interviews to cover all appropriate subjects sufficiently. She will want to talk to your husband and every member of your family who lives at home.

The foster parent usually has a preference regarding the age, sex, and the number of children to be taken into the home. Single women are now eligible to take foster children if their personalities, living arrangements, and their moral character are found suitable to the responsibility. Each prospective parent will be asked to supply as references the names of three or four people who know the family and how they live; these can be friends, neighbors, clergymen, doctors, or employers. The legal requirements of a foster parent differ from state to state, but the basic qualities and conditions considered important by The Children's Bureau, Washington, D.C., are as follows:

- You should have a natural liking for children. You should enjoy playing and talking with them and taking care of them.

- You must be able to give affection and care to a child without expecting him to be loving and grateful in return right away.

- If married, your marriage should be stable and basically happy. Both you and your husband should want the foster child.

- You should accept the fact that your foster child is not entirely yours, that his own parents and the child welfare agency have important places in his life. When the time comes for the child to go back to his parents or to an adoptive home, you should help to prepare him for it. Many foster parents want to adopt legally the children they take, and if the child is offered for adoption, they are given preference if the conditions are suitable.

- Occasionally a widow or a single woman with experience in child care is accepted as a foster mother, most often for temporary care. For most foster children, however, the agency will consider only homes with both a mother and a father.

- If the agency does not have a child who is suited to your home at the time you apply, you will be asked to wait until the right child comes along.

- Representatives of the fire and public health departments of your community will usually be required to inspect your home to check on safety, lighting, fire hazards, space available, and sanitation.

- You must be in reasonably good health so that you will be able to provide constant care for your foster child. Medical examinations of family members are usually required, including tests for diseases that can spread to children. Your foster child will also receive a medical examination.

- Agencies need foster parents of all races. There are many Negro, Puerto Rican, Indian, and Spanish-American children who need foster care throughout the country.

- You will have a chance to meet your prospective foster child and perhaps his parents. The foster child will usually be brought to your home for a visit before becoming a part of the family.

- Your foster child's parents will have visiting privileges, which you will be expected to handle with understanding and tact. A disapproving attitude can be sensed by a child and will damage his ties with his parents, to whom he usually hopes to return.

What You Would Do as a Foster Parent

If you have one or more children of your own at home, the adjustment of a foster child might be much easier than if you are childless. Your own children should be prepared to accept and treat your foster child as a special and welcome member of the family. Love and security are what such children need most, and everyone within your home can help to overcome the initial fear and mistrust such a child is bound to feel.

A foster child can share a room with the family's own children provided the room is large enough and the children are the same sex and approximately the same age. A separate bed, a bureau, and closet space for personal possessions is required for each foster child.

The welfare agency provides for health care in addition to the monthly amounts for costs of basic care. But the day-to-day supervision and rest, the clothing, and the nutrition will be checked when the social worker comes to visit.

The school-age child will need the same parental concern that you give to your own children, including visits to his teachers and participation in parent-teacher meetings.

When you have been accepted by the welfare agency, your home will have revealed good habits, order, and discipline. You must be prepared to take the time and have the patience to help your foster child adjust to his new surroundings. Helping the child to succeed at small tasks and praising him will produce results. Many foster children have the feeling that they are "no good" because they are separated from their parents. These feelings can be overcome by finding out what the child is interested in and likes to do and by providing an opportunity to develop this interest. If behavior problems are persistent, you are expected to call the social worker in to help solve them.

The Social Worker in Your Life

If your foster child needs special medical care, it is your responsibility to let the social worker know at once. You must also let her know if there is a change in your family that could affect the child, such as a serious or chronic illness or an addition to your household.

Foster children can go on vacations with the family, but the agency must be notified as far in advance as possible since permission must be given by the agency. Any absence of the child from home of more than a day or two should be reported to the social worker.

Complete confidence and trust must exist between the social worker and the foster parents. Your privacy and personal problems will be respected, and there will be a deep appreciation all around for the contribution you are making by caring for a foster child.

What the Welfare Agency Pays For

The money paid by agencies to foster parents varies from state to state and agency to agency. It usually covers the minimum expenses of food and shelter, with special allowances for clothing, medical care, school supplies, and the other items that have to be figured separately for each child. Any such money is paid to the foster parent on a monthly basis.

Many agencies pay slightly higher amounts for care of infants and teenagers than for youngsters from ages two to twelve. Rates for care of the handicapped or emotionally disturbed children who need much special attention may be quite a bit higher than the basic rate, which is approximately $135 a month exclusive of clothing and medical costs.

The Importance of a Child

There are couples who, over many years, have dozens of foster children. One such couple expressed the philosophy shared by most: "Even if we never see him again, we know from our own lives that a person's childhood stays with him all his life. If we can help children to be stronger and happier in the years with us, what's more important and satisfying?"

Our Elderly Need Foster Care Too

The defunct tradition in which two and sometimes three generations lived under one roof is being renewed in a foster care program for the elderly, which is becoming an increasingly popular career at home. Today, with our shifting population and with the life-span so extended, families have become widely separated geographically, and the aged are often left behind by sons and daughters whose work and lives take them too far away to furnish protection and care for their parents. This is one of the services most encouraged by the Department of Health, Education and Welfare, which is making this service opportuity known through church and community social welfare agencies. The combined incentives of making a contribution to human happiness as well as supplementing family income are constructive and appealing. From one to six elderly people are permitted to go into private homes, depending on the accommodations and standards of the homes, which must comply with definite specifications.

Foster family homes are not used for persons whose physical or mental condition requires medical or psychiatric treatment. Those chosen for family foster care are physically and mentally normal in relation to their age. They can do simple household tasks and are encouraged to participate in community activities if they can get around independently. The cost of care for the aged varies in different states, but the average is around $200 a month for each foster care resident, which covers all except medical and clothing expenses.

Matching the Family to the Elderly Applicant

There are many more elderly people qualified for family care than there are homes seeking to receive them. The church or welfare agency and the caseworker are essential to a satisfactory arrangement.

An elderly person, if physically and mentally able, can do best with a family that shares a standard of living, educational background, and religious beliefs similar to his own. Advance information on habits, talents, interests, and foibles of the older person joining a family makes adjustment to a new home much easier. The social worker can give these clues to ward off later misunderstandings. Caring for her own room, helping with the dishes, or doing other small tasks that take her into the family life will make an elderly lady feel wanted and needed. An elderly man can be kept useful and happy if he likes to repair things or to help with the gardening.

Retaining Identity Is Important

A few personal belongings and freedom to arrange the furniture in his room help a newcomer to put down roots. Privacy during visits from relatives and friends is important too. The use of the family room at certain times of the day to look at television, listen to records, or to chat with whoever happens to be home makes important contributions to adjustment in the early stages.

Before a home is chosen, a personal visit to the home must be made by the social worker and the prospective foster resident, and a get-acquainted meeting with other members of the family should be arranged.

Whether a private room is provided or the foster resident's room is to be shared, a comfortable bed, sufficient dresser and closet space for clothing and keepsakes, a comfortable chair, a table or desk, and adequate lighting must be provided. For some older residents a room and bath on the ground floor are essential to eliminate the necessity of climbing stairs.

Safety provisions such as nonskid rugs, a banister on the stairs, a screen around the fireplace, a safety bar in the bathroom, and good lighting for stairs and hallways become essentials.

Living arrangements must meet all the local building codes and regulations, and safety precautions against fire must be observed. Inspections by the fire and health departments are usually mandatory.

The Importance of a Medical History

The welfare agency making the arrangement for elderly foster care has the responsibility of providing an extensive health report. Recommendations as to medical needs, special diets, and limitations of activities must be prepared for the guidance of the family that assumes the responsibility for the care of an elderly foster resident. The social worker should be informed at once of a serious illness so that arrangements can be made for a transfer from the foster home to a hospital. Medical checkups should be arranged once a year. The social worker will keep in close contact with the foster family, making weekly visits for the first few months and then monthly visits for the balance of the first year.

Trial Period

The foster care of an elderly person becomes a lifetime arrangement in many homes. When problems of adjustment and care do arise, they can generally be detected within the first six months. If special diet and the supervision of medication are required or if some physical handicap develops so that a family can't cope with the extra care and responsibility, the welfare agency takes over. Additional funds are always provided if a handicap creates dependence and need for partial nursing care. Mild senility is not a major problem if behavior continues to be generally cooperative.

The support and experience of the social worker are always available in any crisis.

The Young Invite the Old

"Frequently it is the young family that is more inclined to offer a home to the older person," says Rose Lichtenstein, author of *Foster Family Care for the Aged,* published by the Bureau of Family Services in Washington, D.C.

"The additional income often provides for future needs such as saving money for the children's college education," Miss Lichtenstein goes on to say. "Also, some young couples welcome the presence of the grandparent figure in their homes."

One such family is described later in this book. Their three young children, all under age eight, will grow up with four foster grandmothers who tell them stories, teach them to crochet and knit, and have time to play games with them. They haven't met their own grandparents in Finland because they are too far away to afford a visit. What a lovely way to bridge that generation gap and make four elderly women's lives full and happy.

10 Fortunes Started in the Home

Fortunes have been made by women whose businesses started in the home. Their ideas stemmed from the woman's world—home, children, and the search for a good life.

Like many average housewives, such women share a strong motivating factor, a missionary zeal to make some aspect of living better or more beautiful. In their wildest dreams they did not envision the profits in store for them. Their special feminine perceptions, insights, and talents provided them with ideas that satisfied the needs of millions of customers.

The successful women discussed in the following pages found satisfaction in being busy and creative above and beyond financial considerations.

The first two of our famous fortunes were made by women whose home careers have outlived them but whose names are still household words.

Let Them Eat Real Bread

Margaret Rudkin, whose Pepperidge Farm bread pioneered in putting essential nutritional qualities back into our daily bread, was motivated first by the health needs of her own nine-year-old son. Thirty years before the national outcry about commercially produced bread, she ground wheat in a coffee mill in her own kitchen to preserve the bran and essential vitamins (especially vitamin B) that were being lost in commercial white bleached flour. She used fresh butter and whole milk in her bread, and she created such enthusiasm that she started to bake the bread to sell. She set up an old extra stove stored in her attic, used a set of baby scales for weighing the dough, invested in a set of mixing bowls, and charged 25 cents a loaf, which was then considered very expensive. She was told by commercial bakers that people would never pay that much. However, neighboring local grocers sold out her bread within hours of its delivery.

Realizing she was satisfying a hidden hunger for good bread, Peg Rudkin ventured beyond her home town near Bridgeport, Connecticut, to a large grocer in New York City. He gave her an order for a dozen loaves a day. Within months the order grew to 200 daily, and the rest is history. Here we have our first example of a career at home that began with a woman's role as caretaker, first to her family and then to the whole community.

Home Sweet Home

The stored memories of a lifetime were the treasures that Grandma Moses drew on when she started to paint at the age of seventy-eight. Her husband had died. The five of her ten children who had survived to adulthood were on their own and living away from home. Even the reduced demands of housework had begun to be too hard, but like most of us, she was a woman who had to be busy. Accustomed to making jams and jellies to sell at local fairs, she had no hesitation about showing her spontaneously painted country scenes at the county fair along with her jellies. (She had never had an art lesson, but she had been a needleworker. Actually, her country scenes began as yarn pictures, but arthritis made that too difficult so she turned to paint.) Only her jams and jellies sold at the fair, so she put a selection of small framed pictures on display in a drugstore, where a businessman who collected Americana bought four small ones at $3 each and two larger ones for $5 each. That was in 1938. A dealer in folk art who met the purchaser of the drug store paintings was so charmed he wanted to see more. He gave her an exhibition in New York City that was called "What a Farmwife Painted." In a newspaper story about the exhibition the reporter referred to her as "Grandma Moses." The name caught on and became her signature. At the age of ninety-three she herself wrote "Grandma Moses" on her Christmas cards.

At first she priced her paintings according to size. But she lived to get $1,000 to paint Eisenhower's Gettysburg home, working from photographs sent to her. The gift painting was a gift to the president from his cabinet. Since her death the prices of her pictures have ranged from $1,250 to $20,000 paid by collectors.

House Dust—Gold Dust

A whirlwind career that began at home, literally with mop and dust cloth in hand, and has stayed there has zoomed to international fame with a column that appears in nearly six hundred newspapers in the United States and goes into twenty foreign countries. Heloise Cruse, known to her millions of newspaper readers only by the name of "Heloise," is an "I'm only a housewife" writer. She captivated a world of women readers who recognized at once that she knew what she was talking about and liked her way of talking—breezily and wittily with remarks such as: "The second wife always has a maid," and "Don't work yourself to death—all the polish in the world won't put a gleam in your husband's eye."

Heloise had never written for a newspaper before early 1959, when she walked into a newspaper office in Honolulu armed with a good idea and faith in herself. She got a job on a thirty day trial basis without knowing how to type. She wrote a column at home, where, as a housewife and mother of two, she had a built-in setup for testing household methods. Her office at home is now an extension of her apartment in San Antonio, Texas, where all the hints and recipes she receives are personally selected for testing.

She is the author of the bestseller *Heloise's Household Hints* and other books, which, in toto, have sold many millions of copies in hardcover and paperback editions.

Black Woman Tycoon

With a beauty business that has climbed to an annual dollar volume of $250,000, Rose Morgan is one of the most successful and influential black business women in America. She has extended the sale of the beauty products under her name beyond beauty parlors into homes in a nationwide door-to-door sales campaign. These are sold by women representatives trained by her to give a beauty lesson with every sale.

A twinkle of amusement and pleasure lit up her warm brown eyes when she told me during our interview in her beauty salon about the first time she was described as a tycoon.

"I was invited to contribute a recipe to the $15 cook book entitled *Tycoons in the Kitchen*. Mine is beef stroganoff—not that I recommend it to my clients on a reducing program!" she said laughingly. "My career did begin literally in my home before I was fourteen years old, when I gave shampoos and sets for 75 cents and used the washbowl in the only bathroom in our house in Chicago."

Rose Morgan knew at that early age that she wanted to have a beauty business of her own. Right after leaving high school she enrolled for one year at the Morris Beauty Academy in Chicago. With her diploma and a beautician's license she could earn a living almost any place in the world. One visit to New York City convinced her that it was her town and her future.

Rose is one of nine children in a close family whose roots are still in Chicago. Her move to New York City at the age of seventeen was a source of anxiety and concern, but her leaving did not sever or weaken her family ties.

Rose Morgan has always run her own show. After being employed only six months in a New York beauty salon, she rented a friend's kitchen and opened a two chair beauty parlor. The stove had to be removed and two secondhand chairs installed— one for shampooing at the kitchen sink and one for setting.

"In those days oil and a pressing comb were used to take out kinks. Today straightening is usually done with chemicals," Rose reports.

Rose stayed in that location for a year. By that time the size of her clientele required larger quarters, so she rented a store front and took on five operators. By 1945 she had acquired the experience and confidence to know she could move into the big time. She also saw advantages in keeping her home under the same roof with her business. A friend who was studying for her Master's degree in science at New York University showed a great interest and aptitude for the beauty business, so Rose asked her to become her partner. They rented a five-story brownstone house at St. Nicholas Avenue and 148th Street in the Bronx. This time thirteen operators were hired to work in the beautiful renovated house.

Rose Morgan is the personification of the silhouette, the grooming, the charm, and the glamour her business stands for. In her beauty salon every employee, whether she is head of a department or a new shampoo girl, is treated with respect.

There is in her shop a dignity and formality that are highly conducive to personal self-esteem and a professional atmosphere.

"Notice how quiet it is here," she pointed out. "All my operators keep their voices very low, and work is performed in the most serene way possible."

Her customers have always included the greats of the entertainment world. Such names as Lena Horne, Diahann Carroll, Ella Fitzgerald, and Mahalia Jackson are often on her appointment books.

By 1955 the Rose Morgan House of Beauty was bursting at the seams again. Her partner had married and left the United States for the Virgin Islands. The five-story walkup, so elegant as a fashionable town house as well as a beauty salon, was unwieldy to manage. Business expansion demanded a wig department; her cosmetics had been so popular that they became mail order items; weight reducing had become an essential part of the beauty business. Besides, Rose Morgan wanted to own the building where she conducted her business. She went to the bank she had used during the ten years her business was building so dramatically. To her chagrin and dismay this well known bank would not even give her credit for air-conditioning at a time when she was doing a $175,000 volume.

She took all her business away from this bank and through the Bowery Savings Bank of New York, arranged a $40,000 mortgage on the new building in which she is presently established. To spare other members of her race this handicap, she resolved that she would organize a savings and loan company that would make funds available to black people who had the proper qualifications. Bethune Savings and Loan was ultimately incorporated in New Jersey. A few years later a similar setup, Freedom National Bank, was established in New York City. Rose Morgan has been on its board of directors ever since.

The year 1955 was a banner year for romantic and business reasons. Rose Morgan had not had time for marriage during the early years of making her reputation, but now she was ready to enjoy her personal life. She loved traveling and on one of her "junkets," as she calls them, she was seated next to Joe Louis at a dinner party. It was instant attraction for both of them, and within six months they were married.

"My responsibilities didn't mean a thing to him. He just wanted to crook his finger and say 'come here' wherever he happened to be. I couldn't just leave everything I had built, so we didn't see much of each other those two years we remained married. We're still good friends, though."

Five years later she married her present husband, an attorney, but she has never changed her professional name.

Over the years Rose Morgan has trained 2,900 employees. Many have gone off to initiate beauty parlors themselves.

"That's the way it should be, and that's the greatest contribution I can make to my people. I believe in on-the-job training and I don't feel abused if, after I invest in training operators, they leave me. I start them the same as I started, doing shampoos, and I take them through every step of beauty training, paying them as they learn. As a consultant for ICBO (Interracial Council for Business Opportunity), I urge training programs in all businesses."

Rose Morgan is a philanthropic leader in the fight against "sickle disease," a blood disease that kills one out of every ten Negroes in this country. She is the president of The Continental Society, consisting of twenty prominent women. These women have already made a start by raising $80,000 to contribute to research into this disease, which was brought over from Africa generations ago and continues to pass from one generation to the next.

Of the more than two dozen awards Rose Morgan has received for her many contributions to the advancement of her people, the Honorary Doctorate Degree in Humanities from Shaw University in Raleigh, North Carolina, gives her greatest satisfaction. Her guiding philosophy is "Teaching hundreds of hands what my two hands can do."

How to Lose and Make a Profit

The highest compliment Jean Nidetch has received, she says, is from the well known writer Jessica Mitford, who was assigned by a magazine to do an exposé on her Weight Watchers reducing business. Said Jean, "Miss Mitford said to me, and I quote her exact words, 'I came to scoff and stayed to applaud.' "

"I'll never get over that I'm making a lot of money," Jean went on to say. Tall, handsome, and full of vitality, she was dashingly outfitted in a Cardin dress and boots to match. It was hard to believe that she had ever weighed 214 pounds.

"Had I set out to make money, I don't think I would have gotten to first base. I didn't invent the idea of losing weight; I just invented the only sure way to do it. Now I spend my life making converts of as many of the eighty million unhappy obese people in this country as I can to try to persuade them to change their way of life."

Weight Watchers has become a publicly owned corporation with an annual gross revenue of well over $5 million. There are branches in forty-seven states and in five foreign countries. Jean Nidetch, president of the company, worked out every detail of her program with the expert advice of nutrition authorities. The company sells franchises in all those states and requires representatives to be trained to conduct the courses. The cost of these franchises varies according to the population of the area. Usually it ranges from $5,000 to $10,000, but in very sparsely populated states such as Montana, a franchise can cost as little as $2,500.

Ten years ago, when Jean Nidetch made a trip to the New York City Department of Health to consult someone in the nutrition clinic, the receptionist took one look at her 214-pound visitor and replied, "Oh, you want the *obesity* clinic."

Jean says this was the turning point in her life and the real beginning of Weight Watchers. In 1961 Jean was "just a very fat housewife" with two young sons, David and Richard. Her husband was a bus driver, her father a cab driver, and her mother a manicurist. A year after her visit to the obesity clinic Jean was down to 142 pounds and had begun her weight loss crusade by holding a series of meetings in the basement of her own home in Little Neck, Queens, New York, to tell overweight people in her community how she had lost weight. She began to get appeals for advice from fat people in other towns with offers to pay her expenses. In Baldwin, Long Island, for example, she was given $1 a week by each member of the group to cover expenses. There were ten couples in the group. It was one of these couples, Mr. and Mrs. Albert Lippert, who suggested that her system could apply to overweight people all over the country. Mr. Lippert joined Jean Nidetch in creating the Weight Watchers Corporation to franchise her method of reducing to trained representatives. In addition to the hundreds of franchises all over the world, the company also has gone into the diet food business. It publishes a diet magazine and cook book and sells the autobiography that reveals Jean Nidetch's own fascinating story.

Art in Industry

A violet patterned linen dish towel introduced me to Vera fifteen years ago. It was so pretty I couldn't bear to dry dishes with it, so I bought three more to match—for $1 each—and used them as café curtains at my kitchen window. My color scheme was delphinium blue, purple, and green. The same café curtains still hang at that window, after countless washings, just as fresh and pretty as the day I first clipped them to the curtain rod. Today Vera's signature appears on countless items ranging from linens to spectacular printed sportswear made of silks, cottons, and polyester fabrics. Her business now grosses well over $10 million a year.

Twenty-five years ago Vera was a young bride, an artist freelancing her designs to textile companies. Her studio was in the kitchen of her three-room apartment. Her husband George Neumann was in the advertising business, and his specialty was printing. He also was his wife's most ardent fan, and it was he who had the vision of extending her talents to the printing of her designs. He suggested that she make some prints for linen table mats, and he volunteered to silk-screen them in their own kitchen. Vera remembers that the design was a two-color print—blue and white—and that the subject was a Swedish wedding.

The first order for the mats was placed by B. Altman and Company, one of New York's finest department stores. The quantity was so much larger than either she or her husband had anticipated that they were totally unprepared to deliver.

"To this day that order hasn't been delivered," she says, "and when I run into the president of Altman's from time to time, he teases me about it, asking me when I'm going to make good on the order.

"We knew we had to borrow money. We managed to borrow $1,000, but that wasn't enough to begin filling even small orders, so we called upon a friend, a former textile merchandiser, to ask him to become our partner, and he put in another $1,000. That gentleman, Mr. Werner Hamm, did more than anyone else to get our business going for us."

Soon they had to have extra space. A small workshop was rented on 17th Street. The rent was less than $50 a month, and they couldn't pay the rent in advance.

"Don't worry," said their landlady, "this is a good luck studio. Henry Luce rented this as his first office when he started *Time* magazine."

Vera's company Printex, is now a part of Manhattan Industries. She is one of the few women in the United States who is on the board of directors of a large conglomerate.

Vera revels in every aspect of femininity. She loves her home, and her garden is her passion. Indeed flowers have stimulated her most inspired designs. She has an outstanding collection of folk art.

"All my best ideas first come to me when I have a fashion need or problem. The bicycle clip scarf, the 'Jolly' top, the 'wing-tip' five-cornered scarf—these were big sellers in my early career."

Vera has gone right on solving the fashion problems of millions of women so successfully that with Mr. Hamm, now chairman of the board, and Vera herself as president, she has built a fashion empire.

From Paper Dolls to Industrial Matriarchy

This story has a "boy meets girl" beginning. Ruth met her husband Elliot when they were both sixteen and in school in Denver, Colorado. Elliot aspired to be an artist and was saving his money to go to art school. They went steady through high school, where Ruth took business courses. When she was nineteen she went to Los Angeles to visit friends. On the spur of the moment she applied at Paramount Studios for a job as a stenographer. She landed the job, and Elliot soon followed her to Los Angeles with plans to go to art school there. The year was 1938. In a few months they were married. Elliot was studying industrial design at night and working for a lighting fixture company during the day. When they moved into a $37.50 a month three-room apartment, they shared a garage, which Elliot and Ruth used as a workshop. Moonlighting from their regular jobs, Elliot first designed and made picture frames. Because there was a lot of extra lumber, Ruth said "Why not design and make doll furniture?" That was when Ruth really started her career at home. One of their friends, a foreman of the lighting fixture factory where her husband worked, helped them to produce the doll furniture in large quantities. This was in 1944, and Elliot Handler was called into the army, so Ruth carried on alone.

When Ruth Handler's daughter Barbara was a little girl, she had preferred paper dolls to all others. Her mother used to take her to the store almost every week to replenish her supply, and she observed that her daughter always chose dolls representing teenagers or adults rather than dolls representative of her own age. This gave Mrs. Handler, now president of the Mattel Toy Company, the idea that a doll with an adult body was psychologically appealing and would have wide popularity. She named the doll "Barbie" after her daughter, trademarked the name, and went to work with designers and production experts to see whether a doll could be manufactured at a price that would be right for big volume. That price, Ruth figured, would be about $3. A wardrobe, sold separately for $4, would also be available. It took three years to put the doll and wardrobe into production in Japan and on the market. If it had been produced in this country, it would have been necessary to charge twice the price. Also, the adult body of the doll was too much of an innovation to be immediately accepted by store buyers, who were afraid that a woman's contours might not appeal to a child. When a few buyers overcame their timidity, Ruth said, "The consumers pronounced the verdict— it was an overwhelming yes." This doll and her subsequent related items are the largest sellers ever known in the toy industry. Barbie now talks, dances, rides a horse, and has a social life known as "The World of Barbie."

Ruth's husband Elliot is chairman of the board, and Ruth, the genius behind the biggest toy company in the world, is its president.

Proud as she is of her brain child, the Barbie doll, Ruth Handler is a bit impatient that her company, which rolls up around $200 million in gross sales a year, isn't equally well known for the more than one thousand other toy items that also have stupendous international sales.

The Mattel Toy Company recently bought the Ringling Brothers Circus. The Handlers have three grandchildren. "Imagine being grandparents with a toy company and a circus too!" says Ruth Handler.

Read Faster—Know More

Evelyn Wood is known around the world for discovering "Reading Dynamics," the rapid reading method that has enrolled 350,000 students. Her career didn't begin to pay off as a business until Mrs. Wood had raised a family and was herself almost fifty years old, but it started back in the thirties while her husband was a bishop of the Mormon Church.

Through the early days of her marriage, Mrs. Wood worked with students and parents, abroad and in the United States, wherever her husband's assignments took them.

"It was at this time that I realized that the real problem people were those who could not read. In working with them I found that they could be helped tremendously. A certificate of merit was granted me by the University of Utah because of the kind of work I did in connection with remedial reading. I wrote a book entitled *Reading Skills,* published by Holt, Rinehart, and Winston, which also won an award."

Having first worked with problem readers, Mrs. Wood became aware that normal readers were reading far below their capabilities. She began to concentrate on methods by which all readers could increase their reading speed. The Evelyn Wood method of dynamic reading was developed, and in 1959 Mrs. Wood visited New York to see what the educators thought about her method. Her reading techniques were demonstrated in Washington, D.C., where "Even the president was impressed. By request I conducted a class in the White House."

People in public life, such as Senators Symington and Proxmire, the Queen of Denmark, and Mrs. Ghandi of India enrolled in her course.

In 1959 the Evelyn Wood Reading Dynamics course was made nationally and internationally available through franchises that are granted to trained representatives. There are 150 institutes franchised, and over 1,200 teachers are employed.

Mrs. Wood believes that in today's world we have to absorb a great deal more information than has ever been required before in the history of the world.

"We are making tremendous progress," she says.

Communication Is the Key

Dr. Joyce Brothers, listed by the Gallup Poll as one of the most admired women in America, prepared herself in college for living a good and satisfying family life by concentrating on courses in psychology and home economics. She has a doctorate in psychology. When her daughter Lisa was born, she stopped working outside of her home to be a full-time mother. Lisa is now a freshman at Princeton University, and Dr. Brothers' office is still in her home. Her schedule of two broadcasts a day, five days a week, takes her to the recording studios frequently, but she writes her daily syndicated column on human relations at home. Two desks and a bridge table are piled high with all kinds of publications used in the preparation of her material. The walls of her home office are lined with files and book shelves. She uses her daughter's childhood formica-topped bed-room bureaus as desks for typing her manuscripts. Although she doesn't see individual patients for consultation, she often serves as a consultant to personnel directors of many businesses, and she devotes some time to teaching and lecturing.

Specializing in problems of human relations and adjustments, Dr. Brothers feels that the greatest lack in the lives of house-wives is someone to talk to. The only talk many of them have throughout their days is with small children. Their husbands, when they arrive home, are frequently "talked out" as a result of the events of their working days and don't want to talk at all. There are only two cultures in the world, she says, that require a mother to spend so much time alone with her young children —the primitive Gussi tribe and the American housewife. A ca-reer at home, particularly one that brings other women into her home, is an ideal solution for women who have the skills and the accommodations to provide a product or service.

In spite of the demands of her schedule and her financial success, Dr. Brothers usually cooks dinner for herself and her husband, an internist.

"I spoiled him when we were first married. He likes my cook-ing, and we both like the freedom to eat when we please and not have to worry about having anyone else around."

Designed for Living

"I don't believe in fashion," says Bonnie Cashin, America's top individualist in the world of fashion and one of the most financially successful.

"Fashion is transitory. I like women to tell me the clothes I design for them are timeless. To see a coat I designed five years ago worn by a smart woman getting off a plane or ship or bus is one of the highest tributes that could be paid me. Fashion is a form of regimentation too often set apart from function or personality. Design is basic, like architecture."

"The layered concept—by that I mean the leotard, skirt, vest, jacket—which I developed years ago, goes on year after year, getting better every year because it adapts to a variety of needs and temperatures."

Bonnie Cashin lives in the same building where she works.

"You should always live over the store," she says. "I like to work at home all over the place. I'm always working whether I'm in my living room, bedroom, or bath. Some of my best ideas are accidental. I'll happen to be walking along the street and see an improvised outfit on a young person rushing to work, and it looks right, so I make a sketch, which is my way of taking notes."

Bonnie Cashin has been called America's fashion maverick. She has been more independent and more original in her use of fabrics than has any other American designer. She specializes in leathers, suedes, tweeds, and canvas.

Bonnie Cashin is a two-time winner of the Coty Fashion Critics Award. These and other honors have come to her because her creations are dashing and spirited and ahead of the times. Her designing career began at home as an apprentice to her mother, who was a custom dressmaker when Bonnie was young. Her father was an inventor. Her home was in California, a childhood setting that has influenced her whole life.

"I'm an outdoor girl, and I like to design with fabrics congenial to nature—tweeds, jerseys, linens, cottons."

How did Bonnie Cashin get her first break as a New York fashion designer?

"Screen credits," she says. After art school Bonnie had a job working for Twentieth Century-Fox. She did the costumes for some hit movies such as *Laura, Anna and the King of Siam,* and *A Tree Grows in Brooklyn.* When she came to New York in 1949, after having designed for the motion pictures, the doors of Seventh Avenue, the garment district in New York City, were thrown open to her.

"The movies were an invaluable background—an education

in themselves, which involved everything from historical research to designing for the problem figures of some of the top
stars."

A Winning Team

Partners who now do business worth millions of dollars and
do not have a single significant competitor are Marianne Mantell and Barbara Holdridge. After graduating from Hunter College in New York City, they had an idea—to record great
literature for phonographs and to use the voices of the actual
authors of the literature that, in their estimation, represented
greatness in our time.

That was eighteen years ago. They were single girls then, and
their homes were the typical New York career girl's small apartments. Barbara was a freelance writer at home who wrote text
for classical albums. Marianne was a girl Friday in the publishing office of a once great company that was on the decline.
Neither was happy with what she was doing. Both were full of
idealism about their mission to bring literary quality to life in
the homes of America.

Being poetry enthusiasts, one night they went to hear the
young Dylan Thomas read his poems. Wouldn't it be a wonderful thing, they thought, for him to put on records his own voice
reading his own poems for people to hear in their living rooms?

They asked the usher to take a note to Mr. Thomas asking
him if he would see them. The poet said he would see them the
next day for lunch. He liked their idea. He said they must get
the consent of his agent. The agent was also in favor of the
experiment.

The girls had $1,500 in their savings accounts; they said, "We
didn't have to borrow a penny." They paid Dylan Thomas an
advance and made a contract through his agent to pay him the
customary royalty on each record sold. The recording they made
was *A Child's Christmas in Wales and Five Poems.* That record
is still at the top of their best-seller list. Another successful recording is that of Sir Lawrence Olivier reciting the eulogy on
the death of King George VI.

They wrote and had printed two inexpensive leaflets, and
with samples of their first records they went to call personally
on record stores in New York City. Almost every store hearing
their records placed orders for from three to five records, which

sold out at once. Reorders began to come in, and their first edition of five hundred records was sold within a few weeks. Caedmon Records was on its way. The name of their company was chosen whimsically from a medieval poem about a swineherd named Caedmon.

Almost overnight their home moonlighting project became a business, and they gave up the other work they had been doing.

"At this point we began to owe everybody money. It took us three years to catch up. Everyone was wonderful except the landlord of the beat-up loft where we had to pack and ship our records. Our lawyer didn't even send us a bill for two years!"

They still speak with awe about how they ever achieved such a miracle. There are now about eight hundred recordings listed in their catalog. Schools are their biggest customers.

Both women have since married. They divide their work week to allow for time at home to supervise their children and domestic lives.

"Being women was no handicap to us in getting started," said Marianne Mantell. "We had a lovely aura of naiveté and crusading zeal when we started—of not being out for a fast buck. This seemed to bring out an element of chivalry in the businessmen we dealt with. We still don't have any competition. Several companies have tried to do what we do, but they don't seem to be able to put it over."

11 Forewarned Is Forearmed

"And what about the risks of a home career?" you may be asking. "You've painted a rosy picture of the successes, but there must be many women who have tried and fallen on their faces."

Believe it or not, few women who have *kept their businesses within their own homes* have been badly hurt. Starting in such a small way, they know very soon whether they have what it takes to be successful. There is usually very little financial risk. If the family situation can't tolerate the diversification of activity that a home career demands, this is likewise apparent early in the game. If the proficiency of the housewife does not measure up to her outside competition, she won't make any money, and she won't have a business.

Conversely, many women succeed who never suspected they had the energy, talent, and resources to enlarge their lives and incomes. For them the discovery is the dawning of a new day.

What's Your Home Career IQ?

Any aptitude test is an oversimplification unless the yes and no answers are prefaced by some deep self-examination and soul searching. The 4 E Career-at-Home Aptitude Test is no exception. As a prelude to scoring yourself on the test at the end of this section, I'm going to prepare you with a background of some of the things I've learned from women who have "made it" over the past few years.

Must one have the self-confidence and brashness of a political campaigner to put over a successful home business? Curiously enough, more of the successful home careers have been started by women who were timid rather than by women who were full of self-assurance. Perhaps it's because they try harder, feeling they must prove themselves. A touch of humility is appealing and encourages others to want to help.

Is the physical power and energy of a steamroller essential in coping with the needs of a family and the pressures of meeting business commitments?

It helps, but it is not necessary. A healthy husband and children are more important than your own unlimited energy. If your time is diverted continuously by nursing the sick in your household, you will find yourself emotionally and nervously torn by responsibilities. However, for those who are housebound by a continuing personal disability or handicap, a career at home can be good therapy.

Many creative people are not the sturdy type. Imagination and talent give what they produce a magic that the public seeks and pays for. Physical stamina and energy are needed more in service businesses such as nursery schools, catering services, or animal kennels than in artistic creation.

How important is experience? Organizational ability—not experience—is the essential ingredient. Learning by doing will be inevitable as your business begins to grow, but you must have some initial ability to sort out your life and responsibilities, or chaos will ensue. This need not be the streamlined routine of an office, and it usually isn't. Women have their own ways of keeping things straight. All women engaging in a career at home *must have some kind of system.*

The following test with instructions for scoring will be a helpful guide in evaluating your own potential for success.

The 4 E° Career-at-Home Aptitude Test

(1) Do you enjoy being busy?
(2) Do you get your housework done early in the day?
(3) Do you like to try out new ideas?
(4) Are you more concerned with pleasing than being pleased?
(5) Do you feel you have a special talent that is a money-maker?
(6) Do your friends and family believe you have a special talent?
(7) Are you a perfectionist?
(8) Is your husband easy to get along with?

  (9) Are your children cooperating?

(10) Did you hold a job before you were married?

(11) Do you throw yourself wholeheartedly into whatever you do?

(12) Can you take criticism and/or rejection?

(13) Do you have a hobby you can turn into a career at home?

(14) Does boredom seem unnecessary to you?

(15) Do you need to make money?

(16) Would having your own money make you feel more important?

(17) Do you have patience?

(18) Do you think a wife and mother gains respect from her family if she can make money on her own?

(19) Are you a good organizer?

(20) Do you have imagination in working out your problems?

Scoring

*The 4 Es are: Energy—Enthusiasm—Ego—Excellence

Score five points for each *yes* answer.

A score of 100% means "what are you waiting for?" Get going.

A score of 50% means proceed with caution.

A score of between 50% and 100% means you can make it if you're willing to face up to your shortcomings and do something about correcting them.

12 Best Sellers Made at Home

120 Careers at Home Reporting Substantial Profits

Of all home careers examined, the following have been found to be the most successful:

Animals: breeding, boarding, selling
Antiques: sale, repair, refurbishing
Apron making
Architecture
Art: creative, gallery, sales
Beading: belts, sweaters, etc.
Beauty parlor operation
Body massage
Bookbinding
Bookkeeping
Bread baking
Calligraphy
Candymaking and testing
Chair caning
Child care
China painting
Clothing alterations
Convalescent homes
Costumes for rent
Christmas ornaments
Christmas tree sales
Dancing classes
Découpage: furniture, portraits, etc.
Dolls: making, dressing, collecting
Domestic employment agency
Designing
Draperies
Dressmaking
Dried flowers
Enamel work, jewelry, accessories
Exercise classes
Fashion boutique
Felt-covered novelties
Flower arrangements
Framing pictures and mirrors
Frozen foods
Furniture moving
Furniture refinishing
Games for parties
Gift shops
Gift wrapping
Glass blowing
Glass specialties: painting, selling, etc.
Greenhouses
Greeting card illustration
Handbags: totes, carry-alls
Hand sewing
Health foods, home-grown
Herbs, raised and packaged
Housemoving

IBM punch machine service
Illustrator
Infants' clothing boutique
Interviewer
Jellies and jams
Jewelled eggshells, boxes, frames
Jewelry making
Kitchen planning
Knitting
Lamps: assembling, wiring, etc.
Macramé specialties
Magazine subscription sales
Mail order selling
Manufacturer's representative
Miniature room furniture
Mobiles
Package designer
Painting and antiquing furniture
Paint mixing
Papier mâché objects
Party favors and decorations
Party menus
Pattern maker and tester
Photography
Pickles
Plaques, wood and plaster
Posters
Pottery
Public relations
Public speaking
Puppet maker
Recipe tester
Remedial reading
Restoring damaged paintings
Restyling jewels
Restyling wardrobes

Retail fabric shops
Rocks and minerals for decorations
Rug braiding and hooking
Sandal making
Scarf making
Screen printer
Signmaking
Slipcover making
Society reporter
Soup kitchen
Speech writing
Stained glass specialties
Stencil making
Stenographic services
Swimming instructor at home pool
Telephone answering service
Ties for men
Tinware painting (Toleware)
Toy making
Translating
Travel agency
Trunks—old-fashioned restored and decorated
Tutoring
Typing
Upholstering
Verse writing for greeting cards
Wall hangings, decorated
Wall shadow boxes
Weaving
Wigs, dressed and sold
Window boxes
Window shades
Writing for advertising, publicity, news media
Yarn shops

Crafts from the Home

The hidden hunger for the handmade and the demand for artistry and individuality in imaginatively designed objects have made best sellers of the items illustrated on the following pages.

A search for regional crafts lures tourists from the jammed highways into small villages and towns, where they can buy a piece of America to take home. In the rural areas marketing cooperatives have been organized to bring the public and the craftsmen together in shopping centers, in which the combined talents and products of a whole area are festively displayed. In urban centers, boutiques and specialty shops search out gifted women who can supply them with the quilting, crewel embroidery, beaded flowers, and unique toys that city dwellers value.

These best sellers are not the mass-produced items that bring profits in the millions to an anonymous manufacturer. A best seller earns the housewife working alone at home about $5,000. However, this can be a springboard to an enlarged business if she takes on extra help and extends her facilities for producing in larger quantities.

In the realm of the highly gifted artist—the potter, the maker of jewelry, stained glass, and other crafts—one-of-a-kind creations can command prices on an extremely high scale. However, there are rare cases; the majority of women will welcome a modest addition of $1,000 or $2,000 to the family income.

It takes more than originality and skill to produce a best seller. It requires perpetual searching and experimenting with new ideas and materials that are encountered through reading, research, and constant exposure to what is going on in a given field.

Window Shades. Nothing succeeds like the interior decorator's touch. Making window shades to match color schemes and fabrics is a creative and profitable home career. Investigate the laminated press-on adhesive shade materials shown above. Also pictured are semisheer transparent shades, which adapt especially well to custom needlework designs.

Press-on Tri-Lam by Stauffer Chemical.

Semisheer transparent lattice we
Photo by George Nordhausen.

Press-on Tontine Tran-Lam
by Stauffer Chemical.

Candles. In a candlemaking business the investment in materials is small, but the appeal and the demand for the product are great. Candles are popular for occasions such as weddings, anniversaries, and birthdays. They often serve as room decorations during holiday seasons and as perennial accessories in the home. Scented candles add a lure that few can resist. Some varieties are bayberry, myrrh, spice, mint, and strawberry.

Wedding candle by The Candle Farm.
Photo by Bill McGinn.

ssorted candles. *Photo by Sam Nocella.*

Jewelry. Hand-wrought sterling silver jewelry, the product of a craft that can attain the status of a fine art, brings prices ranging from $10 to $2,000 and more. Many museums and universities offer special courses in this craft.

Pre-Columbian type necklace by Dorothy S. Benrimo. *Photo, American Crafts Council.*

One-of-a-kind sterling pins by Louella Schraeder.

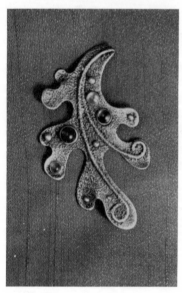

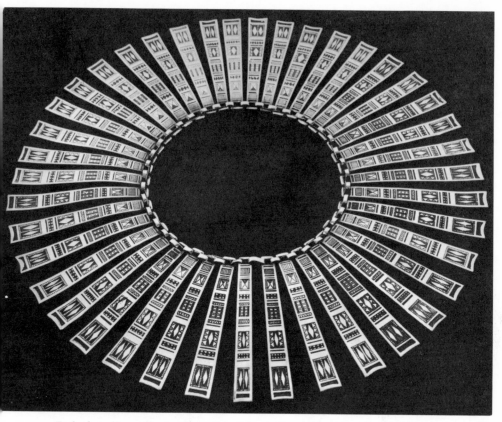

Etched sterling collar by Mary Ann Scherr. *Photo, American Crafts Council.*

by Irena Brynner. *Photo, Craft Horizons.*

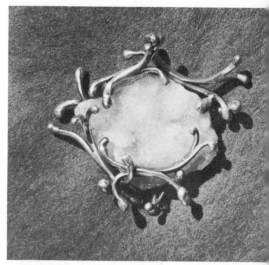

One-of-a-kind sterling pin by Louella Schraeder.

Cakes. Courses in cake decorating are given throughout the country to men and women interested in making unusual cakes for business or pleasure. Professional knowhow enables the student to produce special-occasion cakes such as those pictured here.

Wedding cake by Delores Fillinger. *Photo by Frank Alexandrowicz.*

Child's party cake and matching favors. *Photo by Mel Jacobsen.*

Heart-shaped cake suitable for Valentine's Day or engagement celebrations. *Photo by Mel Jacobsen.*

The perfect cake for a baby shower or christening party. *Photo by John Larsen.*

Beaded Flowers. The basic techniques for making beaded flowers are simple. The beads cost between 75 cents and $1.25 per twelve strands twenty inches long. Finished arrangements are sold in gift shops and boutiques at from $4.50 to $125, depending on the size, the artistry, and the quality of the materials.

Photo by George Nordhausen.

Photos, Nicole Bead and Craft, Inc.

Dolls and Stuffed Animals are easily marketable through gift shops and toy departments if they are sturdy, attractive, and creative in design. The examples on this page were made by a career-at-home housewife.

Fisherman doll by Jeanne Maker.
Photo, Lifetime Career Schools.

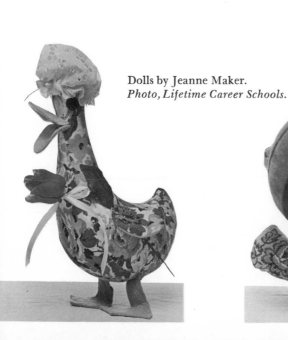

Dolls by Jeanne Maker.
Photo, Lifetime Career Schools.

Christmas Decorations. It's Christmas the year 'round when your home career is making Christmas decorations. First, samples are prepared and advertised. Next, orders are taken. The products should be shipped by early fall.

Merryland Acres, Lake Geneva, Wisconsin.

Photo by George Nordhause

Ceramics created at home can range from quantity-produced small items, such as ash trays selling for less than $5, to sculptural garden pieces, which can be commissioned for thousands.

Wall Fountain by Eloise Harmon.
Photo, American Crafts Council.

Weed pots by Lore Hauptman.
Photo, American Crafts Council.

ate and mug by Michelle Rhodes.
oto, American Crafts Council.

Tote Carry-Alls. Drawing and painting skills of talented career housewives add sales appeal to best sellers such as bags, greeting cards, decorative wall plaques, and painted walls. Tote carry-alls shown here are priced from $15 to $25 each.

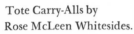

Tote Carry-Alls by
Rose McLeen Whitesides.

Lunch boxes by
Rose McLeen
Whitesides.

Decorated
handbags by
Rose McLeen
Whitesides.

Macramé. The art of tying knots of rope, string, yarn, or other materials to form geometric patterns results in fashionable clothing and home decorating accessories. An ancient craft, macramé has been revived and is now in widespread demand. Art centers, museums, universities, and crafts centers provide courses in this skill.

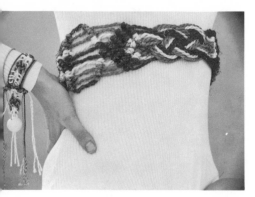

cramé belt and bracelet. *Photo by Jim Dorrance.*

Macramé sandals. *Photo by Jim Dorrance.*

Macramé purse and accessories.
Photo, American Crafts Council.

Decorative wall-hanging. *Photo by Jim Dorrance.*

Needlecrafts. Money is at your fingertips if you can do the basic embroidery stitches—the stem, cross, buttonhole, chain, double running, feather, French knot, lazy daisy, and couching. The demand for handmade crewel embroidery, hooked rugs, patchwork, appliqué, quilting, and other needlecrafts is at an all-time high.

Detail of design in embroidery hoop.

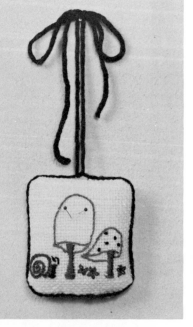

Pincushion. *Photo by Narramore.*

Stitchendipity Armadillo. *Photo by Narramore.*

African Violet Oval hooked by Joan Moshimer.

Stitchendipity Grow Chart. *Photo by Narramore.*

Gorski Lion. *Photo by George Nordhausen.*

PART II
Success Stories

1 Weddings Are Her Business

It was just past noon when Ellen Proxmire, wife of the senior United States senator from Wisconsin, arrived at the chapel of the Fort Myers, Virginia, military base, where the wedding she was to manage was scheduled to take place at one o'clock. She had just come from the rehearsal for *another* wedding.

All was serene and quiet; not a flower had yet been placed on the altar. The beautiful little church overlooking Arlington Cemetery was so deserted it was hard to imagine that within an hour, more than a hundred wedding guests would be going through the church portals to attend the formal wedding of Lonni Hillwig and Major Larkin Spivey, Jr., of the United States Marine Corps.

"Just come along with me while I attend to final arrangements," said Mrs. Proxmire, checklist in hand. "The final church arrangements are always the easiest part of any wedding. At an army base, the flowers always have to be placed on the altar at the last minute because there are other services scheduled there throughout the day."

"Saturday is our happy day," said Lieutenant Colonel James R. Hayes, the chaplain who was to conduct the service. "We save that for weddings. I'll have married five couples by evening."

Two colorful vases of flowers were the only decorations in the church, and no further embellishments were needed. The many rows of candelabra at the altar and the lovely chandeliers hanging from the ceiling would fulfill any bride's dream of wedding day glamour.

Downstairs in the lounge the ushers in Marine dress uniforms, complete with swords, were assembling. When the bridesmaids arrived, they would find facilities for primping. The next items on Mrs. Proxmire's list to be checked out were the white carnation boutonnières for the fathers of the bridal couple (Marine officers who act as ushers wear medals instead of boutonnières) and the white orchid corsages for the mothers of the bride and groom. All the people in the wedding party were lined up exactly where they were supposed to be.

A small tow-headed boy wearing a navy blazer slowly wandered in, carrying a small white cellophane-wrapped pillow trimmed with lace. It was for the wedding ring.

"How does he keep the ring from slipping off the pillow," I asked Mrs. Proxmire.

"Oh, the ring has to be tied and then untied at the altar. Usually we advise a symbolic ring to be on the safe side." Turning to the boy, she said, "Jeff, dear, before you walk down the aisle, don't forget to take off the cellophane cover."

"Where are the flowers for the bridesmaids?" I asked, a bit apprehensive.

"We eliminate all confusion at the church by having the bridesmaids meet at the bride's home. We always supply a tray of sandwiches; most of the girls forget to eat because of all the excitement. Their gloves and then their bouquets are handed to them as they leave the house. The bride and her father are the last to leave. We always make the arrangements for the limousines."

About this time, a slim, young, dark-haired major walked into the lounge, and the waiting photographer said, "Are you the groom?"

"I think so," he answered with a wan smile.

"Before we go up to wait for the wedding party in front of the church, you might like to read our Countdown instruction sheet. It has the hour-by-hour schedule of where you should be and what is to be done at the rehearsal the night before and on the day of the wedding. There have to be three of us on the job the day of a big wedding—one at the bride's home, one at the church, and one where the reception is to be held. There are too many details for anyone to handle alone, so three of us are in partnership at Wonderful Weddings."

Here, reprinted for the benefit of any reader now involved in planning a wedding, is that Countdown schedule.

Rehearsal:

7 p.m.—Friday at Fort Myers Chapel. Mrs. Proxmire and Mrs. (Gretchen) Poston will supervise for Wonderful Weddings.

Wedding Day:

11:30 a.m.—Mrs. Poston will arrive at bride's home.

12 noon—Mrs. Proxmire will arrive at the Fort Myers Chapel with checks for the organist and sexton. Boutonnières for groom and ushers will have been delivered with the altar flowers. Groom and ushers should arrive at this time too. Ushers require no boutonnières, being in uniform.

12:30 p.m.—Limousines will pick up bride, bridesmaids, and bride's parents.

1 p.m.—Ceremony begins. Following the ceremony, after members of the wedding party come down the aisle, they will remain in a room off the vestibule and wait until the guests have left the church. The bride, groom, and wedding party will return to the altar for pictures and then proceed out of the church through an eight-officer arch of swords. The bride and groom go from the chapel to the reception in a horse-drawn carriage. Wonderful Weddings will give check to the drivers.

Reception:

2 p.m.—Receiving line will form. There will be an open bar at this time. The receiving line is to be set up as follows: Bride's mother, groom's father, groom's mother, bride's father, bride, groom, maid of honor, best man.

2:45 p.m.—Bridal table and family table will be seated, and the buffet will be opened for the guests. Bridal table and family table will be served. Guests will serve themselves and choose seats.

3:30 p.m.—One glass of champagne will be served to each guest for a toast to the bride and groom, and the cake will be cut by the bride and groom and served for dessert.

3:45 p.m.—After cake is served, the first dance will be announced. The sequence is as follows: bride and groom dance; bride's father cuts in and dances with bride; groom dances with bride's mother; groom's parents come to the dance floor, and groom's father cuts in on bride while groom dances with his own mother, and the bride's parents dance with each other; general dancing follows.

4:30 p.m.—Drum roll and orchestra leader will announce that those admitting to be the oldest at each table may take the table centerpiece. Bride will throw her garter and bouquet before leaving to change clothes. After changing clothes, bride and groom will return to say goodbye.

5 p.m.—Best man will have car ready and, on departure, rose petals will be thrown at the couple.

After Reception:

Wonderful Weddings will give the following items to the bride's father to take home: The wedding dress, silver goblets, guest book, top of cake, and presents received at reception. Wonderful Weddings will pay all the bills except the club bill. [Author's Note: When a hotel is used for a reception, that bill is also paid by Wonderful Weddings.] It will also pay the initial photographer's costs. Extra prints should be ordered directly from the photographer.

Everything went off just as planned. Later, when I finally sat down with Mrs. Proxmire to talk about the business of running weddings, I asked her how she happened to originate the idea for a wedding advisory service and how long Wonderful Weddings had been in existence.

"My own daughter's wedding three years ago gave me the idea. I discovered how much I needed help and how complicated wedding arrangements are. There was no such service in Washington to advise me or to take over the arrangements. My daughter's was an interfaith marriage, and the groom's family came to Washington from Milwaukee and had to be housed. There were innumerable differences in marriage conventions in the two faiths, and, among the difficulties I had, I discovered that the chapel of the temple in which she was married had no organ. The music had to be taped, and broadcast from the back of the temple! When we arrived for the reception at the Bethesda Naval Officers' Club, there were no plates on the buffet table to serve food to our 150 guests."

When Ellen Proxmire presented her brainstorm to her two best friends, Gretchen Poston and Barbara Boggs, wives of Washington attorneys, they sparked to the idea at once. There was almost no overhead, and each woman took on a separate task, working in her own home. Their only initial expense was for business cards and file cabinets.

The women were very clever during their initial calls on caterers, photographers, hotels, florists, orchestra managers, and tent and limousine companies with whom they planned to work out reciprocal arrangements.

"We didn't know a thing about charging for our services," Mrs. Proxmire said. "We started out with a flat ten percent fee for all weddings, without a minimum charge, and we found ourselves making 10¢ an hour on a $500 wedding. Now we charge 15 percent, with a minimum fee of $200 and a maximum of $1,000. Our charge for giving advice is $25 an hour. Our busiest months are June, August, September, and December."

To get started they kept records of engagements as they were announced in the social columns of newspapers. These were followed up with letters to the prospective brides describing the services of Wonderful Weddings. The business people they had been to see brought them customers too. When some of the Washington columnists began to give them publicity, the phones really began to ring.

"The real response has come because of word-of-mouth recommendations. The wedding today was the result of one we managed a year ago in which today's bridegroom was the best man," said Mrs. Proxmire.

"How far in advance are you consulted by a prospective bride?" I asked.

"Usually three months but occasionally six months ahead. Sometimes, though, we have to whip up a wedding in two or three weeks."

"Do you have a set list of services you undertake, or is each wedding an individual arrangement?"

Mrs. Proxmire said that each wedding is individual. Their most expensive wedding was one for $10,000, and the least expensive was a home wedding that cost $400—before any minimum had been set.

"How do you divide your fees?"

"We split what we make equally. Actually, we've been putting as much money as possible right back into the business. This year we had to take on a small apartment for office space. Our rent there is $150 a month. Now that we're grossing around

$65,000, we can afford secretarial and telephone answering services. The first year, three years ago, we only took in $5,000—that was the year we figured we made 10¢ an hour!"

For most weddings, Mrs. Proxmire and her partners take care of the invitations, arrangements for the decorations at the church and the reception, the catering, flowers, music, photography, publicity, and transportation. They also handle other services when requested, such as shopping with the bride for her gown and assisting in the selection of the gifts for the bridal party.

"For many brides we become substitute mothers if for any reason there is no real mother to take care of the usual details."

"How do you protect yourself financially?" I asked, thinking of the bills that would come pouring in after the wedding was over for which Wonderful Weddings was responsible.

"At first we required a deposit, but now we can make an accurate budget and require advance payment, with an adjustment when the accounting is submitted if a rebate is indicated or the charges are slightly over our estimate."

"What future do you foresee for your business?"

"We've already gone national," said Ellen Proxmire. "We're being franchised." She explained that Wonderful Weddings branches were being offered to women in other parts of the country for a $6,000 investment.

"What will an investor get in return for her $6,000?" I asked.

"Instead of doing it the hard way—spending three years as *we* did, learning how to get started—she will receive a one-week training course and the equivalent of a home-study course, through a 300-page manual. In addition, the investor will get a regular newsletter that will keep her in touch with every aspect of the wedding business. Also, printed material for the business will be provided. What we get is a percentage of her fees in return for our services."

"What do your husbands think of all this?" I asked.

"They're impressed. They just warn us not to make too much money, or it will cost them on our joint income tax returns!"

2 For Sale: Candies, Jams, and Bread

"We live on a 119-acre farm named Hi-Ho Acres in the beautiful hills of Parke County, Indiana. I make and sell fifteen different kinds of candy, jelly, jams, fruit breads, and yeast bread. Some of my best sellers are apple butter, pumpkin, persimmon, and rhubarb breads, sassafras hard candy, corn cob and dandelion jellies, and butterscotch fudge. Last year I made $3,000, most of it during the ten days of the Covered Bridge Festival held in front of the county court house square in Rockville," wrote Kittye Hiland before I flew to meet her for our interview.

When the Hilands came to meet me at the airport I didn't expect Kitty to look like an airline hostess with an Audrey Hepburn haircut. The welcoming party included the whole family. Her husband George was carrying two-year-old Rourke, and the two teenaged sons Ben and Kern showed up as we crossed the road to their car.

"What I make doesn't sound very profitable, but most of my items sell for 60 cents or $1," Kitty told me as she showed me around their house. Then we walked over to her "store," perched on a slope just 150 feet behind the house.

"By converting the chicken house, which had for years been used for storage, into a store, I can have a career and be with my family at the same time," Kitty went on to explain. "I made the outside sign with lettered stencils I bought at the dimestore."

The transformation from chicken house to workshop and store was complete and beautiful. Kitty had hung red and gold fabric from the counter top to the floor over the entire length of the room. An open pine cupboard at the far end of the store held rows and rows of jewel-colored jelly in old fashioned glasses, labeled temptingly with names such as Corn Cob, Dandelion. Red Clover, Sassafras, and Sarsaparilla jellies. Gift-packaged display groupings adorned the counter.

"The Covered Bridge Festival and Maple Fair taught me that the way to catch the tourist trade was to package everything like gifts to be taken to the folks back home. Customers taste first with their eyes, then with their noses, and finally with their mouths," observed Kitty, "but it's the taste that brings them back for more."

Kitty's recipe awards are set apart in a display panel of blue, gold, red, and white satin ribbons, which she has won at fairs over recent years. A purple rosette with streamers tops the exhibit, representing the overall triumph of victory in the grand prize sweepstakes for excellence and originality in creating new varieties of candies. A color picture of a loaf of home-baked bread in an oval frame hangs like a family portrait at the entrance to the shop. Mimeographed copies of recipes are stacked on the front counter for customers to pick up with the compliments of the house.

The unexpected thing about Kitty Hiland is that she didn't grow up on a farm, though her husband did, and she never held a job in her life. She was brought up in a small town, "a spot in the road," surrounded by farms. Kitty credits her high school home economics teacher with giving her the basic knowledge and love of cooking that eventually led to her home career. She met her husband, who was a telephone company cable supervisor, on a picket line. Her sister, an operator, was marching in the picket line too. George Hiland still works for the Indiana Bell Telephone Company, but he has been promoted to construction supervisor. On the farm he is building up a herd of Black Angus beef cattle ("You don't have to get up at four A.M. to milk 'em") and has forty acres of his land planted in crops— corn, beans, and hay. His neighboring farmer works his land in exchange for its use on a fifty-fifty profit sharing arrangement.

"Parke County is the Covered Bridge capital of the world," I was told. Tourists come from all parts of the United States and abroad to buy crafts and take part in the festivities that are held all over the county. In front of the county court house building in Rockville, the stands are as colorful and exciting as sideshows at a circus. George Hiland always takes his vacation during the ten days of the Rockville festival to help out at their stand. The Hilands pay $5 a year dues and ten percent commission on all sales to the Parke County Corporation, which uses the money of exhibitors to build new projects and to maintain the reconstructed early American town called Billy Creek Village. This is open to the public daily for eight months of the year. Authentic old buildings, including a general store, a country church, a bandstand, and other buildings, have been moved to the site of Billy Creek Village in order to provide the historic and traditional setting for the crafts that are demonstrated and sold there from May to Thanksgiving. Kitty's products also sell at the General Store in Billy Creek Village. No outside commercial products are allowed. The crafts include weaving, candlemaking, pottery, flax spinning, and others. The goods are offered for sale by men and women volunteers from the community. They are dressed in jeans, long calico dresses, and sunbonnets. Kitty has made herself three costumes, which she also wears in her own store.

If Kitty could package her housekeeping system, her profits would be in the millions instead of the $3,000 it is. She has no housework schedule except meals on time. The men in the family keep everything picked up as they go along from day to day. Even baby Rourke picks up his toys because he sees his father and brothers putting away their boots, guns, ice skates, sleds, and bows and arrows.

"My husband says he doesn't mind if our feet stick to the floor and we can write our names on the table as long as the house looks neat."

The new wall-to-wall carpeting makes shedding shoes on the back porch and walking around the house in stocking feet irresistible to everyone, especially Kitty herself.

"I never have to say a cross word. The boys' father can't stand disorder, and the boys follow his lead. Everyone makes his own bed in the morning and gets his own breakfast, and in the evening everybody takes a turn at loading and unloading a daily wash. They smooth and fold the clean clothes too. By 7:30 every morning everyone is out of the house except me and the baby."

That means that Kitty can tackle any job she feels like doing that day. Often it's housepainting and carpentry instead of cooking.

However, cooking goes on all winter in Kitty's second kitchen so that enough candies, breads, jellies, and jams can be frozen for the three big regional events—The Covered Bridge Festival, the Maple Fair, and Billy Creek Village.

Kitty makes 2,000 jars of jellies and jams, 1,500 small loaves of fruit breads, 700 pounds of fudge, and 700 pounds of sassafras hard candies. For the Maple Fair, held in March, the maple candy she sells adds $500 to her income. Candies are sold by the half pound, 55 cents for the hard candies and 60 cents for fudge. Jellies in old-fashioned jars are $1.25 each. Apple butter is 80 cents a pint and sells faster than Kitty can make it.

Her rule of thumb on pricing is to charge three times the cost of the ingredients used. This ratio pays for her time as well as the ingredients and allows a profit of around twenty-five percent. Her teenaged boys pitch in and help during the fairs, and she pays them each 50 cents an hour.

This year Kitty went into her big production, and she insisted on swinging the added expense entirely on her own. She went to the Parke State Bank and borrowed $1,000 to remodel an extra bedroom into a kitchen with an outside entrance, required by the state health department. She spent $19 on insurance ("Just in case I died, I wouldn't want George having to pay back my loan").

Quantity purchases of ingredients are just as inexpensive at markets as they would be if bought at wholesalers since Kitty doesn't have to buy on the scale of a commercial food factory. She buys 120 pounds of sugar at a time, 80 pounds of flour, and apple sauce for apple butter by the case. Nuts and creamery butter she seldom uses—"The public is too cholesterol conscious—they don't want those ingredients."

Packaging is a baffling problem to the majority of women who produce products to sell outside of their homes. Kitty's approach to finding packaging resources is direct and effective and recommended to all beginners. Whenever she sees packaging she likes, she looks at the label to find out who manufactures the product and writes to that company for information. If the company is in her vicinity, she phones.

"You know, big business executives have been very nice to me. They're not stingy about giving me names and addresses and prices."

She often goes right to the owner of a food or gift shop and asks where the container, the basket, the transparent wrapping, or the plastic jug, jar, or barrel can be bought. Florists provide many materials useful to her in wrapping and making displays or stuffings in which to protect things that might break. Many of her candies she wraps individually in vividly colored florists' foils so that in a glass jar the candies shine through like Christmas tree ornaments. She uses Styrofoam balls bought from florists and spears hard candy sucker sticks through them like porcupine quills. Miniature bushel baskets, little brown plastic kegs, and transparent gift bags were all tracked down with the help of local merchants.

It is hard to believe that a girl with the imagination, the organizing ability, the energy, and the enthusiasm of Kitty Hiland ever had a problem with insecurity and mental depressions.

"I was so frightened I couldn't learn to drive a car. I didn't think I was any good at anything, and I was terrified my husband would leave me when he couldn't stand how awful I was. I even went to a psychiatrist for help and after months he confessed he couldn't help me because we all loved each other. We were normally intelligent and physically healthy, and there wasn't a clue to why I had these phobias."

It wasn't until Kitty joined Recovery, a self-help program founded by Dr. Abraham A. Low, of the University of Illinois Medical School, that Kitty began to believe in herself and to discover that she could respect the abilities she had. A rather gruesome comment that another psychiatrist made to her—and she can laugh about it now when she tells it—was that she really wanted to kill her husband and children.

"Imagine my angelic husband and boys inspiring any such idea!"

Kitty used to think that anyone could cook.

"Now I know it's a talent, and when people come back again and again to buy what I make and praise me, I love every minute of it. I call my chicken house my playhouse. Every day I read Dr. Low's book *Mental Health Through Will Power Training* like the Bible. [Published by the Christopher Publishing House, Boston, Massachusetts.] I became the leader of a Recovery group myself and helped others. Dr. Low has died, but his book should go on forever."

The self-expression and recognition that Kitty didn't even suspect she needed now finds a way to fulfillment.

"Other people want to see the world. I never want to be anywhere else. This is a beautiful place, full of hills and the beauties of nature. We have deer come right up here behind my
chicken house store. The stand of sassafras trees over there
bursts into a blaze of color in the fall, and the redbud trees
around the house are a lovely garland of bloom in the spring.
The people are the kind that say 'if you need me, call me' and
they mean it."

3 Stitching for Fun and Profit

Everything about Jan Henson Carter is understated — her voice (which is soft), the way she seems to get things done without fuss or bother, and the simple quiet manner in which she tells about her work. She has set up a needlework shop in her house in Austin, Texas. She conducts a mail order business that sells stitchery kits, and she teaches the techniques in classes at home. And she talks of it all as if there were nothing extraordinary about her. The things about Jan that are *not* understated are her flair for designing and her love of color. The walls of her house, the tops of her tables, the covers on her beds, and the cushions on her chairs surround her with her own inventiveness and talent.

The room that would otherwise be the living room of her gabled white brick home is her showroom and shop. With framed stitchery pictures on white walls, it looks more like an art gallery. Whimsical lions, calico cats, sophisticated abstracts, and colorful flower motifs combine to create a young contemporary look—a considerable departure from traditional embroidery and needlepoint.

A sign outside—STITCHENDIPITY/ART NEEDLEWORK BOUTIQUE— invites the public between the hours of ten and four. Indian chimes at the front door summon Jan from her laundry, kitchen, or garage workroom ("my cozy cave" she calls it) whenever a visitor enters.

Though Jan's career at home began two years ago, "I'm still just getting started," she tells you. "I brought in only about $1,500 last year, but this year the amount may double. I had to put most of what I earned last year and the year before into paying for my catalog and materials."

Now, about that word "stitchendipity." "It's my own invention," she says. "It means a variety of unexpected stitches and techniques all combined in one needlework piece. Most of my pieces are simple. As a matter of fact, I measure the time it takes me to make each piece I design. I have a symbol composed of the words 'quick to stitch,' and anyone who buys one of my kits knows beforehand just how much time and work she is taking on."

"Who are most of your customers?" I asked.

"The young marrieds. Many of them want dramatic effects—designs that can be made quickly to give their rooms individuality and to reflect their own personalities."

Jan's college degree was in home economics, but until she married Richard Carter, she preferred the liveliness of a business office. They met where both of them worked—in the district executive offices of the Boy Scouts of America, in Los Angeles.

It was loneliness in a small town that later led Jan to discover her creative talents. Dick was promoted and transferred to an executive post with the Boy Scouts in Olympia, Washington, and the Carters moved to a quiet village nearby. Jan read about an exhibition of creative stitchery at the state museum in Olympia. One day she finished her housework, picked up baby Andrew (who is now a handsome lad of six), climbed into the car, and went off to the exhibit. What she saw thrilled her. This was much more than the painstaking filling-in of ready-made designs with tiny stitches; this was an art form. And Jan felt it was within her capabilities.

"Creative stitchery is to needlework what free verse is to poetry," she explains. "The rigid rules and time-consuming labor of traditional needlework never appealed to me. Now, after seeing that exhibition, I felt free to make my own designs and color combinations. I signed up for courses at the museum and took three in succession."

The first sign that stitchery might become a career at home came to her when she woke up one night with the word "stitchendipity" ringing in her ears.

"I realized," Jan recalls, "that a lot of other girls would love to start with designs, instructions, and materials all assembled and then go on to their own original designs if they had the urge. My friends were so enthusiastic that they asked me to start some classes. I charged $1 an hour and usually had at least four pupils for periods of up to three hours at a time, earning me about $12 an afternoon. Then I started to experiment with kits. I took sample ones to needlework stores on consignment and filled orders as they came in. In addition, I put a fifty-word mail order ad in a small needlework magazine. The local library gave an exhibition of my work and my pupils' that stirred up so much interest I knew I needed a showroom at home."

In pricing her kits, Jan has a rule of thumb. The first step is to find out what the competition is charging. "Then," she explains, "I assemble everything and figure out the cost of the materials—the cost per square inch of my fabrics; the cost per square inch for yarns used; the cost of different needles, trimmings, and findings (handles, frames, and the like).

"The cost of the printed directions and the kit's plastic container have to be figured in too, and also my labor in making the stencils and the tracings of the designs. Then I add in overhead, which means the expenses of my workroom—electricity and so forth. I compare the total with the prices of similar kits and then decide what I should charge.

"I learned that in the early stages of a business you have to have a sliding scale of profits. There will be some items that justify a profit of only five percent, but you'll go out of business if that's all you make on all of your items. You must take a higher profit on many of them—so high that you double your cost price. You're entitled to charge for your taste and creative talent. But you still have to price things so your customers can afford to pay for them.

"My least expensive item sells for $1—a miniature crewel design on linen, four and a half inches square. My most expensive item is a king-size quilt for $68. Every kit contains stenciled or traced fabric, yarns, needles, and instructions. Some also contain trimmings and findings.

"I learned many of my stitches and techniques before I was ten years old. They are very simple. These are the embroidery stitches I use: stem, cross, buttonhole, chain, feather, French knot, lazy daisy, and couching. Aside from basic embroidery, I work with appliqué, needlepoint, and quilting. It's as much fun to experiment with new stitches as it is to play around with mixing paints. Needle and thread are to me what brush and palette are to an artist."

4 One-Woman Beauty Parlor

As I drove along a residential street in Somerset, in the dairy farm country of south-central Pennsylvania, looking for a white house with two front doors and a small sign reading MARY BOWLIN'S BEAUTY SALON, I counted five churches within six blocks—Catholic, Methodist, Church of the Brethren, Grace United, and Church of Christ. I kept an eye peeled for special hairdos, imagining they might be the work of the enterprising housewife whose home career we were about to explore.

Mary Bowlin's sign is so modest I almost missed it. It is the only business sign in a several-block area of closely built, well kept homes. I climbed the porch stairs and pushed open a door bearing a welcoming COME IN.

Mrs. Bowlin greeted me wearing a crisp white uniform and looking more like a trained nurse than the beautician she is—except that her elaborate hairdo, pulled up from her ears into a French twist in back and with a smooth bouffant puff over her forehead, is unmistakably the work of a professional.

I had arrived as she was doing a set in the room's single hydraulic chair, facing a wet unit that includes a shampoo bowl, mirror, and cupboard.

"I'll be with you as soon as I put Mrs. Sailor under the drier," Mary said, flashing a warm smile. "Wouldn't you like to go into the living room and get acquainted with my daughter?"

The living room is the other half of the same beauty parlor room, but to reach it, one must return to the porch and reenter the house through another door. Inside I found sixteen-year-old Kristy Bowlin, her long pale blonde hair rolled in big curlers, sitting cross-legged on the stair landing with two high school chums. I joined the conversation about an upcoming school basketball game and dance.

Three sharp knocks on the partition that divides the living room from the beauty parlor signaled that Mary had put her customer under the drier and was free to tell me how her home career started.

"When the Tri-County School of Beauty Culture opened a branch in town, I was the third to enroll," Mary reminisced, adding that, at the time, both of her youngsters were in school all day. "My husband Jim had said that if I could find a way to pay the $450 fee, I could go ahead and take the course."

Figuring how to get the money took some ingenuity. Mary had to find work that wouldn't interfere with her class hours. The junior high school cafeteria turned out to be just the thing. She went to her beauty school classes every morning from 9 to 11:20. Then she worked in the junior high kitchen until 1:15. At 1:30 she returned to the beauty school until 4. She arrived home a little later—about the same time as her children.

"I was allowed to pay for the course in monthly installments," Mary explained. "It took me nine months to complete, and by then it was paid for. I could have finished in six months if I hadn't been working."

The cost of equipment—which she bought on the installment plan from the company that runs the training school—came to about $1,500. She needed a hydraulic chair, a wet unit, two hair driers, and a manicuring table and stool. Her appointment desk and two chairs for waiting customers were additional expenses, as was a movable supply caddy containing rollers, pins, lotions, and sprays. These supplies run about $30 a month. Paneling her thirteen- by fourteen-foot room with wallboard and installing new lighting and special plumbing fixtures set Mary back about $450.

The Bowlins own their house, so they had no trouble getting credit through a finance company. Mary said the investment has taken about five years to pay off, at the rate of about $400 a year. Her gross annual income averages $2,500, from which she must deduct her expenses.

Tuesday and Wednesday seven customers represent a good day's volume, but on Thursday, Friday, and Saturday, this number can soar to eleven, and Mary's business hours are extended into the evening. The shop is closed on Monday, when Mary takes care of her weekly housecleaning, washing and ironing, and other domestic chores. Now that Kristy is in her teens, she is a big help with the homemaking, even sewing her own clothes.

Beauty shop appointments are made by phone, allowing seventy-five minutes for a set. A shampoo and set cost $2. A permanent wave is priced from $7.50 to $12, depending on the head of hair and the type of permanent. A haircut is $1.50; a manicure, $1.25; coloring, $6; a facial, $2. Almost all of Mary's customers use rinses, but only about ten percent dye their hair.

High school girls, Mary finds, get their hair done only for big occasions such as proms and graduation parties, but then they want "the works." They show Mary pictures of hairstyles from magazines and often ask for a "rehearsal" hair set the week before the big event. Sometimes they bring artificial flowers to weave into braids or to tuck into chignons. Week in and week out, though, it is not the teenagers but their mothers who are the regular customers, and they usually stick to conservative styles.

To care for her own rather elaborate hairstyle, Mary sleeps on a satin pillowcase. This keeps the setting intact for days, she says, with only a bit of brushing required.

Jim Bowlin is a postman and must get to work early in the morning, so he and Mary are too busy for a very active social life. However, they do occasionally join their Somerset neighbors for card games or church socials.

"I love to dance," says Mary, "and before we were married, Jim told me he could dance up a storm. But my grandmother used to say that such idleness is the work of the devil. As far as Jim and I are concerned, though, we've never had time to find out!"

5 Raising Pups for Love and Money

Ann Mesdag's at-home career began when she couldn't resist buying a female German shepherd that had no tail. Despite the missing part—it had been lost during a run-in with a car—the dog, Siren, was a magnificent animal, whose parents were both champions. And Ann could have her for just $100.

In those days, however, $100 was quite a bit of money to Ann, her husband Matthias, and their growing family. "We were just starting a new life in America after having been Dutch prisoners of war in Indonesia during World War II," recalled Matthias, whose nickname is Theis (pronounced *tease*).

"I had never had a dog," Theis continued, "but Ann had lived on a plantation in Java, and her mother had raised prize-winning dogs as a hobby. Well, Ann loved dogs and she *had* to have Siren. And I can't say no to anything Ann really wants, so we got the dog."

Siren's first litter produced four puppies. Ann sold three of them for $50 each, keeping the fourth for breeding. All the pups from Siren's second litter were sold in just one night after the Mesdags placed a classified ad in a local newspaper. One of these puppies became a champion.

The first two litters were born and raised in the basement of the Mesdags's rented house in a project in Seattle. It was possible to fence in a run just inside the door of the basement, and Theis built a couple of four by six-foot whelping boxes where Ann's dogs gave birth to their litters.

The Mesdags's early days in America were a struggle — but they were nothing compared to what Ann had undergone as a prisoner of the Japanese. Just a teenager at the time, Ann had been living with her parents in Java when that island was over-run by the Japanese early in the war. She became a member of the Dutch underground, relaying vital information to the United States army in Australia. Eventually Ann was captured. She was tortured—kicked and burned. But she survived.

After the war Ann and Theis met, married, and came to America, settling in Seattle. Though he had received excellent schooling in Holland as an engineer and had served as an officer in the Dutch army, Theis had to take a $2,700-a-year job while learning English and going to the University of Washington at night. Meanwhile, Ann, who had to stay at home during the day to tend to the family and the dogs, worked nights in a cannery. Ann's mother, Mrs. Ann Braekens—who has lived with the Mesdags ever since they came to America—also pitched in, working as a practical nurse.

Through the combined efforts of the three, the family was able to move to a home in the country, in Bothell, Washington, where Ann started a real kennel.

Within seven years Ann's kennel was producing 150 puppies a year.

Ann's business, officially known as the Van Nassau Kennels (a name chosen because of its aristocratic Dutch connotation) now includes nine seventeen- by nine-foot runs and a long shed made of fiberglass, with twenty five- by nine-foot rooms that sleep two dogs each.

The construction and operation of the kennel was strictly a family affair. Under Theis's direction, facilities for the dogs were built by the four Mesdag boys, all of whom are now in college. (In addition, Theis and Ann have four daughters, three of them adopted. "As our children started to grow up," Theis explained, "we found that we couldn't face the future without children at the dining room table.")

Labor has never been a problem at the kennel. "We have never had the money to hire anyone," Ann said, "so all the work had to be done by the family. The boys would clean up the kennel every morning before going to school, and then they would clean again in the afternoon after they came home. They also fed the dogs once a day—at five P.M.—a diet of boiled beef poured over dog biscuits or kibbled dog food, plus multiple vitamins. Now, with the boys away at college, the two oldest girls have taken over these chores."

Sitting in the Mesdags's spacious ranch-style living room, I asked Ann if she felt raising dogs at home was a practical, profitable idea for the average woman.

"First, of course," she replied, "a woman must have a great love for dogs. Also, I feel that such a career is better for a woman than it is for a man. Women have stronger stomachs for this sort of thing; they don't mind being midwives to a litter or taking care of sick animals. I guess it's their maternal instinct that fortifies them. If a husband is against having a kennel at home, though, I'd advise a woman to drop the whole thing."

Running a business of this sort requires a great deal of patience, Ann pointed out. "Before a kennel can succeed in making a profit, years have to be invested in establishing top bloodlines. In the early days any money I made went into acquiring and producing fine dogs, so that during the first seven years of operation, my kennel produced twelve American and Canadian champions—and I didn't make a dime.

"Now," she continued, "ten years later, I have owned or bred close to a hundred champions, and on gross alone it might appear that I'm getting rich in the dog business. But you have to subtract my expenses for shows, travel, and handling. Actually, I net between $10,000 and $12,000 a year."

Another factor to be considered by anyone thinking of following in Ann's footsteps is state and local licensing and zoning regulations. For example, in Ann's state, Washington, kennels are restricted to rural areas with a minimum of five acres of land. The kennels have to be forty feet away from the owner's home and any adjoining property lines, and adequate indoor facilities for the dogs are required for wintertime operations. Public health regulations include giving all dogs shots for rabies, distemper, hepatitis, and leptospirosis. In addition, there is a $30 annual license fee.

When training and showing her dogs became so demanding that she couldn't supervise the care of the puppies, Ann persuaded two housewives down the road to start puppy nurseries. Neither woman had any previous experience in caring for puppies, but under Ann's direction the plan has been very successful. Ann provides the food and medical requirements, and her neighbors get $5 a month for each puppy.

Ann's goal is to reduce the number of dogs currently in her

kennel from forty to thirty and to produce about sixty high-price puppies a year that would sell for at least $250 each. Ann has sold a few dogs for as much as $2,500 apiece.

A stud fee is clear profit to Ann, and it accounts for about thirty-five percent of her business. (German shepherds are the second most popular breed of dog in America—the first being poodles.) Registration papers go with the sale of each dog.

My talk with the Mesdags was interrupted several times by phone calls. One was from a man in Venezuela who said he was flying in the next day to pick up a show dog Ann had raised for him. Another call was from a woman who was making a plea for a gift dog to a crippled child.

"Each year I give away many dogs to the blind and disabled," Ann said. "One of my pleasantest experiences occurred about two years ago. A jalopy pulled up in front of the house, and a young man got out. He had a German shepherd with him. It seems the man had been drafted, and he wondered if I could find a good home for his dog while he was in the Army. I promised I would and that when he got back, I would give him a German shepherd puppy.

"Well," she continued, "just last month the young man got back from Vietnam, safe and sound, and he came to claim the pup I had promised him. That's a promise I was delighted to keep!"

For Ann and her family this gesture was a small repayment to this country for the bounty and good fortune they have received from it.

Theis summed up their feelings: "America to us is the symbol of everything that's good in life. We love the air we breathe and the space and the freedom—where we can raise children and dogs to our hearts' content."

6 Housewife's Invention Hits the Jackpot

The Animal Fair showroom looked like a setting for a Peter Pan party, but there wasn't a child in sight. There wasn't a mother in sight either. There were men picking up cuddly bears, innocent looking white woolly lambs, nut-eating squirrels, plush skunks, and giant stuffed animals that seemed to be looking pleadingly for approval. The men were toy buyers for department stores all over the country, and they pulled ears and tails, squeezed animal middles, and looked for some gimmick that would have special sales appeal.

I had accompanied the buyers, and we were all ushered into an office at the far end of the showroom. The president of the company that manufactures the fanciful line of stuffed animal toys we had seen was host to the many buyers who were attending the Toy Fair week in New York City and placing their orders.

Also in the office was a dashing-looking woman in her early thirties, waiting to see the president. I had no idea then that the woman, Harriet Johnson, was to be the subject of this story. I was to learn that she is an inventor-housewife who made $25,000 in royalties in one year.

"Are you connected with this company?" I asked.

"Heavens, no! I'm a housewife. But the company did buy one of my ideas last year, and I'm here to see a Toy Fair for the first time in my life. I never knew how important a trade show could be if you have something to sell."

Harriet handed me an advertising leaflet with the photograph of her invention on the cover.

"This is it," she said. "Sears Roebuck has decided to feature a version of it in its catalog."

The photograph showed the head of a boy peering out from between the jaws of an alligator sleeping bag—with a white saw-tooth rickrack effect simulating the teeth. The material was a dark green quilted wool. The alligator had red-rimmed orange eyes, and the hard black shiny-button pupils stared right out of the page.

"Perfect!" I exclaimed. "I want to interview you for my careers-at-home book. Where do you live?"

Her eyes looked as surprised as her alligator's. "In Falls Church, Virginia, just outside of Washington, D.C."

A few days later, Harriet told me, step by step, how the alligator sleeping bag she had run up on her sewing machine became a best seller—with the prospect of still another boom year ahead.

Her husband Nelson, a major in the army, was in the house, and soon their two sons Nelson, Jr., age nine, and George, age eight, came trooping home from school.

"The boys were my built-in proving ground," Harriet said. "By the time I was ready to show my animal sleeping bags, they'd been field-tested by my own children and their friends. I used their sizes for measuring, and when we'd go visiting for an evening, I used to roll up a bag for each of my sons and put them to bed in them when they got sleepy. When we were ready to go home, my husband would carry them out to the car still asleep. The first two alligator sleeping bags—Slumberchums, as they were finally called—are still like pets to the boys. Even now they like to set up a tent in the back yard during warm weather and sleep out in their alligators."

"Have you ever had a job or done any designing before?" I asked.

"Nels and I were married two weeks after we were graduated from the University of Wyoming, and he's been my only boss, literally.

"At college I was preparing to go into commercial art and planned to do post-graduate work at the Chicago Art Institute. I'd been brought up in nearby Winnetka. Nels had joined ROTC in college and was obligated to go into the service for two years after graduation, so my career as a commercial artist was side-tracked to become an army wife. That was in 1960, and in 1963 Nels was sent to Korea as a first lieutenant. I was left with two babies in the house near Fort Meade, Maryland.

"Moving around to various army posts and having two babies had kept me very busy until Nels went away. But then I was housebound and alone, and I had to find things to do to keep me busy and interested.

"I began thinking up ideas and making models of things for the children. I remember one of them was something I called a Keep Busy Box—a learning box with all kinds of household gadgets that toddlers could learn to put together. The box included an electric plug that they could pull apart and put together, and it turned out to be a real menace. I had to run around the house covering up all the baseboard plugs to keep my bright little boys from electrocuting themselves. I made a dozen things and didn't know what to do with them. I'd seen similar ideas advertised in catalogs, and I realized that this kind of thing could pay off if I only knew how to go about it.

"It wasn't until four years later, after I had been making one model after another, that I had a brainstorm. I became determined to try to sell my idea. No, it wasn't the animal sleeping bag, but it did lead to what became the sleeping bag. It was a crawl-in giant plastic ball. I made two versions and called them Holey Rollers. The children had a wonderful time crawling in the holes in the sides of the balls and rolling around.

"When I went to visit my family in St. Paul, they thought I should see a local manufacturer. I didn't know how to find one, so I looked in the Yellow Pages under *Toys—Plastic,* and I went to see the manager of the only firm listed. I was advised to try to finance the manufacture of the Holey Rollers myself, and the manufacturer said he thought enough of the idea so that if I supplied the money, he would make and sell them.

"My heart sank. I didn't have that kind of money and couldn't raise it. The company designer came to my rescue and said that if I would go into a fifty-fifty royalty arrangement with him, he would produce the item and put up the money himself.

"The sad part of the story is that I agreed to this arrangement and never saw a cent of profit. There was a lot of confusion because the company was sold and the toy never did get produced in a large enough quantity to make money. But I had learned a hard lesson. I then decided to set up my own workshop.

"It was while I was shopping for materials for Holey Rollers that I saw the fake furs that gave me the idea to convert my brainchild into animal sleeping bags. I made ten different animals—a Saint Bernard, an octopus, a ladybug, a dragon, an alligator, a dolphin, a snake, a leopard, a cockatoo, and a hound dog.

"By the time I had finished all of them," she continued, "I knew that producing more than one of each would be agony. Making up just a single model was worse than labor pains at childbirth. I would *have* to find a manufacturer."

I asked her if there was any way she could protect her ideas through a patent or copyright.

"Oh, I thought about it, but it's expensive just to find out if you have an idea that can be patented. A patent is usually based on the uniqueness of a construction feature, and I didn't have that advantage. What I had was an idea that would have to be converted into a mass-produced item.

"My children were so crazy about the animal sleeping bags that I was convinced that this time I had a great idea. Again, it was a visit to my family with the models that got me going. On the way to St. Paul, I stopped off at the Merchandise Mart in Chicago, where I knew I could visit a variety of showrooms for stuffed toys. I became interested in Animal Fair because it was in Chanhassen, not far from St. Paul, and I was told to get in touch with the president. This time I took the precaution of finding out about the reputation of the company and its president through my stepfather's lawyer and other business associates. I was assured of the reliability of both.

"I called the president's office and made a date to fly out with my models the next day. When the president himself said he would see me, I was in a panic. I put my animals in garment bags, hung them up on the coat rack of the plane, struggled with them at the airport when they had to be transferred to my family's car, and arrived an hour and a half late, just at lunchtime. Instead of telling me to unload, the president took me to lunch.

"By the time lunch was over, I had created interest enough to be asked to show some of my monsters in his office. He seemed to fall for the alligator right away. That was the one he decided to have his designer make up in several versions. He asked me to call my lawyer to arrange for a letter of agreement. I didn't have a lawyer, but my stepfather did, and they attended to the preliminary formalities with the understanding that a contract would be drawn up if the company decided to go ahead. It was established that I would get five percent net on the wholesale price of each animal sold.

"The company salesmen took samples to various stores to get individual reactions. One department store chain really liked my alligator, but they wanted it in a less expensive version; the original was made to retail for $25.

"My first royalty check came in September; it was under $100. The second one in October was for $500, and then, in November, it suddenly jumped to $1,500. Between August and December I had received about $3,500."

"Who owns the idea now?" I asked.

"The manufacturer bought the idea and owns the designs and name, but I am protected by a contract that says I originated the idea, and I am entitled to the five percent royalty on all sales. This company—and most toy companies—have their own designers, and I was told that most of the ideas that come in from outside are not novel enough to buy. I was lucky enough to be first with this idea. The next month a man brought samples of a very similar sleeping bag that he had been trying to perfect for two years. But I was ahead of him and hit the jackpot. That only happens once in a lifetime, I am told."

7 She Quilted Her Family a House

Salt of the earth with a savor—that's Eula Kircher.

"The sale of one of my quilts made enough to pay for the new roof on our house, with 60 cents left over!" she said as we started the house tour. "I'm on my 381st quilt since I began to sell them fourteen years ago. My husband retired eleven years ago, and we sold our farm and bought this tumbledown four-room Ozark cabin with the idea he'd rebuild it as we lived in it."

Eula's eyes twinkled, and she smiled broadly as she introduced her lean, tanned husband John, who had come in to make me as welcome as she had.

"This seventy-year-old kid has designed every inch of this house, driven every nail, laid every floor, put on the roof, and, within six months, the siding will be on the outside and the house painted white and the kitchen and bathroom will be finished and the fireplace blazing!" Eula's nonstop enthusiasm was tempered a bit by her more conservative husband.

"Here's hoping," said John.

In addition to Eula's quilts and approximately $200 a month from Social Security, John adds to their income by raising sweet potato seedlings and selling them at the rate of about 100,000 a day for three weeks to seed houses during the season.

"My job is to wrap and pack 'em," said Eula.

During strawberry season the Kirchers sell about 240 quarts and share the profits with the dozen pickers who help them.

"We work like killing snakes!" said Eula Kircher, whose conversation is punctuated with what she likes to call hillbilly talk.

148

"We put as little cash in building as possible. We just spend it as it comes in from my quilts and John's extra projects," said Eula.

Her daughter Maxine, who had driven us over from Joplin, forty miles away, where she lives with her industrial engineer husband and three children, explained, "They have a ball, those two. They're on the trot about a week out of every month. They pile in their camper to visit fairs and friends all over this state and in Arkansas and Oklahoma."

Another married daughter lives in Idaho. When letters come addressed to "Granny and Granpa Kircher" from their three grandchildren in Idaho, the mailman starts blowing his horn as he comes driving up the hill.

Several years ago Eula was invited to Washington, D.C., to exhibit her quilts at the Smithsonian Institution.

"The most thrilling day of my life was the day Mr. and Mrs. Lester Elliott, who run the War Eagle Fair in Rogers, Arkansas, came to relay the invitation."

The Missouri Farmers Cooperative had asked to sponsor Mrs. Kircher and pay the expenses of the trip. This is an annual crafts exhibition arranged by the U.S. Department of Agriculture and the Farmers Cooperative Service, and it includes the outstanding work of women from all over the country.

"I was supposed to fly, but I wanted my husband to come with me, and he wanted to drive. So we compromised by taking the bus and shipped my frames and quilts by express."

Mrs. Kircher went on to tell us that the booth at the War Eagle Fair, which she rents for $5 for three days (and pays a ten percent sales commission on each spread), brings in additional orders throughout the year. She always sells the dozen quilts she takes to the fair from $80 to $150 each. "I have to turn down about 300 orders for quilts every year. Three a month is my speed."

The most important room in the Kirchers' house is Eula's quilting room. The room is twenty-five feet long and twelve feet wide. Her rectangular quilting frame looks as big as a single bed in the center of the room. Her 381st quilt was stretched on the frame where she was working on it the day I met her. The windows of her quilting room look out over a sloping hill that is planted with 1,200 different varieties of iris. "I'm weak-kneed about iris," said Eula. "I can't resist collecting and planting the bulbs, even if the flowers come and go in a month during the spring.

"I've been quilting for forty-two years," she continued. "My mother and grandmother used to quilt, but nobody taught me. I just watched and started quilting on my own. I never began to count how many I made until I started to sell them."

Mrs. Kircher makes an original design for every quilt. No two quilts she makes are ever identical, but she does identify six of her quilts by names, and these can be ordered to look like the originals with slight variations. "Dogwood" is her biggest seller, at $150. This features a spray design with brown branches, deep pink blossoms, and green leaves against a delicate shell-pink quilted cotton background. "The Plume" is a quilt with printed calico appliqués outlined in the shapes of plumes against a beige background. "Looks old-timey," said Eula, but it struck me as a strikingly sophisticated quilt. "Whig Rose" was inspired by a Civil War story and features a rose appliqué with four layers of petals in graduated shades of pale pink to red. "Poppy," "Morning Glory," and "Water Lily" take their designs and colors from their title flowers. All of Mrs. Kircher's quilts are large enough not to require dust ruffles. A separate design is made for the section of the quilt that covers the pillows.

"Before I start a quilt I don't make a drawing; the idea is in my head. I use newspapers to cut out the designs first, and I fool around until I get the right proportions. Then I cut out a master pattern from cardboard sheets (nineteen by twenty-eight inches) that I buy at the dimestore. Some quilts will have as many as seventy-five or eighty flowers and leaves, and the scale has to be right. After the appliqué design is cut out, I turn the edges under with a basting stitch and pin the flowers in place on the material, which is spread out on a four- by eight-foot plywood board. I discovered that the zigzag stitcher on my sewing machine was stronger than hand-stitching for sewing the appliqués on the fabric before I begin quilting.

"With the zigzag stitching, the appliqués can stand machine-washing forever. The same is true of dacron batts for padding. Dacron never lumps when it is washed.

"After I have sewed the design on the fabric, I put the padding between the layer of fabric with the appliqués and the plain bottom layer and tack the work on the poles on either side of the frame. The far-side pole is used for the roll of fabric to be stitched; the near side is the pole onto which the finished quilting will be rolled section by section. The part being worked on is stretched out in the middle." Eula demonstrated as she talked to me.

"My frame was made by my brother-in-law from a diagram that was ordered from the manufacturer who makes the batt padding. Anyone can have a quilting frame made by using one of these diagrams. The poles at the sides come in different sizes and can be changed according to the size of the quilt you're making. I've made every size from quilts for cribs right up to king-size beds.

"The needles and the thread I use for quilting are very important. I use a #9 *sharps* needle, which is long enough to go through the thickness of the padding so that the design is as even and finished on the underside as it is on the top. That way my quilts are reversible. The thread I use is heavier than ordinary sewing thread and is coated with silicone. I make eight running stitches to the inch. It is always the same color as the background material. A silky, fine percale and cotton-and-dacron mixture are the best fabrics to quilt-stitch. Calico prints are my favorites for the appliqué cutouts."

Mrs. Kircher explained how she uses a #6 draftman's lead pencil to draw the lines that become the pattern for the quilting on her spreads. "I never use a soft pencil; it smudges and shows through."

The high point of the Kirchers's year is the War Eagle Fair held in October. Eula starts sewing quilts for the fair in June and makes 12 to 14 to sell. The fair is attended by 80,000 people during the third weekend in October. Eula said, "You drive in on a country road lined by trees so thick with autumn leaves it's like you're driving through a tunnel of fire."

That's why the fair is advertised as "the flaming fall review." Two giant circus tents and a fair building hold the exhibits. There are huge barbecue pits where chickens are cooked and sold. There are reunions with old friends, and new friends who have heard about Eula's famous quilts come to see her display. One year the wife of the governor had to be turned down on some quilts she wanted to order, but Eula had so many orders already that she could not promise a delivery date.

"I felt bad about that," she said, "but the next year she came back, and I sold her quilts for every bedroom in her house!"

Eula Kircher's talents are in demand more now than ever. A labor of love has become a profitable career.

8 Secretarial Training in the Home

The motto over the entrance to the Mason School of Business reads, "Enter to learn; go forth to serve." Thelma Mason, its founder, carries her message like a torch, with the proud zeal and faith of a true crusader. The secretarial school she founded as a home career on her back porch has become co-educational and is qualified by the Manpower Development and the Youth Opportunity government programs to train veterans and disadvantaged young people to go into business offices to hold clerical, secretarial, and accounting jobs.

"Honey, they were just asking to learn," she told me when I went to interview her at her school. "The last thing I ever dreamed of starting was a secretarial school. My own dream of becoming a secretary was coming true, and I loved every minute of it. I've come a long way, baby, since that day in the eighth grade when my teacher asked me why I wanted to learn to type since I'd never be hired to work in an office as a secretary. Colored girls couldn't get jobs like that in those days. Now I can't train enough of them to keep up with the demand."

Thelma Mason, born in Pittsburgh, Pennsylvania, was the twelfth in a family of sixteen children.

"My father was a laborer. My mother was a good mother," she said as she pointed to the enlarged tinted photograph of a fine looking couple that hangs on the wall of her classroom. "The ten of us children who survived all graduated from high school. The other six died before they grew up. By the time I was sixteen, both my parents had died, and I was on my own."

Thelma was the only member of the family who was bound and determined she was going to go to college. It was the typing she learned in the eighth grade that helped her to pay her way through the University of Pittsburgh at night. She had to earn extra money as a domestic servant, and it took her five years to get her degree. During those five years she lived in the YWCA.

Thelma Mason, a handsome figure of a woman, five feet and nine inches tall, an imposing 180 pounds of energy and radiant good health, is married to Tessie Mason ("Don't ask me, honey, where he got the name Tessie"), who is a retired U. S. Post Office employee. He now runs the Mason Snack Bar just down the street from Thelma's business school. They have two sons in their teens, Michael and Robert.

"We met as pen-pals during the war. He fell in love with my picture one of his buddies showed him. He was a sergeant and an army cook. When he was sent home after he was wounded, his mother asked me to visit them in Athens, Alabama."

The Masons were married and moved to Nashville. "I never will forget how awful I felt the first time I saw those signs on the street cars and soda fountains separating the whites from the colored people, so different from Pittsburgh," Thelma said sadly.

Thelma doesn't like calling Negroes "blacks."

"They're not black, they're all shades, so why isn't "colored" more descriptive?"

Independent and forthright, Thelma doesn't allow any group to dictate her standards, philosophy, or styles. She doesn't go along with the Afro hairdo "It's a symbol of violence," she says. She has been active in the Urban League and believes the National Association for Advancement of Colored People (NAACP) has the best approach to civil rights problems.

"Equal pay for equal work and quit making excuses. Learn!" That's Thelma Mason's credo, though she is realistic enough to tell students they'll have to be better on their jobs than whites to get equal pay.

One day at the Sunday School Publishing Board, where Thelma was working as a secretary, two friends at lunch asked her if she would teach them how to type in the evening.

"Sure, if you beg, borrow, or rent your own typewriters," was her challenging answer. They did so, and the lessons began on summer evenings on the back porch of her apartment. Her charge was a dollar a month until the word got around and she was swamped with girls, all wanting to learn to type.

"That was my destiny. The good Lord puts us on this earth to do a job, and most times we don't even suspect what that job is. But when the time comes, we know. I knew."

All pupils had to furnish their own typewriters, and the classroom was eventually moved indoors from the back porch to the living and dining rooms. She took her classes in shifts, and the charge was increased to ten dollars a month, with lessons in bookkeeping and shorthand included. When the enrollment increased to sixty-five, the Tennessee State Board of Private Business Schools heard about the classes and informed Thelma that she would be required to pay a license fee of $25 a year and have fire and sanitary inspections.

The Masons faced the necessity for expansion and outside financing to comply with the regulations and to buy the equipment needed. This was in 1960, a year and a half after the classes had started on the back porch. Thelma had already gone to the Nashville Office Machine Company in the hope of persuading the manager to let her have five used typewriters on credit. She was permitted to rent them and to apply the rental fee to the purchase price. A cafeteria had gone out of business in the neighborhood, and she bought twenty-five chairs and twenty-five tables for next to nothing, jamming them into her house to accommodate her students. But the city regulations required that two lavatories be available to students in a school that size. They reported further that she must install a drinking fountain and a new fireproof front door. These were just a few of the changes that had to be made.

Fortunately the Masons owned the three-family house they lived in. The lot behind it was a hundred feet deep, so they decided to borrow money to put up a shell house with heat and the facilities required by city regulations. The Postal Credit Union extended two loans to them to do the necessary remodeling and building. The first loan was for $2,000, and the second was for $4,000. The curriculum was to be greatly expanded, and the tuition cost had to be raised accordingly.

Her career's darkest moment came just after these changes were made. Half of her students quit school. The change was so sudden they didn't feel equal to the work or to the increased cost of tuition. Never one to take defeat, Thelma started a recruiting campaign with the help of the twenty-five students left in her school. Within a year the enrollment was back to sixty-five. The school continued to operate as a night school because Thelma had never felt secure enough to give up her secretarial job at the Sunday School Publishing Board.

In 1966 Thelma decided to devote all of her time to the Mason School of Business, with day classes scheduled in addition to the night school program. In 1968 junior accounting, higher accounting, and business administration courses were added. The following year medical secretarial training and courses in consumer economics and business law became available to students. Her staff was increased from two to five teachers, and she had to advertise for a college professor to take over the courses in advanced accounting, business law, and economics. A white professor who had taught at business colleges in Arkansas, Kentucky, and Mississippi qualified for the position and now lives with the Masons Monday through Friday, joining them for meals and teaching a full day and night schedule. On weekends he goes to his own home sixty miles away, where his wife and family live. When asked whether racial issues were discussed with him at the dinner table, Thelma said,

"Actions speak louder than words. Why discuss the subject? I wouldn't want to embarrass him."

A complete secretarial course is offered for about $525, and for daytime students the course can be completed in one year; for night students it takes eighteen months.

The junior accounting course is approximately $600, and the tuition for higher accounting is around $750.

The additional students sent through the Youth Opportunity Program and the Metropolitan Action Committee made it necessary to add two rooms to the classroom at the back of their house and to invest in electric typewriters, dictaphone machines, adding machines, calculators, and copy machines. Raising the $5,000 needed was made possible by the Small Business Administration; no private bank would advance the loan without a government guarantee.

Every girl enrolled in the Mason School of Business is required to take the course in beauty and grooming included in the tuition.

"Lots of my girls have come from very poor homes. No one has taught them how to take care of themselves. I have to say to some of them, 'Honey, you smell. You have to learn to use a deodorant and take a bath every day.' I don't bite my tongue to avoid the unpleasant truth. They take it from me like they would from their own mothers—maybe better—and they love the beauty contest. Most of the girls, though, with the spark of ambition that brings them to me, care about looking nice. Some of them are real beauties."

Thelma Mason belongs to Weight Watchers, which she attends once a week to check her tendency to get heavy and to learn to "stand proud."

"We must teach our colored parents to send their children to business schools to get training in everything from typewriter repair up to the operation of data processing and key punch machines. No part of the job is too small or too big for my school. Knowing how to change a typewriter ribbon is a must even for a business law major. Tardiness and absenteeism are two things all youth have to overcome, and learning that your word is your bond is the cornerstone of character."

There was fervor in her voice as Thelma recounted a heartbreaking experience with one of her most promising students.

"My only failure was a character failure. This girl was smart and pretty, and I recommended her highly to a big corporation. When I heard she was caught stealing, I just broke down and cried like a baby. The money she was handling was treated by a chemical so that there was no room for doubt about her guilt.

"I'm not interested in the too-smart girl. She'll make it anyway. I'm most interested in a dumb, lost girl who doesn't know she has a chance. I say to these girls—the big slobs who don't know they have a chance, 'Prepare yourself—there's a place for you.'

"I tell my students they are the future leaders of our race, and they have to learn to do one thing very, very well and they'll get along just fine.

"I don't believe in aptitude tests or psychological testing. Inhibition is the enemy of learning, and insecurity can block confidence. Young people must conquer their fears, and the way to help them is to motivate them and make them believe in themselves.

"I stay close to my students for six weeks after they enroll. I try to work with the total person and bring her personality and brain into some kind of harmony until she is relaxed and ready for the discipline of hard work. This is very important because many of my students come to me through government programs;

they have been limited by their environment and education. I guarantee jobs to every graduate. One day I had fifteen calls for a job I couldn't fill. Baby, there's a place for you if you have the right training and the right attitude."

Thelma was so eloquent that I asked her why she had not gone into politics. She said:

"My life is very rewarding. I haven't lied, I haven't cheated, I haven't stolen, and I haven't kicked anybody. Politics is a rough game, and I'd rather see results day by day rather than promise results in the distant future."

Having achieved a gross income of $25,000 with a net profit of $8,000 annually, Thelma has been putting most of her profits back into the school, drawing only enough money to meet her immediate family needs.

Writing about Thelma Mason in the *Pittsburgh Courier*, a leading national newspaper devoted to the interests of Negroes, Toki Schalk Johnson wrote back in 1960 about the first anniversary of Thelma's school:

"Thelma Mason has a great big faith, as big as her heart. She believes in what she is doing, and she believes that the way will be opened for her to add all of the new machines she wants, the new building, and teach hundreds of students who need her schooling. . . . Thelma Mason's faith and determination to help Negro youths will pay off in rich dividends."

Today Thelma has made this prophecy come true.

9 Family Room Nursery School

I tiptoed into the big darkened living room, which had two braided red oval rugs on the floor. Fifteen small children, each sound asleep on colored plastic mats, lay limp as rag dolls. In their multi-color shirts, overalls, and cotton dresses they looked like piles of confetti.

Carleene Johnson, slim and tall, her smooth black hair swept back from her ivory-skinned face, took stock of the slumbering small fry and then led us to the nursery school playroom, formerly the Johnson's family room. It's twenty-one by thirty feet, with a high-beamed ceiling. On one side of the room hung a three-foot paper clown—a handmade cutout holding a group of balloons, each with a school child's name on it. A large cardboard basket brimming over with paper flowers was pasted on the opposite wall. Sturdy small tables and chairs lined the middle of the room, and low shelves holding toys, blocks, and books were within a child's easy reach.

"I bought the children's tables and chairs secondhand from stocks of discarded public school equipment, and we refinished them," Carleene explained to us. "I did the same with some of the other indoor and outdoor equipment. When I started this nursery school with five children, my investment in equipment was only around $30. Now parents leave us toys their children have outgrown. It's a welcome dividend."

Carleene smiled as she told me, "Barter plays quite a part in my home career. One mother did my entire maternity wardrobe in exchange for her child's fee, and another made curtains for my living room. One year a mother set my hair every week to help pay for her child's tuition."

The monthly income from Carleene's school is about $600. She charges 25¢ an hour and another 25¢ for lunch. The children also get morning and afternoon snacks of juice and cookies. In addition, there's a $2 annual charge—plus a four percent tax —for craft materials used by each child. Carleene's husband Charles—more often called Chuck—keeps the books and sends out the bills.

I didn't meet him at first. He was at the physical science laboratory of New Mexico State University, where he designs missiles and rockets — from his wheelchair. When Chuck was twenty-one and training to be a runner in the Olympics, he contracted polio.

While we were talking, Chuck drove up in a large blue station wagon. Carleene slipped out of the front door and went to meet him. She took his collapsible wheelchair from the car so he could wheel himself into the house to join us. He had come home early to take over the school so that Carleene would be free to tell me her story. She started with the daily schedule.

"The first child arrives at 6:30 in the morning," she explained, "and the rest from 7:30 to 9:00. Their mothers pick them up between 4:00 and 5:00 in the afternoon after they leave their jobs. All of the mothers work. Some do secretarial and clerical work and others teach school. Most of their husbands are doing graduate work at the university."

I asked Carleene about discipline at the nursery school.

"Children need discipline, of course," she continued. "They need order, routine, and, most of all, time — especially when they're little. Parents today don't seem to have enough time to listen to a very young child or wait for him to work out a situation or problem on his own.

"I'm with fifteen children all day, and I believe I know something about them. A child knows when he's been naughty and deserves a spanking; he won't hold it against you. The important thing in handling children is the disposition of the adult. If you're impatient, nervous, or tense, you shouldn't be around children all day, every day. I don't think a working mother should feel guilty if she doesn't have the temperament to spend her time with little children all day and chooses to work part time and put her youngsters in a nursery school. But she should be sure that a patient, loving substitute mother takes care of her children in a limited group.

"I love children, but I'm also *interested* in them. They fascinate me a good deal more than working in an office ever did. An office job would pay me as much as I make at home and wouldn't be so physically demanding. But neither would it be so satisfying. I don't have a single degree behind my name—I never went beyond high school—yet the university has asked me to be a consultant to an experimental nursery school it runs.

"Getting inside a little child's mind—seeing the outside world through his eyes—is a daily adventure," Carleene continued. "Here's an example: one three-year-old at the school went home and told his mother that every day when the mailman came he kissed me. The story was relayed to me by the child's mother (maybe *she* was curious, too!), and I realized that in that child's world his father never came home in the middle of the day bringing in the mail. My husband Chuck does. Anyway, I made a point of having my own older children come in when my husband arrived, and I asked them to call him 'Daddy' loud and clear. That made clear the 'mailman's' relationship, and my respectability was instantly restored!"

During the time we were talking, daughter Teri had come home from her school to help with the nursery school children who were waking up from their naps. Hands and faces were washed; each child had an individual washcloth hanging on a peg. Then each was given orange juice and a cookie, and all were taken outdoors for an hour of play.

New Mexico law requires that an outdoor school play yard have seventy-five square feet per child, with the playground enclosed by a four-foot fence. (Sandboxes, two swing sets, two seesaws, and a slide are Carleene's play equipment.) The indoor space required is thirty-five square feet per child. There must be one toilet for every ten children, and each youngster must have a health certificate attesting that certain shots have been given. As the teacher, Carleene must have a tuberculosis test every year.

"How about accidents and sickness?" I asked.

"Children can arrive in the morning and appear well — and then start running a temperature during the day," she said. "I have become quite expert at detecting an oncoming fever. When this happens, I isolate the child at once in our bedroom and phone his parents to pick him up. I do have to carry expensive accident insurance, but so far I've been lucky—nothing more than bruises and scratches. When one child was first enrolled, he had the habit of banging his head on the floor when he was angry. Before he came to us he had actually suffered a brain concussion. I had to watch him every minute until he'd been broken of the habit."

Carleene encourages the children to become familiar with crafts materials, but she doesn't concentrate on teaching them these skills. She feels they are still too young and will acquire such skills when they go to primary school. She does emphasize games such as charades and dancing and singing. Another important activity is what she calls "spoken-word-story" sessions. These are more than merely storytelling periods. As Carleene tells a story, the children do not just sit by passively listening; they are encouraged to act out the stories and relate them to things in their everyday lives.

"Too often," Carleene explains, "today's children, who are brought up on an unending diet of television, simply see situations and fail to relate to them the way youngsters did in earlier generations. For example, years ago if a child saw a fireman in action, he would react—that is, he'd go home and playact at being a brave fireman. Now, largely because of passivity brought on by television, children just sit. Here at the school, and especially during the spoken-word-story sessions, we get the children to become involved—to describe things they see and feel and hear."

Watching the children during these sessions and seeing them come alive with new-found wonder are among the many joys Carleene has realized from her job. Still another has been the growing sense of closeness it has brought to her family. "Every one of us—my husband as well as our children—has pitched in to help with the school," she says. "From five to six every day, the house is cleaned from attic to basement. We all have a particular job to do. Six of us do the scrubbing, vacuuming, and dusting while Teri is busy cooking dinner, which is ready just about the time the cleanup brigade is finished. Everything around here is done with teamwork—and affection.

"I feel that what I have is not just a career at home for myself; it has become a *family* career."

10. Fashion Designing: Earn as You Learn

Five generations of Dabney brides have been brought to Pine Top Farm in Rockville, Virginia. Today, however, the entrance —a half mile or so from the antebellum white house—bears an innovation that would have startled the early Dabneys. Instead of the single traditional sign identifying the farm and its owner, there are two signs—one of them to introduce F. Bruce Dabney, farmer; the other to identify his wife Thelma, fashion designer and dressmaker.

The novelty of Thelma's wood sign attracts immediate attention. It's cut in the shape of open scissors and shows a spool of thread speared by a needle.

Turning onto the property, I drove up the lane to the house, approaching not at the front but by a side door that serves as the entrance to Thelma's shop and workroom. From the threshold I had a panoramic view of the Dabney's 356 acres, three-quarters of which are planted in soybean and corn, with the rest turned over to grazing sixty-five head of cattle. A long row of pines on the horizon gives the farm its name.

The scene does not suggest urban life or the world of fashion; nevertheless almost every day prospective brides, bridesmaids, flower girls, housewives, and career girls find their way here from the city of Richmond, twenty-three miles distant, to select the designs and fabrics that Thelma will convert into special outfits for them. They all make a second trip for a fitting and, if the occasion is a wedding, sometimes two or three more visits. About a hundred names, complete with measurements, are now in Thelma's customer file. "My clients' ages range from eight to eighty," she says. "One twelve-year-old has been coming to me since she was six."

Starting as a dressmaker whose primary job was to make alterations, Thelma has developed into a full-fledged creator of original designs for clothes and millinery. The society sections of Richmond newspapers often feature studio photographs of brides outfitted in wedding gowns she has made.

A striking brunette whose five feet seven inches is considered the ideal height for a model, Thelma inspires confidence in her customers by the way she wears her own clothes. At the age of eighteen she became the first Virginia girl to win a 4-H dressmaking contest—with an outfit she designed, made, and modeled. As a prize she got a week's trip to a 4-H congress in Chicago. She recalls it as "the most thrilling thing that had ever happened to me. I still have that outfit I made as well as the newspaper stories about me."

"Did you take home-economics training after high school?" I asked.

"No," she replied, "I went to business school and then into accounting. I continued this for six years after I was married —until my son was born. Then I started concentrating on dressmaking. I'd known how to sew since childhood. I learned from my mother, who still teaches sewing, and from my grandmother, who gave me my first lesson. She stood patiently by as I tried to turn up a hem. I was only five years old."

Four correspondence school diplomas are framed on a wall of Thelma's workroom, and another is due to join them. Her first diploma—from the National School of Dress Design—took her two years to earn and cost $109 for the tuition.

"My training was interrupted by sickness in the family," she recalls. "That's why it took so long; I should have finished in half the time."

A six-month follow-up course in advanced tailoring came to $100. In addition, she spent another $100 for six months of millinery instruction. A course in costume designing, which involved sketching and creating original patterns, cost $64 more. "It was worth every penny," says this enthusiastic student, who won numerous honors during the four years it took her to complete these various studies.

"Did the customers you were making clothes for know about the courses you were taking?" I asked.

"Yes, and they took a great interest in my progress. While I was studying I used commercial patterns unless customers asked me to make special designs for them. I still use commercial patterns when a customer brings one she wants me to follow. But now my clients rely more and more on the designs I sketch for them. I always make them up first in muslin."

"Why did you take special courses after you were established?" I asked.

"Because I wanted to go beyond routine dressmaking and learn about textiles. I wanted to study anatomy and learn to design for the individual figure with all its variations. I wanted to study the history of fashion and the techniques of workmanship that make the difference between a homemade dress and a custom-made original. It's quite a challenge to find ways of concealing figure defects. Every woman has them, including those on the ten Best Dressed list. Look at Jacqueline Kennedy Onassis: Why does she wear so many sleeveless dresses? Because her shoulders are slightly broad, and the sleeveless dress gives her figure the right proportions."

"How can most women improve the way they look in their clothes?"

"By studying what the shoulder lines do to their figure," said Thelma. "There are some women who should never wear a padded shoulder, no matter what the fashion is, and there are others who have disappearing shoulders that make their hips look a mile wide. Tricks of design and careful fitting can improve the appearance of posture, give the illusion of height, and make an inexpensive dress look like a Paris original."

How did Thelma actually go about getting her business started? First, Thelma's husband Bruce was persuaded to convert one of his tool sheds into a combination shop and workroom, and then to join the shop-workroom to the end of the house. Once the project was started, it got more and more ambitious, adding a modern kitchen and bath/dressing room. Bruce did all the outside construction himself, with Thelma pitching in to help with the inside work, including wall paneling, painting, and laying wall-to-wall carpeting.

"I'll never forget those two months it took to do the job!" Thelma recalls. "We were exhausted, but it turned out fine."

Although Thelma's workroom is only ten feet by fourteen, the clever use of wall space accommodates a folding metal table;

a nine-drawer cabinet for patterns, plastic garment bags, trimmings, and samples; an electric sewing machine that, says Thelma, "does everything but talk"; a nylon-mesh dress form that can be squeezed or pulled to individual measurements; two full-length mirrors; an ironing board; a tailor's board; and a steam iron. A boutique atmosphere is provided by various hats that Thelma refers to as "whimsies" because most of them are simply decorative bits of veiling, flowers, or feathers.

Thelma sees customers by appointment only, four days and one evening a week. This leaves her free on weekends to go to football and basketball games with Bruce and their fourteen-year-old-son Walter. Her day begins at six o'clock. After breakfast she loads the washer, does the routine housework for an hour, and, on days when she has late appointments, prepares a casserole for dinner.

"Fabrics are the excitement of my life," Thelma confesses. "I have 500 samples to show my customers, and I subscribe to three wonderful services: Fabrics Around the World, which costs $2 a year and sends me a page of samples a week; the Fashion Fabrics Club, which, for the same fee, mails a folder of samples accompanied by fashion sketches every six weeks; and Designer Fabrics by Mail—six reports and dozens of samples of national brands every month, for $3 annually.

"Samples of woolens and Thai silks are sent without charge by various manufacturers. And there's a free service for wedding fabrics—samples of laces, satins, peu de soie, sheers, and brocades—sent twice a year. It would take me months to see such a range of samples if I made the rounds of the fabric markets in person."

Thelma's price list for work on major clothing, exclusive of fabrics, starts at $10 for a skirt, $12 for a dress, $14 for a two-piece dress, $25 for a suit, and $30 for a coat. Wedding dresses start at $40 and go up according to the amount of detailed hand needlework required. Hats begin at $5. Her income from all this ranges from $2,000 to $3,600 a year.

"In addition to my career at home," Thelma told me as I was leaving, "I'm a substitute home economics teacher at our local high school. It's a good change of pace for me—and I don't object to the $10 a day it brings in!

"Also," she added with a smile, "it helps keep me from being idle."

11 Window Shades Raise Profits

The rain was coming down like a burst water main, and I was lost just off highway 91 on the outskirts of New Haven, Connecticut. Betty Zeidenberg was the one-woman rescue mission who drove over to the lonely gas station to guide me to the shelter of her home and fireside for the interview that was two hours delayed by stormy weather.

Two boys—Clint, eight, and Todd, seven—left the television show they were watching to rush to the door to greet their mother and her visitor. The entrance from the garage into the seven-room split-level house opens on a pine-paneled family room, carpeted wall to wall in red; the sofa and chairs are covered in a black linen with a red-rose floral design.

Betty Zeidenberg's house has been her showcase, ever since she hit upon the practical and profitable idea of making decorative window shades to coordinate with color schemes and fabrics.

"We'll start your tour where I started my business — in the kitchen," Betty suggested. "Our house was quite new, and I was having the fun of fixing it up. I decided to make the kitchen window shades match the curtains by sewing the curtain fabric onto standard shades. It was a complete flop! The fabric was too bulky, and the shades wouldn't move!"

Betty led me from the kitchen to Todd's room—a typical boy's room, with a wild animal theme. On the windows are dramatic leopard skin pattern pull shades that match the studio bed. Clint's room, next door, has black and white houndstooth check shades with a bed cover and bolsters to match. The master bedroom features an orange and gold floral print in the quilted bedspread, the draperies, and shades. Skill, imagination, and love of color are evident in these rooms and in the others in the house.

"Did you have to go through much trial and error before you made a shade that worked?" I asked Betty.

"No. I quickly realized that it would be necessary for the fabric to adhere tightly to the material of the shade," she told me, "and for a number of years I used an iron-on backing that worked beautifully. Then a new material came on the market— a room-darkening shade material that has adhesive on one side and can be ironed onto the fabric. This is, of course, the process called laminating."

"When did it occur to you that your hobby might become a business?"

"My neighbors thought of it before I did. I began taking a few orders, and before I knew it, I had all the work I could handle. I cleared about $2,000 the first year. Now that I've added other decorating, shopping, and coordinating services, I make four times that much, but the window shades are my real home career."

Betty laughed and shook her head, seemingly still amazed at her own talents. "Believe it or not, I was a bookkeeper for a camera specialty company for about six years after Mel and I were married. All I knew about making things was the occasional sewing I did on my own clothes. I never had a day's art or decorating training in my life."

Glancing around Betty's house, you would never suspect any work was going on. Her rooms are so immaculate they look like stage sets.

"Where do you work?"

"My husband converted the basement into a workroom-play-room-laundry center," she explained. "He went to a lumber yard and got a four-by-eight-foot plywood panel and four ready-made legs, which he put together for a cutting-and-pressing table. Then he installed an eight-foot fluorescent light over it. I have a standard sewing machine with a zig-zag attachment for the side hems of the shades, a steam iron, a special window shade staple gun to attach the shades to the rollers, and good scissors. I use a hacksaw to cut the shade rollers to the right dimensions. A desk, a telephone, and a buzzer (so I can hear the front door-bell) complete my workshop. I do a load of laundry every day; the washer-drier is right across from my cutting table."

"What goes into making a window shade?" I asked.

"First I take the window measurements and design the shade. Many of my finished shades have border outlines and applied decorative treatments. Sometimes I use fringe, braid, or tape. I cut a design out of cardboard and trace the outline on the shades. The actual cutting, decorating, and completing of the shade, including the roller and pull, take me only a half hour."

"How do you charge—by the hour or by the shade?" I asked.

"By the shade—$18 for a small one, $25 for a standard size, and up to $40 for the wider shades. This includes all materials except the matching fabric. The customer supplies that. I buy the backing material by the thirty-six-yard bolt. When the shade is finished, I install it myself."

"Doesn't this take you away from home a good deal?"

"I'm always here when the children are home. I spend a lot of time working when my husband is away weekends on singing engagements. His regular job is as a plumbing supply salesman, but he was trained to sing professionally, so he has two jobs. This is another reason my home career is so important to me. I'd get very lonely without it."

Betty says women want and need a lot of help in decorating. They are insecure about their own taste, but they are not timid about responding to new looks, colors, and patterns. This season she has found them receptive to French and Mediterranean motifs and furniture styles. They love the new "wet look" in wallpapers—like patent leather.

We were sitting in Betty's favorite room, her living room. The walls are white; the fireplace, black brick. The decor is Spanish, with colors of antique gold, avocado, and black; touches of apricot show in cushions and accessories, and there are many black accents in bookends, vases, and ashtrays. A low rectangular table of shiny material resembling tortoiseshell stands in front of the sofa. At the windows are tieback draperies of avocado sheer dacron batiste; behind them are gold window shades decorated with a Spanish scroll design.

It is a becoming setting for Betty—and testimony to her original way with windows.

12 Cooking Classes in Home Kitchens

The white stucco house, one room deep, stretched like an arm clinging to the curved side of a steep wooded hill overlooking a winding country road. Flowering blue plumbago vines spilled over the roof and onto the terrace, where crimson geraniums, oleanders, and pungent lavender splashed their vividness among the outdoor furniture.

Shirley Freeborn, slim and blue-eyed, broke off a clump of lavender and handed it to me in greeting.

"Tell me, how did you happen to start a cooking class in your own kitchen?" I asked.

"Four and a half years ago," she said, "I was still trapped in the nursery. My youngest was under three, my oldest was eight, and I was needed at home by all four of my children around the clock. I was desperate for adult companionship, so I turned to the thing I know best—French cooking."

"Had you had special training as a gourmet cook?"

"Well, yes and no. I married a man who had been brought up in Paris; his mother was French, and his father was American. We lived in France several years after we married."

"Did you work before you married?"

"Yes, I was a ticket agent for an airline."

"That seems remote from the kitchen!"

"Perhaps, but my growing up wasn't. My grandmother, mother, and stepmother were all good cooks and bakers. Cooking was the only part of housework that interested me in the slightest."

"How did you happen to live abroad so early in your marriage?"

"My husband was a representative of an international insurance company. The first six years of our married life, before we had any children, we were sent to Paris, Saigon, and Hong Kong. Now his work is completely different: he is in marine biology, doing oyster seed research. Oysters, you know, have been dying from polluted waters around the world."

"When you decided to start a home cooking school, did you place advertising in your local paper or send out printed announcements?"

"I've never depended on one line of promotion or advertising copy. I started with five women who heard I was organizing a class. In the beginning an eight-lesson course cost $25. I didn't make any money, but I thoroughly enjoyed the work. The second year my price went up to $35. Since then I've been charging $40 for eight weekly lessons. Word-of-mouth praise from pupils has made my school successful."

"How long is each lesson?"

"From 9:30 to 11:30 in the morning. One class meets Tuesday; the other, Thursday. I do the shopping for both in one day and the preparation the day before each class."

"Are your classes for brides or for more experienced homemakers?"

"My pupils are what I would describe as middle-young—from thirty to forty-five. When their children are very young, women do only the most casual entertaining, I find. Then, as their husbands progress and their children go off to school, homemakers have extra time and start entertaining in a more important and challenging way. That's when they want to broaden their culinary knowledge."

"Is there any one thing you teach that makes a special hit with them?"

"When I show them how to bring a curdling hollandaise sauce back to perfection! That sends them marching home with new courage!"

"How do you divide your courses?" I asked Shirley.

"I have four types of courses during the year," she explained. "My first is a beginners' course in French cooking—not, mind you, for beginners *in* cooking. The women who take this course know procedures, but they don't know the difference between American and French ways with sauces, seasonings, stews, soups, or desserts. My second and third courses are advanced versions of the first, with more complicated and elaborate dishes, including soufflés and pastries. The fourth course concentrates on food for entertaining. I hope to add a special course for brides and one for men. I get lots of requests for both."

"How many do you take in a class?"

"Never more than eighteen."

"Then your maximum weekly enrollment is thirty-six. That could bring your cooking school income to $5,760 a year. How much has to be spent for supplies and overhead?"

"About one third of that figure."

"What cooking weaknesses show up most among your pupils?" I asked Shirley. Her answer was revealing: "Most women are poor at putting together a menu. Their constant lament is 'I'm so bored with my menus!' "

Each pupil in Shirley's school receives a copy of the recipe for the dish she will learn to prepare and an interesting menu to go with it. Pupils sit, notebook in hand, on folding chairs on one side of the kitchen and watch Shirley demonstrate the preparation of the dish. By the time a course is completed, each pupil has collected a fine repertoire of distinctive recipes.

Shirley says the average woman does best with meats, salads, or desserts. Curiously, though, most of them are eager to learn how to prepare fish dishes. Skill in seasoning vegetables and in making sauces is rare.

"Did you have to make any major changes in your kitchen or invest in extra equipment for your school?"

"No. When we built this house, I took over the kitchen planning myself. It hadn't even occurred to me then to have cooking classes, but I did want a roomy kitchen designed for family eating as well as cooking. Also, I'm left-handed, and the arrangement of the equipment had to take that into account."

"How big is your kitchen?"

"About fifteen by eighteen feet. I studied women's magazines and manufacturers' catalogs, and my husband promised me that finishing the kitchen as I wanted it would come first; we'd hold off on other rooms. I have only one oven and one refrigerator-freezer. The wall oven is electric, lined with stainless steel, and I have a four-burner cooking unit with a gas grill for broiling in the middle. The cupboards are custom-made of redwood, and all the counter tops are maple chopping boards kept bone-white with bleach detergents."

One of the striking features of the kitchen is the forty-eight-inch square chopping block table. Its top is laminated because the Freeborns use it for dining as well as for food preparation. Cooking utensils are mostly heavy aluminum pots, pans, and skillets. Some are enameled cast iron.

"What household help do you need to run your school?" was my next question.

"Twice a week I have a housekeeper for three and a half hours to clean," said Shirley. "She is my good angel. I do everything else, including the laundry, shopping, cooking, sewing, and weeding and watering the garden."

"Does this leave you with any time for community activity?"

"Only as a room mother for school parties and as a helper with church sales."

"If you could make one reform in food for entertaining—say, at a dinner party—what would it be?"

"I'd cut down on hors d'oeuvres and elaborate appetizers. When a well prepared dinner is to be served later, it's a shame to dull the appetite."

"When you were a girl, would you have dreamed you'd be turning to cooking as a part-time career?"

"Heavens, no! I was going to be a dancer or an actress."

"Is your home career a satisfactory substitute for the applause you might be getting from an audience?"

"Taste buds are as important as pitch is in music, and cooking is one of the arts you can share. It's an expression of love and friendship."

Shirley offered me one of her pastries, made of sour cream and lingonberries. The experience was totally rewarding.

13. Parties à la Carte

Carol Weindel, mother of two daughters and a son, turned to what every housewife knows—cooking—for a home career to help pay her daughter's college expenses. I had heard a lot about Carol before I flew to St. Louis to meet her.

Mrs. Weindel, pretty and petite, greeted us at the door of her home, a two-family house with wide white stones leading to the entrance. I almost mistook Carol for her daughter Karen, whom I met a few minutes later. Karen had just entered her first year at Missouri State College for Teachers, and Carol told me she hopes her home career will net $1,000 this year toward Karen's expenses.

Robert Weindel, Carol's husband and an X-ray technician at the City Hospital, is, like his wife, a dynamo. In addition to his hospital job, Robert works two or three nights a week as a salesman.

"I feel I'm very lucky to have a wife with so much talent," he says. "And she's so modest she probably won't tell you that she was chairman of a project to write a cookbook for the St. Louis Junior Women's Chamber of Commerce."

It is true: Carol *is* reticent. "I have always had a terrible inferiority complex," she explains, "because I never finished high school. But catering is helping me to get over it. The women for whom I arrange parties virtually plan their social lives around me. They ask me to check my calendar so that they can decide on a date when I can take over. They act as if cooking were a rare talent and I'm the only one who could do it properly for them."

One of her most enthusiastic customers, Mrs. Thomas Benson, had Carol cater a housewarming for 150 people, a pre-prom dinner for her son's prep school class, and a bridal shower luncheon—all within three months. "I think Carol could go in a park and serve a meal without a range or sink," Mrs. Benson claims.

Sticking to parties involving range and sink, we asked Carol where she *does* prepare the food.

"Right in my own kitchen," she answered. "I'll show you."

She has an eleven-by-fifteen-foot kitchen with a two-oven gas range that has four burners. There's a sixteen-cubic foot refrigerator that holds about two hundred pounds of food in its freezer compartment. Her plug-in electric baker is big enough to hold a twenty-two-pound turkey or large beef roast. She also uses it for making casseroles to serve as many as a hundred people.

The desserts, vegetables, and salads that Carol prepares are transported to her customers in large rectangular Styrofoam containers, which she buys in a market. She delivers appetizers, pies, and cakes on big square trays.

A forty-eight-inch kitchen table where her family eats doubles as Carol's work table for her party preparations. A desk, phone, and bulletin board are also part of her kitchen facilities.

Except for a few large kettles, mixing bowls, and pans, Carol hasn't had to invest a cent in new equipment for her business. Her customers sometimes ask her to arrange for the rental of extra plates, glasses, or silverware, which she has delivered directly to their homes. In addition to preparing the food, Carol does the shopping, makes the centerpieces, and hires butlers, waitresses, and supplies. We asked her what she charges for all these services.

"I have a basic rate of $2 an hour for the time it takes me to make all preparations. I work on a big party for two days—but not all the time. I still have housework to do and my family to take care of. I feel it wouldn't be fair for me to charge a customer by the day. I keep the sales slips for the food and materials I buy; these are billed separately."

"How expensive are the types of parties you cater?" I asked.

"It depends on the food I serve, of course. A formal dinner for twelve or more, individually served, with cocktails and wines, is the most expensive kind of entertaining. With careful planning $10 per person will cover the cost of everything—including liquor, a butler, a waitress, and the food. I charge $15 a hundred for hors d'oeuvres in addition to my regular hourly charge for cooking. Appetizers are very fussy and time-consuming to make. Getting them to look pretty takes a great deal of effort.

"A wedding buffet with a nonalcoholic punch," Carol continued, "can be managed for $1.25 to $1.65 a guest, exclusive of the wedding cake. These are strictly stand-up parties that require only fork and finger food. A dinner buffet for twenty-five people runs to about $3 a guest, exclusive of liquor. A cocktail buffet with just appetizers will cost $1.50 per person, also not including liquor. A good church dinner featuring a main dish such as pepper steak or chicken, plus everything that goes with it and a hearty dessert, can be served to about a hundred guests for $1.75 each if the actual serving is done by unpaid volunteers."

"How do you gauge quantities in ordering provisions?" I inquired.

"For a dinner buffet, I figure on about four ounces of meat per person. For a cocktail buffet, I usually recommend four appetizers per person, plus relish trays, dips, and salted nuts. For a wedding punch, count on eight ounces per guest."

As we talked, Carol's conversation was sprinkled with tips on shortcuts for quantity cooking, such as her formula for preparing rice. This is it: setting the oven temperature at 400 degrees, she combines the required amount of boiling water, salt, butter or margarine, and rice (Carol uses the instant type) in a 13x9x2 pan, which is then covered. In fifteen minutes the combination is cooked to perfection—dry, fluffy, and ready for a party.

The homemade seasoning salt that brings raves from Carol's customers when she uses it to coat a rolled roast beef is just as simple to make—one cup of coarse salt (the easiest to find in a supermarket, Carol says, is usually kosher salt) combined with three tablespoons of coarsely ground black pepper and one tablespoon of garlic powder. Her broiled pineapple slices with mincemeat in the center make a delicious garnish surrounding a baked ham, turkey, or roast beef.

"Where and how did you learn to cook professionally?" I asked.

"Right out of cookbooks and magazines."

"You mean you never had a lesson?"

"No, but I was the second of eleven children, so I grew up knowing a great deal about quantity cooking. Also, I worked as an assistant to several caterers, among them the famous Miss Hulling's establishments in St. Louis. I didn't do the actual cooking, but I was exposed to just how it was done.

"The minister of my church here helped me more than anyone else to get started," Carol went on. "He recommended me as the cook for wedding buffets that were held in the church parlor. Weddings now make up half of my business. As I branched out to take on catering for parties in private homes, one customer would tell another. They have taught me a lot about interesting food. We plan meals together, and they share recipes with me.

"When Bob is free on the evening of a wedding, he helps me deliver the food and makes the 'innocent' punch. Even when champagne or liquor is served at a wedding, a nonalcoholic punch should always be on the buffet. Bob's recipe is tart and refreshing: To make twenty-five cups of punch, he combines three large bottles of ginger ale, one large bottle of seltzer water, one sixteen-ounce can of frozen lemonade, one package of frozen sliced strawberries, and forty-six ounces of water. The concoction is poured over an ice ring or block of ice."

"When do you have time for your own social life?" I wondered.

"Catering is seasonal," said Carol. "During July and August and in the early months of the year there isn't much going on. That's when my own social life picks up."

"What are your own plans for the future?" I asked.

"I'd love to open a tearoom that I could decorate myself," Carol replied enthusiastically, "with a whole new range of menus. *That* would be fun!"

14 Hooked Rugs Designed for Profit

The round work frame rested on a stand in the middle of the sturdy New England barn. The design being hooked was almost completed, and Joan Moshimer, showing us around her studio-showroom, took time out to explain it. "This is one of my latest patterns," she said. "It's the Apollo 11 insigne and makes a stunning rug or wall-hanging—or, in a smaller version, a framed wall decoration, chair seat, or pillow top."

The design *is* striking. It shows an American eagle landing on a moon crater, while in its talons it clutches an olive branch of peace. And in the black background, the distant sphere of the earth glows dramatically. Yet despite its space age theme—commemorating the first lunar landing—the overall effect of the work is as traditional as if it were in celebration of the landing of the Pilgrims, more than three hundred years earlier.

In fact, meeting Joan and taking a tour of her barn-studio in Kennebunkport, Maine, was like telescoping hundreds of years of history. First there was the house itself. Colonial style, it was built in 1810 by a sea captain. Then there was the craft of rug hooking (the room was literally filled with its charm), which came to this country with the Puritans. Finally there was Joan herself. A World War II bride from New Zealand, she was born in Auckland, where in 1944 she met Robert Moshimer, an American soldier who later became her husband. ("The luckiest blind date a girl ever had!" she says.)

Joan, a tall (five feet ten), handsome brunette, has become a real Yankee; she even talks with a Down East accent. And she has become a Yankee trader too; she makes close to $5,000 a year by selling the patterns for the hooked rugs she designs.

"How many designs have you made?" we asked as we glanced at the rugs on the floor, the wall-hangings, the chair seats, and the piles of samples stacked on long pine tables—all displaying Joan's handiwork. "Personally," she said, "I've originated two hundred designs, but my catalog features more than six hundred, including patterns by a number of others. Designs sell for from 50 cents for a table pad pattern to $75 for a room-size rug pattern."

"You must have been in the business for years to have built up such an extensive catalog," I opined.

Joan shook her head. "I've been selling patterns for less than four years. I began by taking orders for designs from pupils in my YWCA rug hooking classes. Actually, I started as a student in a YWCA class myself. I'd never seen or even heard of rug hooking in New Zealand; it's a typically American craft. It appealed to me because it's so easy and so beautiful in a practical way. I wanted to make for my house the kinds of rugs I couldn't afford to buy. When you make a hooked rug, you make something for posterity.

"Traditionally," Joan continued, "hooking is done by using narrow strips of wool that are cut from flannel-weight cloth. However, almost any weight of closely woven wool can be used. The heavier the wool, the narrower it should be cut. Loosely woven wools and tweeds are not good for hooking. Fabrics from clothing as well as mill ends and remnants of yard goods also can be used. I get great effects dyeing one color over another Beginners often skip the dyeing and stick to colored fabrics but not for long. Dyeing mellows and harmonizes effects, and it isn't all that complicated."

Backtracking a bit, I asked: "Were you paid when you taught at the YMCA?"

"Yes, $16 a day, and I taught two days a week for five years," said Joan. "In New Zealand before I was married, I had sketched merchandise for department store newspaper ads, so the urge to create my own rug hooking designs was irresistible when I came to this country and discovered the craft."

Joan showed us her 121-page catalog, containing nearly 400 of her pen and ink outline drawings. The catalog sells for $2 and includes instructions on the techniques of hooking and dying. Her patterns, printed mostly on burlap (with some done on monk's cloth) are sold from identifying numbers listed in the catalog.

"Don't you need machinery to print these?" I asked.

"When I have to make several copies of a pattern I use an electric stencil," she explained. "I transfer the pattern to the fabric with an inked felt stamp pad, something like a blackboard eraser. I silk-screen some of my designs for rugs, using frames as big as six or ten square feet. I also use an edging machine—I bought one secondhand for $150—for casting the outside edges of the patterns."

Joan then led us up a steep stairway to a series of workshop rooms that connect with the barn. In her design room a working potbellied stove stands on old wide floorboards. The horse stalls at the back of the barn have been converted into storage units for rolls of burlap, homespun wool, and monk's cloth. The finished patterns are laid flat on metal shelves resembling wide bookshelves, with each shelf labeled with the pattern number for speedy location.

"I couldn't have tackled this kind of career at home without the help of my husband Bob or until my children were into their teens," Joan told me.

Joan respects her husband's administrative skills with the mystified awe with which an artist usually regards a mathematical wizard. As branch manager for a glass and paint company, Bob Moshimer has had extensive experience in conducting a business. It was Bob who arranged to take on the patterns from other designers to add to Joan's catalog.

"It took me six months to draw the sketches and hand letter the text for my new catalog," Joan continued. "Until now the catalog had contained only twelve pages. I used $150 from my earnings to help pay for the printing. I've taken four classified ads in needlework pattern books, so I really don't make much profit from the sale of my catalogs. But they do sell my patterns."

"Were the classified ads expensive?" I asked.

"The first two cost $20 and $56, respectively. The results from these encouraged me to be more daring, so, for a total of $260, I bought two ads in a nationally distributed pattern book."

"Do you have patterns for beginners?" I inquired.

"I've developed simple kits that contain a pattern, a hook, wool swatches, and an instruction sheet. The average price for these is $5.95, but the more elaborate designs, such as Apollo 11 (which I don't recommend for a beginner), run to around $10."

The only outside help Joan has in her home career is a part-time assistant, a girl who, for six weeks in the spring, is paid $1.60 an hour to cut and edge burlap for patterns. Joan writes her own business letters in longhand, and she and Bob label and stamp each package as they fill mail orders.

"Where do you get your inspiration for new designs?" I asked.

"All over the place. For example, here is a bluejay feather I picked up in the yard; I'll design a bird kit from this. A photograph of a thirteenth century Persian bowl inspired me to design a turquoise and apricot wall-hanging. Emblems are popular, and I have patterns for the Seal of the United States, the American Legion, Harvard University, the 4-H Club, and the Boy Scouts and Girl Scouts."

"How about your collaboration with Leonardo da Vinci?" interjected Bob, who had joined us. Da Vinci's "Last Supper" was the inspiration for a 30"x82" wall hanging, printed on monk's cloth. That pattern costs $25 and is usually a joint effort by church groups. (Joan's catalog gives the "seating plan" for the design, with the name of each apostle written on the drawing, but only for reference—not to be worked into the hooking.)

As a "touch for posterity," Joan recommends that each rug hooker work her initials—usually on the border—into every design she makes. Such identification forms a link with future generations, Joan feels.

"It is important," she told us, "to build your reputation in a craft by teaching and by exhibiting at fairs and expositions." Her rug designs won first prize at the Eastern States Exposition in 1962. Joan has also participated in shows in Fairfield, Connecticut, and at the North Carolina Craft School. A summer school class in rug hooking in her own studio is planned for the coming summer.

"Young wives are eager to learn rug hooking, in contemporary designs especially," she observed. "So I think I'll try adapting some Picasso and Klee abstracts."

Yesterday, today, and tomorrow provide enough ideas for Joan Moshimer's designs to keep the shelves in her barn piled high with patterns for many years to come.

15 Beauty School for Three Generations

It was ten o'clock on a Saturday morning when I slipped into my seat in a new kind of classroom—a beauty classroom—at the home of Marjorie Young. She is a thirty-five-year-old homemaker and mother of two boys, John and Robert, and a daughter named Jennifer.

Marjorie was busy recording the week's progress of each of her six teenage pupils, the routine she follows at the beginning of every session. The girls had taken off their shoes when they came into the room, put them neatly under their stools at the makeup counter, and had gone straight to the scales where they were weighed.

"What happened to your diet this week, Marie?" Marjorie asked.

Pink-cheeked Marie, a model height at the age of fifteen, with lovely long, slim legs, weighed 130 pounds and needed to lose 15. She was a diet dropout for a week, and her posture, checked in front of a full-length mirror, revealed a fanny bulge.

"Have you been sitting on the floor and 'walking' on your bottom?" she was asked. This exercise is especially effective in reducing the lingering fat so common to girls in their early teens.

"By the way," Marjorie said, turning toward the entire class, "every one of you should have a full-length mirror in your room. If you don't, ask for an advance on your birthday present. A standard one costs about $14 in any home furnishings shop or department store. Your homework depends upon seeing yourselves as others see you—how you stand, walk, sit, wear makeup,

181

wear your clothes—everything. Your full-length mirror is your best friend and severest critic."

The first lesson in each course for all three age groups enrolled (classes are conducted separately for preteens, teens, and adults) concentrates on exercise and diet; the second, on posture and walking; the third, on skin care; the fourth, on hair styling; the fifth, on makeup; the sixth, on manicuring and hand care; and finally, on how to wear clothes and choose colors. At the completion of the course, a fashion show and party are held in the Youngs' living room to give a final flourish to the "new you" promised at the beginning. In seven weeks each pupil is expected to be able to walk and wear her clothes like a professional model.

"It took me a year of weekly lessons in a New York City modeling school, and it cost my family $500 for me to learn the basics that I teach my pupils in seven lessons for a total of $25," said Marjorie. Her father insisted she go to a school for professional models when she was only twelve "because I was such a clumsy child!"

Before her girls took their seats at the beauty counter, Marjorie made a check on their sitting techniques.

"Sitting down is an awkward maneuver for most women, so I think it's important to establish a conditioned reflex early," said Marjorie as she performed a personal demonstration to her pupils. "Don't start sitting down until you get right up to your chair and have turned around; then let yourself down into the chair. Keep your knees together and your feet together unless you cross your legs, which you should learn to do sitting sideways on the chair."

Each girl then did a sit-down of her own. One chunky youngster grabbed the arms of her chair and pushed herself out of it with a gusty sigh.

"No, no, Joanie," Marjorie said. "Getting up is as important as sitting down. You never push yourself out of a chair; you rise."

These preliminaries over, the girls took their places on stools at the makeup counter that stretches around two sides of the nine-by-twelve-foot room. Marjorie's husband Bob installed the twelve-inch shelf that is supported by wrought iron brackets against the two walls. Standard door mirrors were hung horizontally above the makeup counter and framed by two rows of forty-watt frosted light bulbs. A built-in bench, cushioned in Paisley corduroy and slipcovered by Marjorie, stands against the wall in one corner of the room, and Marjorie's desk, which matches the blue walls, actually conceals a sewing machine. Between sessions the classroom doubles as Marjorie's sewing room. A downstairs bathroom, just outside the classroom, serves as a dressing room and washroom after practice facials.

The day I joined the class, the lesson on skin care and makeup was in progress. A sheet of blank white paper and a pencil were handed to each girl, and she was instructed to study her face in the mirror—using the paper to cover up first one side of her face and then the other—to observe that both sides were not necessarily identical.

"Now," Marjorie told the class, "I want each of you to draw an outline of your face, and to write down any feature you dislike."

There was much rustling and girlish clowning at this point. Some of the comments on the papers were: "I look like a squirrel." "My ears stick out." "I hate my nose." "My chin is too big." "My skin looks like mud."

Each girl then was given individual instruction, including a demonstration on how, with the proper use of makeup, she can minimize her facial faults and play up her best features. None of the girls in this class used powder or lipstick, but all used colorless lip gloss, cake blusher, and eye makeup. Powder was recommended for some of the girls, and those who needed to tidy straying eyebrows were taught how to use tweezers properly. Pupils supply their own makeup and equipment, with Marjorie supplying the facial tissues and cleansing creams used after practice sessions. Preteens pay $5 less for the course because makeup instruction is not included for them. Marjorie stocks demonstration creams, makeup, and shampoos, but she sells nothing. She recommends solutions for special skin and hair problems, but her pupils do their own shopping.

For example, the girl who hated her big chin was told that it was further accentuated by the way she held her head. She was instructed to "hold your head as if you have a string in the middle of your scalp holding it up."

The high point of the morning was an oatmeal facial. The recipe for this calls for a cup of oatmeal, one-fourth cup of warm water, and a tablespoon of honey. This mixture is blended into a paste, applied to the face, and allowed to dry. Then it is removed with a warm, wet washcloth.

Another enthusiastically received beauty recipe was a milk bath formula for dry skin. This consists of one-half cup each of powdered skim milk, oatmeal, and powdered laundry starch, which is tied up in cheesecloth or a big cotton handkerchief so it can be swished around in hot bath water. The usual soap routine was recommended for scrubbing.

"You'll come out of your bath as sleek as an eel," promised Marjorie.

The home facial for adult classes combines two teaspoons of fuller's earth, which is mixed with about a tablespoon each of water and witch hazel to form a paste. After witch hazel pads are put over the eyes, the woman applies the paste to her cleansed face and lies down to let the paste dry. (Don't laugh until the paste is softened with warm water and wiped off, Marjorie warned.)

Classes for adults put more emphasis on the nourishing aspects of skin care than the teenagers' classes, which stress soap, water, and cleansing creams.

For the amusement of her adult groups Marjorie has a cartoon hanging over her desk that depicts a woman creaming her face while her husband watches her, saying: "Your complexion *should be* flawless; it gets fed better than I do."

Before Marjorie initiated the beauty classes in her home, she started teaching good grooming to thirty-five girls in a Commack, New York, high school twice a week. For the seven-week course—which she still teaches—Marjorie receives $300. In addition, she has added an adult education class to her busy schedule. At this once-a-week, two-hour session she teaches twenty women; she is paid $14 a week. Aside from these outside interests, Marjorie's income from her home career this year should be about $1,200.

"I keep Monday, Tuesday, and Wednesday free to take care of my home and to do the shopping and cooking for the rest of the week."

Her two Thursday classes are for adults. They consist of mothers who usually haven't changed their makeup or the way they wear their hair since they were in high school. These classes last for an hour and a half. The early afternoon class is followed by an evening class at eight o'clock. On Friday from

2:30 to 3:30, she takes high school juniors and seniors. The teens and preteens come to her on Saturday in the morning and afternoon. Individual private consultations, at $5 a session, are fitted in between classes. The private consultations are appointments for advice on hair styling, wardrobe coordination, or figure problems. Often these women enroll in a class to follow through on the program Marjorie has prescribed in the consultation.

Enrollment in her school has been stimulated by two classified ads that appear alternately once a month in a local shopping newspaper; these cost her $8 a month. The ads have brought an enthusiastic response. They read:

"Wives and mothers! It's time for a change. Update your looks and create a 'new you' with hair styling, makeup, and wardrobe advice given by a professional model." And: "Preteens and teenagers! Register now for a seven-week course in posture, diet, skin care, and hair styling given by a professional model. Classes limited."

Marjorie Young's own professional modeling career began when she was thirteen, after the one-year course at the school for professional models in New York City. Her first calls were to model at teen fashion shows, for which she was paid $25 and an additional $12.50 for the preliminary fittings.

"The rate of pay for professional models has zoomed since then!" Marjorie noted.

At college Marjorie majored in fine arts, intending to become an art teacher. But when a football player on the Hofstra College team took one look at the drum majorette, Marjorie's life was destined for many changes.

She married J. Robert Young while he still working for his degree in engineering. They had their first baby a year later and moved to Freeport, Long Island, where she registered with the Nassau Model Agency. Two years later she bought the agency for $500 and booked twenty-four models from her three-room apartment—all the while caring for her babies. She ran the agency for six years, until the family moved to East Northport, where Bob is an aircraft design engineer at the Fairchild Hiller plant.

Marjorie's glowing good looks and outgoing personality give her the confident look of a country club sportswoman rather than that of a professional model; there is no hint of anything artificial or theatrical in her appearence. She is 5'7", weighs 125 pounds, measures a compact 36-25-36. (Her hips are only one inch up from her professional modeling days.)

"I check my weight every other day," she said. "Whenever I put on two or three pounds, I cut down on calories right away—especially carbohydrates—and I eat lots of fresh grapefruit. It seems to have a chemical effect on my system that makes me lose weight fast. For my overweight adult pupils I have a stand-ard quick-weight-loss diet that takes off a pound a day. I always have them check with their doctor first. 'A pound a day away!' is my motto, and here is the diet:

Nine-Day Wonder Diet

FIRST DAY

BREAKFAST	LUNCH
½ grapefruit	Chicken sandwich on rye toast
Black coffee	(no butter)
	Raw tomatoes

DINNER

Stalk of celery
Steak
Tomato salad
(no dressing on any salads)
½ grapefruit

SECOND DAY

BREAKFAST	LUNCH
½ grapefruit	Jelly omelet or scrambled eggs
Black coffee	3 saltines

DINNER

2 thick lamb chops
Stewed carrots
Lettuce and tomato salad
Pineapple or ½ grapefruit

THIRD DAY

BREAKFAST	LUNCH
½ grapefruit	Minute steak
Black coffee	Stewed tomatoes

DINNER

Minute steak
Spinach
Lettuce and tomato salad

FOURTH DAY

BREAKFAST	LUNCH
½ grapefruit	2 lamb chops
Black coffee	Stewed tomatoes

DINNER

Tenderloin steak
Stewed tomatoes
Carrots
½ head lettuce (lemon juice may be used on it)
½ grapefruit

FIFTH DAY

BREAKFAST	LUNCH
½ grapefruit	French toast
Black coffee	

DINNER

2 lamb chops
Any vegetable
Stewed celery and 2 olives
1 raw apple

SIXTH DAY

BREAKFAST	LUNCH
½ grapefruit	Ham, cheese, or chicken
Black coffee	sandwich on rye toast

DINNER

Chopped meat
Mixed vegetable salad
½ grapefruit

SEVENTH DAY

BREAKFAST	LUNCH
½ grapefruit	Omelet
Black coffee	3 saltines

DINNER

2 lamb chops
Stewed carrots and celery
2 olives
½ grapefruit

EIGHTH DAY

BREAKFAST	LUNCH
½ grapefruit	Scrambled eggs
Black coffee	Sliced tomatoes
	1 raw apple

DINNER

Broiled halibut
Green salad
Celery and olives
Any vegetable
Sliced orange

NINTH DAY

BREAKFAST
½ grapefruit
Black coffee

LUNCH
Jelly omelet
3 saltines
Choice of raw fruit

GRAND FINALE DINNER

Any appetizer
Any meat, vegetable, and salad
½ portion of any dessert

"Good luck! Do not substitute," is Marjorie's advice. "Everything is planned so that you should lose a pound a day. Try to limit your salt intake and stay with the vitamins. Drink plenty of water between meals. This diet is for nine days and *nine days only.*"

16 Patchwork Styled to Sell

When Dorothy Weatherford met me at the airport, it was not difficult to pick her out of the waiting crowd. Her plum-colored, midi-length skirt, violet sweater, navy blue shiny boots, and hoop earrings had the unmistakable stamp of the artist and the flare of the fashion designer. She designs and makes all the clothes she wears.

"I spend practically nothing on my clothes," said Dorothy, the gifted fashion designer of Mountain Artisans, Inc., as she drove me to the mountain village of Sod, West Virginia. There we were to meet some of "my mountain lady seamstresses," who stitch the patchwork and appliqué dresses, skirts, accessories, and decorative pieces that have risen to high fashion in the most exclusive shops all across America in the past two years.

Two years ago Dorothy was an oil painter and sculptor who spent her days on the top floor of a rambling ten-room house that she had converted into a studio. Her three youngsters could be supervised as they played at one end of the room, and she could paint and sculpt at the other.

"My work seemed like play to the children," she said, "so they imitated what I did—we had our own little 'Headstart' program before they started school; now they're all in school."

Sam and Sara are in school most of the day, but four-year-old Ann goes to nursery school three hours a day. Dorothy picks her up at noon and brings her home for lunch and a nap. Dorothy's husband Sam is a safety engineer for a chemical company, where his life is like sitting on the rim of a volcano about to erupt.

"Sam tells them how *not* to let that happen, but he's the one who knows what to do if it ever does."

Dorothy's huge thirty by forty-foot studio has been converted into a workroom in which she devises her sketches and selects the fabrics and patterns for the patchwork squares that she first stitches together and then cuts out according to the garment she's making up into a model. A table big enough for ping pong stretches across one end of her workroom, where she does her cutting. Heaps of fabrics—calico prints and stripes, velvets, satins, taffetas, and ribbons—surround the table, and yards of unbleached muslin stand in rolls for use in making up samples before beginning an actual garment, accessory, or decorative item.

After the models are approved at the Charleston headquarters of the Mountain Artisans, they are added to the line that is shown in New York to store buyers twice a year. When the orders are brought back, patterns in different sizes are taken to the fifteen sewing centers to be made up by the mountain seamstresses, who are paid $2 an hour and work on an average of five to eight hours a day. At present 250 women are employed, with a waiting list of 500 more who will be put to work as soon as Mountain Artisans can expand to take on additional orders.

The day we visited the sewing center in Sod we met Blanche Griffen, the leader of the group, whose daughter and granddaughters have been brought up in the quilt sewing tradition.

"We live for the day when our girls are old enough to hold a needle, and we're mighty proud to make things folks around the country like and use," Blanche said. They have even invented "bread-wrapper" cellophane braided rugs that sparkle with the red, yellow, and blue print that appears on the wrappers of the bread they buy at the supermarket. These are not included in the Mountain Artisan's line, however.

The Sod sewing center, typical of the other fifteen, is a weather-beaten clapboard two-room house that clings to the side of a mountain. A potbelly stove, two industrial sewing machines, a cutting table, an ironing board, and half a dozen wooden classroom chairs compose the furnishings. Diagrams of patchwork with fabric swatches pinned on them are tacked to the walls. An order for twenty-eight beach bags for Lord & Taylor's in New York City was being completed at home by needleworkers who had dropped into the center earlier in the day to pick up materials and patterns.

The Mountain Artisans project was started only two years

ago by a group of women from The Village Stitchery in Harrison County. The story is as inspiring as an Horatio Alger legend —with women as the heroines. They have overcome the obstacles of no money, no organization, no fashion knowledge, and no selling prowess. They had the intelligence to seek help from the Department of Commerce of West Virginia, which supplied the imagination that brought them together with a group of local artists to contribute ideas and designs. Florette Angel, employed by the West Virginia Department of Commerce, was the moving spirit behind this collaboration between artists and needleworkers. Dorothy Weatherford was one of the artists who volunteered to cooperate. A sucessful young painter, whose work was already represented in several museums and private collections, she had not envisioned a switch to fashion designing.

"I find it very difficult to draw a fine line between painter, sculptor, designer, and craftsman. In my mind they are synonymous, each expressing an individual's method in the search for beauty. When I design clothing I am essentially a sculptor. A quilt or pillow becomes a painting with fabric," she says.

This credo netted her a commission from John D. Rockefeller IV, who ordered an animal quilt about seven by nine feet, which hangs on a wall in their home like a painting. Sharon Rockefeller, wife of West Virginia's young secretary of state, has brought the same faith and zeal into her support of Mountain Artisans as Dorothy Weatherford has into her designing.

"As an artist and designer, I view the concept of Mountain Artisans and what it can do for the 250 women presently working for us (and many more in years to come, I hope) as not only economically rewarding for them, but also as a means of stimulating the women to try little experiments on their own that can be incorporated into my finished designs. The cross-fertilization of ideas is what I find most rewarding. These women are wonderful; they'll try anything," Dorothy said.

The Department of Commerce sent Florette Angel with a dozen and a half completed garments to New York to try to break into the fashion and home decorating world. There was no expense money to pay Dorothy's way, so she borrowed the fare from her parents in order to join Florette. Contrary to all predictions, store buyers and fashion designers were receptive and enthusiastic about what they saw. The first orders were placed by the resident buyer for the famous Neiman Marcus

store in Dallas, Texas. Mrs. Henry Parish II, the celebrated
New York decorator who restyled some rooms in the White
House during John F. Kennedy's administration, placed orders
for quilting upholstery. When Dorothy and Florette flew back
to Charleston, they reported, "We were awed by what had happened to us and scared to death. We had no idea of how we
were going to find the money to finance those orders or even
pay the needleworkers. We hoped local citizens who were board
members of Mountain Artisans would invest personally, but
they steered us to the bank to raise the necessary $5,000. With
our orders in hand, we went to the Kanawha Bank and Trust
Company and arranged a loan.

"Those first hectic weeks of having to cope with delivery
dates, packing, shipping, billing, and getting our organization
set up were hair-raising," recalled Dorothy. "We had to rely on
the New York buyers' patience and forbearance, qualities for
which they are not exactly noted—but somehow we made it!

"Our next trip to New York really made a splash. A fashion
press party was arranged in the ballroom of the Beekman Hotel,
and Rosemary Sheehan, fashion director for Galey & Lord fabric company, was the commentator for our show. The company
had previously given us a lot of fabric for experimental designs.
Society women volunteered to be models; we served sassafras
tea and cornpone for refreshments. Our New York publicity was
fabulous!" Dorothy's voice recaptured the excitement of the
occasion.

Their triumphant return was tense with the same kind of
anxiety that had attended their first homecoming. Dorothy and
Florette knew there wasn't enough money in their account to
fill the sheaf of orders they'd brought back. Unsuccessful at-
tempts were made to enlist the aid of foundations such as Ford
to help perpetuate the craft for which Appalachia is famous.

The only remaining chance to get the necessary funding was
to apply for a grant from the Research and Demonstration in
the Crafts Division of the Office of Economic Opportunity,
Washington, D.C. The statement in the charter of Mountain
Artisans, which had been incorporated as a nonprofit institution, was a major factor in clinching a favorable result for their
application. The objectives were described as follows:

"To educate, instruct, train, or retrain persons in the state of
West Virginia and the Appalachian region in various arts and

crafts, particularly mountain arts and crafts products within and without the state of West Virginia, in order to improve and raise the educational, cultural, and economic life of the people and to preserve the unique cultural heritage in various arts and crafts, thereby preventing these skills from being lost or abandoned."

Neighboring counties had succeeded in arranging an Office of Economic Opportunity grant and had asked Mountain Artisans to supply some of the labor required; with this as a link the first grant of $180,000 was arranged with Mountain Artisans in October, 1969.

By the spring of 1970, sales had more than doubled, and store listings included twenty-nine stores from coast to coast. At least as important as money to the success of Mountain Artisans was the marketing and technical counseling provided by the U.S. Department of Commerce.

"I could design clothes, but I didn't know a thing about adapting them to the standard sizing required by the Washington Bureau of Standards," said Dorothy, who received this technical help from the Washington counselors who came to Charleston twice a month.

A management consultant firm was hired to set up a production, finance, and marketing organization that could handle the ever-increasing volume of business. Pricing, bookkeeping, production schedules, and merchandising plans were arranged by the same firm so that orders, purchasing, and deliveries could be handled on a professional basis. By the fall of 1970, orders had more than tripled, and the Mountain Artisans' line consisted of eighty items including fashions, pillows, toys, quilts, and other accessories.

A staff of seven field workers now go from county to county, giving guidance at the sewing centers, delivering new models and patterns, and checking quality standards. Miss Sally Wells was appointed general director at the Charleston headquarters. Florette Angel became sales and publicity director, and Dorothy Weatherford was named fashion designer. The OEO grant pays all salaries, including the hourly wages of the needlewomen; Mountain Artisans assumes the expense of materials and traveling.

"If we had not had the government grant, we'd have had to fold up at the very moment we were successfully launched as a craft center, and 250 women would have been out of work. Now we have a chance to grow into a full-fledged self-sustaining business. When we reach that point, all additional profits will go to increasing the wages of the women, who now work for $2 an hour," said Director Sally Wells.

As I boarded the plane back to New York, Dorothy Weatherford was on her way to teach a class at her children's school. The project involved making what she called "a story telling rug." Contrasting twenty-inch blocks were to be sewn together —a block for each child to sit on during story telling time. The children were assembling the rug themselves.

"We've had orders from New York's top designers—Donald Brooks, Oscar de la Renta, Scaasi—which is exciting, but I find helping to raise our children in the tradition of our native crafts the most rewarding activity of all."

It's how Dorothy gives her own children roots—and wings.

17 Heirloom Christmas Treasures

"This Christmas, with any luck at all, I expect to hit my stride and sell a thousand of my wreaths and swags and little cone trees, but I've learned every step the hard way," said Marilyn Parker as we talked in her living room, where a large picture window overlooks beautiful Lake Geneva in Wisconsin.

Brimming with enthusiasm, good looks, and vitality, Marilyn told about Christmas five years ago, when she got off to a disastrous start in a home career that she had expected to launch on a big scale overnight.

"For years I had been making wreaths as presents to my friends and family. When they kept coming to me to ask me to sell them, I didn't take it too seriously at first. But when a congressman's wife came to place an order, I decided I really *did* have the professional touch and that I would go all out into business for myself the next year.

"So the whole family got into the act. We took rakes and poles and went out into the woods and gathered thousands of cones and pods, and I made up 125 wreaths. In the middle of November I ran an ad in a Chicago newspaper and waited for the orders to pour in. Chicago is only one hour away from here, and I figured I would reach the entire area through a newspaper that had a large circulation. Would you believe I got only one order?

"That Christmas my house and the houses of my friends and relatives were the most decorated in town. What I didn't know was that I first had to start building up my local following and acceptance through flower and gift shops. I also learned that

195

my wreaths had to be unique. I figured I needed a greater variety of materials and colors than our countryside could provide. In order to get the price I had to charge to make any money, the wreaths had to have permanence. Their construction had to be very strong; I couldn't use glues that would dry out and loosen. From the beginning, my wreaths have had permanence because my materials have always been dependable. I never use paints and sprays that will fade or flake off.

"First I had to hit on a design that was unusual. From the time I was a child I liked to draw. When I was thirteen, I won a scholarship to the Chicago Art Institute for one term and learned about combining colors and how to go to art books for design ideas. So I took myself off to the town library to look and learn more about dried leaves and pods and grasses and how to combine them in decorative effects. Then the Della Robbia design idea burst on me, and I felt sure I had something. The forms, the colors, and the repeat clusters would make beautiful designs for swags and centerpieces as well as wreaths. I even got an idea for making a miniature wreath around a vesper-type candle and glass that could be used on end tables.

"The book that helped me most at first," Marilyn continues, "was *New Decorations with Pods, Cones and Leaves,* by Eleanor Van Rensselaer. From it I learned that exotic materials from Africa, Australia, and India could be bought from a wholesaler in the state of Washington. I still gather cones and pods in the nearby woods, and it doesn't cost me a cent.

"I had everything I needed, so I went to work on sample wreaths. These I took to show a buyer at a gift shop, 'Flowers by Connie,' in Rockville, Illinois, about fifteen miles from home. She placed an order and included one of my wreaths in her mail order catalog. Other gift shops in my area bought too, and that year I must have had $4,200 in orders. But I had to sell wholesale, which meant that 50 percent of the price went to the shops. I hope to make my own retail business bigger eventually so that I can make more money."

Life suddenly became pretty hectic for Marilyn and the whole family. Her father, a retired policeman from Chicago, came to her rescue. He became her volunteer helper—cutting wires, putting together frames, and gluing on the burlap backings. During rush periods her mother takes over with the girls. Eleven-year-old Kelly and nine-year-old Candice can help with the housework, but baby Kara is only a year old and needs a sitter.

Husband Bernard's job keeps him away from home quite a bit, so his contribution is making deliveries to gift shops on weekends in November and December.

"I keep out of the way as much as I can," he says. "Once I came home before I was expected and found Marilyn sleeping with Candice in her bed. Our bed was covered with milkweed pods. When I sat down on the corner of the bed, a cloud of white fluff filled the air and got into my nose, ears, and mouth. I found a haven for the night on the living room sofa. I never know when I'll find a batch of pine cones drying in the oven instead of a batch of cookies."

Marilyn was quick to correct him. "I don't dry cones in the oven any more. It makes them too brittle. I never varnish them either."

Christmas at the Parker home lasts from June to December. Vacation time for Marilyn is January and February. Before Easter she has shown her samples to gift shops and to clubs that are planning Christmas bazaars for the following November.

"For the Christmas bazaars I assemble the materials in kits, and the volunteer women make them up to sell at their bazaars, which brings in a nice profit for the charity."

Orders from clubs running bazaars are stimulated by free one- and two-hour lecture-demonstrations in Marilyn's home. Groups of up to thirty women book their dates in advance, see an exhibition of her decorations in the family room, and get instructions on putting them together. By the time they leave, they have usually placed their orders.

To the whole family Marilyn's enterprise is a hilarious adventure. All of them have stories to tell about the funny things that seem to keep happening. They can even laugh about the time Marilyn's father's car was hit, and bushels of lotus pods were strewn all over the highway. Instead of getting the vital statistics from the man who had rammed into him, he rushed out into the middle of the highway to rescue the lotus pods.

"How about that for an ex-policeman!" laughs Marilyn.

Marilyn's workroom was moved from the top of the garage to a nine- by twelve-foot room next to the living room. Bernard, who studied to be an architect, has rebuilt the entire house over the years and introduced such innovations as a sunken fish pool in the floor of the living room (now drained to protect the baby) and a gravel cactus garden under the stairs leading to the second floor. He added a pine-paneled room for Marilyn and her father to work in; the room is off limits to everyone else. The only furnishings in the room are a desk, a chair and a tripod easel, where Marilyn hangs the frames on which she designs her wreaths and other decorations. Other tools in the room are scissors, two pairs of pliers, and an electric drill with a bit the size of a needle. It is used to drill the holes in the cones and pods through which the wires are inserted.

Rows of large empty ice cream containers line the workshop floor. These containers, obtained free from a local ice-cream parlor, are used to store fifty varieties of dried cones, seed pods, and flowers. The bulk of the other supplies—about 100,000 local pine cones, stacks of cartons stored flat, and big metal garbage cans for sphagnum moss—are stored in the garage.

"All the dirty work is done in the garage," says Marilyn. "The cartons that the wreaths are packed in have to be substantial enough to hold up year after year. After the holidays, the wreaths and other supplies are put away until the following Christmas season begins."

All decorations are made on frames padded with damp sphagnum moss and wrapped with a four-inch plastic flower tape. The cost of each wreath frame runs to about 40 cents. The cones, pods, and fruits to be used are prepared for wire insertion with the tiny drill. The wires that attach the cones and pods to the moss-covered frames keep the arrangement very firm and secure. The names of some of the materials sound like an Arabian Nights' dream—dried gold wild artichokes, devil's claws from Iran, dried purple hanha fruit from Australia, dried red pomegranates, velvety "elephants' ears" from Africa. The variety seems infinite as you see canister after canister filled with exotic shapes, patterns, and colors that can be clustered to make beautiful designs. Assembling each wreath after the frame is prepared takes at least an hour and a half. A small cluster can be assembled in fifteen minutes, and a cone tree can be made in half an hour. The time involved for swags and wreaths depend on their size and the elaboration in design.

Merryland Acres is the name printed on Mrs. Parker's card along with her telephone number, address, and "Holiday Decorations, Imported Pods, and Kits" under the name. "My card is the only printing—except for labels—that I've spent a cent on since that newspaper ad," Marilyn says ruefully.

In pricing her goods, Marilyn follows a rough rule of thumb; she adds up the cost of her materials plus about $2.50 an hour and doubles the amount to arrive at a wholesale price. Eventually she hopes to increase production and sales to a point at which profits will justify her skillful efforts.

"A chimpanzee can be trained to do the boring routines of housework." says Marilyn. "I made Christmas decorations for years before I began to sell them because I loved doing it. I still love making them, and the money I make gives me a sense of real professional accomplishment."

18 Foster Grandparents Welcome!

The one- and two-story ranch homes down the block looked fresh and inviting as we approached the cream-colored house with turquoise trim where I was to interview Salme Kopperoinen. The social worker who accompanied me from the San Mateo County Department of Public Health came along to introduce the thirty-nine-year-old housewife who had found room in her home and her heart to care for "my four elderly ladies," as she calls them, in addition to her own three small children and her forty-one-year-old husband, who is a senior engineer with the Arthur McKee Company.

The front door chime was answered by a tall, beaming young woman wearing a white nylon shirtdress and white shoes. A little boy about four years old was right behind his mother. He was dressed up in a navy blue replica of a sailor's uniform.

"Please, will you come in? I will show you, first, the house."

Salme's accent betrayed her Finnish background, but her words were clear and her voice was vibrant and friendly as she introduced three of her "ladies" who were watching television, seated comfortably on a sofa and chairs in the living room. The oldest was seventy-nine, a lively, slim little woman who said, "I'm a widow with no children of my own, but I raised my sister's three boys after she died. They come to see me and often take me out riding."

A metal walker was standing beside one of the chairs, and a dark-haired woman, seventy-two years old and also a widow, told me she had suffered a stroke within the year and could no

200

longer manage alone in her own home. She had become paralyzed from her shoulder to her foot on one side, but she could get around with the support of the walker. Her four grandchildren are still quite young, and she is taken to see them by her son as often as she feels up to the trip. Her hair looked freshly set, and though she was handicapped in her movements, she was thankful that her thinking, her speech, and her face had not been affected.

"Let me show you my room," said grandmother number three, who left the television soap opera she had been watching to lead me into her room, which opened into the living room.

The first floor of the house has two double bedrooms for four elderly occupants with a bath between. Each room opens onto a patio at the back of the house.

"We spend more time outdoors most months than we do inside," said my guide.

Her bureau and the walls around it were covered with family photographs, the most recent being of the wedding of her oldest granddaughter.

"You all like television, but I don't see any in your rooms. Why not?"

"Two of us share a room, and it's better to go into the living room so that if one of us wants to sleep or rest, we won't disturb the other."

"How about choosing programs? Do you and the family agree on the same ones?"

"There's a family room right next to the kitchen where the children can play and watch their programs and where my husband and I can sit in the evenings," explained Salme. She had joined us again to conduct the tour through the rest of the house and to show me the structural requirements that had to be met in order to get a license for foster private home care for elderly tenants.

"In the bathroom we had to place chromium bars on the wall next to the tub and by the toilet so our ladies can hang on to them. I am always near if they need more help. I usually help them out of the bathtub.

"The ramp you see outside of their doors to the patio was built by my husband. This makes walking safer and easier for them."

Fire department regulations require each bedroom to have

an outside exit. We walked down the ramp and into the patio, which has a covered trellis, outdoor chairs and benches, and two picnic tables at one end.

"We have lots of meals outdoors," said Salme. "We can all be more relaxed with the children."

We went upstairs where the family has its own bedrooms and baths. A sewing machine was in one of the rooms, and it was piled high with bright woolen fabrics.

"Do you have time to sew with three meals a day to prepare for eight people and the house to keep clean?" My wonder and admiration were evident.

"Oh, yes. The ladies tidy their own rooms and make their beds, and I give the house a thorough cleaning weekly. I'm used to big families."

In Finland Salme, one of a family of ten children, grew up on a dairy farm. Seven were girls, and three were boys. Her own mother has twenty-four grandchildren. Before she was married, Salme worked in the alterations department of a clothing store in Finland. She was trained in a vocational school and left home to live with her sister in the city when she was sixteen years old. The business course she added to the studies in domestic science has come in handy in keeping the records required to run a licensed home for the elderly.

"Before we were married, my husband and I took the same train to work every day. Finally one day we spoke and started making dates. We went together for five years. He is a university graduate in mechanical engineering. When he had a chance to go to Australia, he decided he'd like to see what life was like there, so that's where we spent the first four years of our married life and where our oldest child was born. Then the company my husband worked for in Australia said we could go to the United States, where they had a branch in Massachusetts. We lived there for two years, but it was too cold. We decided to come to California; engineers can always find good jobs here."

Their wanderlust was appeased in California, where they felt they had found the end of the rainbow. Salme and Kysti decided they wanted to settle down in their own home. Finding the kind of a house in which they wanted to bring up their children turned out to be very expensive. Because their standards were high and their energies and skills great, the home they wanted was going to cost them at least $32,000. This was more than even

Kysti's good job could swing. Salme was determined she was not going to work away from her home and leave the rearing of her children to someone else. The foster care plan for elderly people was the ideal solution. This would add to the Kopperoinen's income a minimum of $220 a month for each elderly person cared for. When multiplied by four the cash would help the financing of their new home and start a savings account to educate their children. She talked it over with Kysti, who had every reason to know that his wife has the temperament and capabilities to make the plan work without too much stress on their family life. They agreed that the elderly people they would care for must be mentally and physically sound and ambulatory and that their only handicaps must be due to the limitations of old age. (Many private foster homes for the elderly include nursing care for those with the mental problems of senility.) While the Kopperoinen's is not a nursing home, Salme is expected to provide care for minor illnesses, and she also supervises the medication prescribed by doctors. In the case of the woman in her home who had a stroke and uses a walker, Salme receives additional money for the extra work required. The Department of Public Health must approve all applications for admittance whether the payment is made through the welfare department or through private means.

The first step taken by the Kopperoinens in establishing a foster home for the elderly was a call to the San Mateo County Department of Public Health to inquire about procedures. They were informed that a personal interview must be arranged. Qualifications of character and temperament and responsibility had to be judged. There were many city and county departments involved, including zoning, building, health, fire, and welfare, but contact with these had to follow the initial approval of the couple's personal suitability to the project. Before the license could be issued, there had to be an inspection of the premises to recommend any alterations that might have to be made. Salme and Kysti did not buy their house until they were sure that the house would meet these requirements.

Salme described and pointed out the safety and fire prevention precautions involved in the regulations before we ended our tour of the house in the kitchen. The table was spread with a sumptuous feast of home-baked breads, cakes, cookies, and coffee. After refreshments were served, Mrs. Foote, the social

worker, said goodbye, leaving the two of us to continue our interview alone. A baby's cry from upstairs announced that nap
time was over for tiny Eiri, just two months old. We went upstairs where the baby lay in her wicker bassinet, a bundle of
pink under white linen sheets trimmed with lace.

"Isn't that handmade lace?" I asked, and Salme said yes, adding that learning to make lace was a tradition in Finland. She
had made the lace for her baby's sheets in the last month of her
pregnancy. While we were upstairs, six-year-old Eija, her oldest
child, burst in the downstairs front door, home from school. She
looked like the cover of a fashion magazine, dressed in a turquoise jumper made by her mother, bright red leotards, and
a sweater. Her eyes matched the blue of her dress, and her hair
was the color of ripe wheat.

The kitchen, like every other room in the house, was immaculate and equipped with the latest appliances, installed to make
Salme's housework and cooking easier. Her husband had made
the kitchen cabinets with the help of a carpenter friend. The
refrigerator, the largest two-door home model, made with
shelves from top to bottom on the left side, held a supply of
frozen foods sufficient for two weeks. Shining copper baking and
cooking utensils hung on the wall. One of the kitchen doors
leads into a dining alcove, which is at one end of the living
room. The dining table is kept set for "my ladies," who eat their
three meals a day there, joining the family on special occasions.
Kysti gets home after six at night, which is too long for the
elderly people to wait for their dinner. Salme looks forward to
ending the day with a quiet dinner and a visit with her husband
alone.

"He is a very good man, my husband. He helps me a lot,"
said Salme appreciatively.

"Our new baby was born on December 14th, and he took his
vacation after that so that he could stay home and help me. We
put the Christmas tree up the day I went to the hospital. It was
sooner than we would have normally, but I didn't want our children or my ladies to miss the excitement of trimming the tree
with the family. I had done my Christmas shopping, wrapped
the presents, and baked cookies ahead.

"My husband saw me start to watch the clock as we were trimming the tree, and he knew the labor pains had started. Finally,
he just couldn't stay calm any longer. He went to the telephone

to call our doctor but couldn't reach him, so he drove me to the hospital anyway. Two hours later, before our doctor returned, our baby girl was born. Everything was fine, and I came home two and a half days later. When I came into the house, my ladies gave us a great reception. The baby's crib was all ready for her, and my husband had hired a woman to cook a dinner to celebrate.

"Then days after the birth of our baby we had a Christmas Eve party. The relatives of our ladies and some neighbors were invited. There were about twenty of us. We opened presents, served turkey, ham, fruit punch, cake, and cookies. My husband played the accordion, and everybody sang and danced. On Christmas morning everything was so quiet I couldn't believe it. My big Christmas surprise present was from my ladies. All day they were away with their relatives, who had come to get them early in the morning and didn't bring them home until after dinner that night. My husband took the children to the Lutheran Church, where they go to Sunday School.

"I spent the whole beautiful Christmas day in bed with my baby!"

19 The Growth of a Food Business

Mary Forester, a slim, trim woman who wore her gold-color dress with style and her short silver hair brushed close to her head, talked with me in the Victorian parlor section of her Butternut Farm kitchen. Here Mary, her sister, two local women, and a young man can turn out a thousand jars of her secret formula hollandaise sauce in a day and dozens of jars of other sauces—bearnaise, mustard, bordelaise, barbecue—and herb jellies.

"When did it all start?" I asked Mary.

"Back in the fifties, after my husband and I bought a lovely old farm in Ghent, New York. That was the original Butternut Farm. We had kept our small apartment in New York City since my husband still worked there, but it was at the farm that I started experimenting with sauces and jellies—as much for fun as for making money. Whenever I wound up with more bills than cash, my husband dug into his pocket and made up the difference."

"What gave you the idea to concentrate on hollandaise?"

"Actually, I got it from the manager of a distributing company selling my very first item, which was called Bouquet Garni. My friend Dorothy Curtis and I had come up with the idea of turning out those little cheesecloth bags filled with dried-herb seasonings that are found in so many French recipes. It was on one of our expeditions to see the distributor about Bouquet Garni that the hollandaise idea came up.

"The distributor was emphatic. He told me: 'If you can produce a hollandaise sauce that won't curdle when heated and will

206

keep fresh in the refrigerator just like mayonnaise, then, lady, you've got it made.' "

Things went along beautifully for Mary until 1960; the demand for hollandaise from her one-woman operation was growing steadily. Then her husband Arthur became seriously ill, and it was necessary to sell the farm and move back to New York City. During her husband's illness, a food company in Brooklyn filled the orders that continued to come for Mary's product. After six months, Arthur died. Mary's farm was gone, and her once promising home business was foundering.

Fortunately, Mary still had the secret of her hollandaise. She also had faith in herself, and she was determined to find the backers needed to build a profitable business.

Mary's sister Blanche ("Babe") and brother-in-law asked Mary to live with them in Connecticut and reestablish her hollandaise operation in *their* kitchen, with Babe's help. They soon found, however, that hollandaise doesn't mix with four young children as well as it does with asparagus. There simply wasn't enough available room to produce the quantity needed to make the business pay.

"So," Mary continued, "we rented an extra kitchen nearby, with living quarters attached, and I moved in with my sauces and jellies twenty-four hours a day. The sauces liked it fine—they increased and prospered—but I needed a change of scents and scenery, so I eventually moved to a place a mile down the road."

Production problems—how to ship out five thousand jars a week—had to be solved. What was needed, Mary decided, was special equipment. Top-of-the-stove kettles and hand-pouring would never do. Either Mary would have to borrow money or she would have to find stockholders and incorporate Butternut Farm. Eventually she did incorporate and so acquired the necessary funds for her growing business.

A steam-jacketed kettle with a sixty-gallon capacity was purchased for $500 (a new one would have cost $2,500), then a jar-filling machine (it looks like a giant funnel and is attached to the kettle by a hose, was bought. A machine that pastes labels on jars was much too expensive to buy outright, so one was rented, with the cost being applied toward the eventual purchase of the machine. Next came a freezer that could hold three hundred pounds of egg yolks. This equipment, plus supplies of jars and ingredients, were the basics for increasing production.

The overall area of Mary's kitchen is twenty-five by thirty feet, with a ten- by twenty-five-foot space for storage. A walk-in refrigerated room was already on the premises; the place had previously been a meat market. The original building was a granary on a farm that dates back to the 1700s.

"What does incorporating yourself involve?" I asked Mary.

"You have to get a lawyer to apply to the state government for a certificate of incorporation, which will permit you to sell stock. Laws in various states differ on incorporation regulations. Incorporating simply means ownership by more than one individual. Our little home business has always been a closed corporation. When I found I had to incorporate in Connecticut in order to raise money to equip my kitchen, I had stock certificates printed up for $10 a share. I have since bought back the shares owned by my family and friends, who had been my only stockholders. Last year I had an offer from an outside company to buy a third of the stock, and I decided to share the ownership again, as long as I was able to retain two-thirds. I liked the two young men who wanted to come into my business. They own an advertising agency, and I thought they could help the business grow.

"There have been times in the past when I needed $2,000 or $3,000 fast. I never had any trouble getting a few thousand dollars from our local banks; they knew me, and my credit was good."

While we were talking, Mary was called into the kitchen to supervise the mixing of the hollandaise. Babe was there, stirring sixty gallons of sauce in the steam-jacketed kettle—with a canoe paddle!

"You should have come the day the hose sprung a leak under the table," Babe said. "None of us knew what had happened until there was a sea of hollandaise sauce—gallons and gallons, all over the floor. What a mess! Robert, our Jack-of-all-trades, bailed us out."

Getting back to drier areas, I asked Mary about the payroll. "Are all of you paid by the week?"

"My sister and Robert work regularly and are paid by the week," Mary answered. "Two others, Ruth Lockwood and Karen Schenning, come in only when we need them and are paid on an hourly basis. I keep the books and have a drawing account for our expenses and my personal needs. Some weeks I draw less pay than my workers. But because I am a stockholder, the money I draw is considered part of my salary, and I share in the profits at the end of the year."

"How much business do you do in a year?" I asked.

"Our gross is about $60,000 in orders, but by the time our overhead is met, our net profit only amounts to about $5,000. Would I ever sell? Of course, if the price were right. But as long as Butternut continues to grow, as it has for the past ten years, my investment in the business makes it worth hanging on to."

The six-ounce jars were being filled from the hopper now, and Robert was twisting on the tops by hand. "We had a bottle-capping machine," Mary said, "but Robert's hands were quicker than the machine."

Next, I observed the machine that sticks the labels on the bottles as they are conveyed electrically on a belt. They are then placed in cartons. These are addressed with stencils and piled up by the door, ready for the trucks that will carry them to the distributors in New York City and the rest of the country.

Thirty food brokers and distributors take orders from retail markets and then relay their bulk orders to Butternut Farm, where they are picked up daily. Mary herself delivers orders to nearby gourmet shops in one of the two station wagons the farm owns. She likes to keep in personal touch with store managers in order to gauge customers' reactions to her products.

In addition to the sauces, Bouquet Garni and the jellies are a part of Butternut Farm line. The jellies are the most expensive items to produce. They have to be poured by hand and, consequently, are made in much smaller quantities. The clove, rosemary, marjoram, and cranberry-celery seed jellies are for meats and poultry; the two glazes, for ham and poultry; chutney, for curry and cold meat; and the mint, for lamb.

"What is your biggest overhead, next to salaries?" I asked.

"Insurance! It's horrendous! There is product insurance, and the law requires us to carry fire, liability, and workmen's-compensation insurance. Our equipment has to be insured too."

"Even if you work in the kitchen a third of the time, your title is president of Butternut Farm, isn't it?"

"Yes, and Babe is the secretary and vice-president."

I observed that, to the outsider, the division of labor at Butternut Farm is so democratic it's hard to tell who's who. "Just how does the work week line up?"

"Two days a week I'm out selling and making local deliveries," said Mary. "Once a week I drive to New York to see the distributors and get orders outside of Connecticut. (Butternut Farm sauces go to New York, Chicago, California, Dallas, St. Louis, and Detroit supermarkets.) I work on the books once a week. My accountant checks them every two weeks and does all my tax work. My employees' withholding taxes for five people alone run over $1,500 a quarter.

"These requirements seem routine compared to other factors in getting going. For example, there's the permission you have to get to open a business in a country town like Cannondale. You have to go to the local planning board commission to find out whether your location is zoned for business. You are required to have fire and sanitation inspections regularly. A state agency and the federal Food and Drug Administration come unannounced to inspect the premises once a year and to see that the labels on your products state the ingredients properly."

I wondered, "Looking back to the very beginning, in 1952, can you say what the high points were in getting your career started?"

Mary laughed and said, "Would you believe that two grown women have gone along the streets of New York ransacking the wastebaskets on corners to find copies of a day-old newspaper? That's what a friend and I did when we found out that Clementine Paddleford had written up our Bouquet Garni in her food column in the *Herald Tribune*. We found the clipping, took it to Vendôme and Maison Glass, two famous New York gourmet shops, and got orders for four dozen packages from each store. It was like finding gold!"

Although Mary Forester's home career is turning into quite a business, it is her fascination with food and flavor that is a perpetual source of fun—not work—to her and her friends.

20. Candlemaking Makes Money

Candlesticks have been part of religious ceremonies from earliest days. Moses was commanded to make Holy Candlesticks of pure gold for the Tabernacle. There were golden candlesticks in Solomon's Temple. And, of course, candles are widely used for religious observance today — especially at Yuletide — as a symbol of the Everlasting Light of Heavenly Love.

Three thousand candles with the trademark "Chesapeake Colony Candles" over this printed message have found their way into the homes of hundreds of army families in Fort Rucker, Alabama, as well as others throughout the world. And back of it all is an army wife, Emily McGowan, who took up candlemaking as a hobby.

In 1967, with Lieutenant Colonel Frederick W. McGowan's retirement as an army pilot just two years away, Emily decided to make candlemaking her home career. "I put my candles on sale at Fort Rucker before we retired," she recalls. "It was something of a trial run to help prepare me for my life as the wife of a civilian. At age forty-five, my husband was going to start a brand-new career with the Insurance Company of North America, so why shouldn't I have my fling at something new—something that would make money? Four of my five children had already flown from the nest, so I was going to have plenty of time on my hands."

211

That experiment confirmed what Emily had always suspected about the business possibilities of candlemaking. She made $800 right in her own kitchen, where she was able to improvise with kitchen utensils and work at odd hours of the day and night. Her years of teaching and exhibiting at craft shows helped to facilitate the launching of her new career.

She taught candlemaking classes for service wives at army posts. They were given free until four years ago, when Emily realized she could no longer afford to contribute the required classroom materials—paraffin, beeswax, stearic acid, wicks, wax coloring crayons, and one mold for each student. The $10 that these cost and the classes themselves had been her personal contribution to the craft and hobby workshop program at the army base.

When the base chaplain heard what she was doing, he ordered wedding candles from her for the marriage services he performed on the post. As a present, Emily always gave the bride and groom a wedding candle to burn on each anniversary. Even now, anyone celebrating a twenty-fifth or fiftieth wedding anniversary is entitled to a free anniversary candle from Emily whether or not they are relatives or friends. "I'm a sentimental soul," she says. "I guess that's why candlemaking appealed to me in the first place."

Today, in what Emily calls her "forever house"—a two-acre farm in Mt. Laurel, New Jersey, seventy-five miles from New York City—a roadside sign invites the public to visit "The Candle Farm." Emily's winter workshop is a converted sun porch, but in the summer "I move my workshop to the basement, where it is cooler."

The total space needed to make candles consists of little more than the length of an average kitchen counter and shelves for storing supplies and finished candles. On the counter Emily has two portable electric stoves with two burners each, ($10.98 apiece) and a $40 electric candle-dipping machine.

"You could start making candles with no equipment other than the stove and utensils in your own kitchen," she says. "All kinds of household containers can be used as molds, especially empty milk cartons and orange juice cans. I have a variety of commercial molds in the shapes of cylinders, stars, hexagons, squares, and short, round forms. These average $4.25 each and last forever. Kits are available that combine materials for learning, and I stock these for sale.

"If you're going to start a candlemaking business, you can make twenty candles a day, using ten molds twice," says Emily. "Some candlemakers use double boilers for melting wax, but I save coffee tins so that I can keep a dozen going on the two stoves at the same time. They must be placed in water in square baking pans, because the double-boiler principle is essential to the operation. Of course, dipped candles don't require molds. My machine dips sixteen candles at a time, which takes about an hour to an hour and a half. I only dip bayberry candles, but for molded candles I use a variety of waxes and materials.

"The waxes, the scents, and the wax coloring crayons are the ingredients that produce the magic. Paraffin can be bought for 23 cents a pound at supermarkets, but I buy mine by the case—twenty one-pound packages for $4.28 wholesale.

"Bayberry, beeswax, and spermaceti whale wax are carried by handcrafts companies, as are spools of wicks, boxes of wax coloring crayons, and metal molds. The rolls of transparent plastic wrappings I buy for 50 cents, six rolls at a time. Scents added to the melted wax have great appeal, but they increase the price I must charge accordingly. Bayberry is the most popular, at $4 an ounce retail. Some scents, such as lily of the valley, sell for as high as $10 an ounce.

"I had to get a retail license in order to buy my materials wholesale, so I applied to the Tax and Licensing Department at the state capital. The license was free.

"I started selling individual candles to the wives of army officers on the post as well as to flower shops. Then I began showing in craft exhibits and at art festivals. I won a blue ribbon at the Ozark Boll Weevil Festival. When I offered to match candle colors to room schemes, special orders began to come in, and word-of-mouth publicity brought more orders. My candles range in price from 75 cents for a pair of dipped bayberry candles to $6 for a candle with a five-inch base.

"Candlemaking is a year-round business," Emily says. "I turn out candles for weddings, anniversaries, birthdays, children's parties, baby showers, room decorations, and in quantities for holidays such as Christmas and Easter. For Christmas one of my most popular candles is a white cylinder with a red poinsettia showing through from the inside. I use a wax or plastic flower for this and pour the paraffin over it. Foliated candles, those that spread to become petals as they burn, have become very popular. Wax coloring crayons that are melted at 150 degrees with the paraffin produce beautiful shades. I sometimes use oil paints for shades that I can't match with crayons only."

Emily gets a great variety of decorative effects on the inside as well as on the outside of her candles by using diamond dust, sequins, gold angels, spray paints, wax and plastic flowers, decals, and ribbons.

She finds making her own molds for special candles very exciting. One mold that requires the highest degree of skill is a raised, embossed exterior design. Emily saw an antique cover for a pressed glass sugar bowl that she just couldn't resist. The mold was made by pouring liquid latex over the top, one layer after another. Each layer had to harden before she poured the next, and when she had nine layers, she decided she had a mold strong enough to peel off and pour hot wax into. The result looked like a fairy tale castle turret.

Hospitality radiates from the McGowan home, and Emily is her own best customer for her candles. The Monday we arrived for our interview the dining room table was still adjusted to seat nine people, with flowers and candles as the centerpiece. Friends from Taiwan, her son, daughter-in-law, and two grandchildren had been guests for the weekend. In the living room an antique chopping bowl overflowed with an arrangement of fruits, flowers, and a handsome green bayberry candle.

Blonde and slim, with a spontaneous manner, Emily says: "I love people, and I love to entertain in my own home. To me, candles are a symbol of friendship and warmth."

21 Partners in Paper Flowers

If you'd asked either Sharon Hart or Bonnie Livingstone a week before they met whether they had a home business in mind, the answer would have been, "Who, me? With a houseful of babies? You have to be joking."

Little did they dream that in less than four years they would be splitting a $2,400 annual profit from making paper flowers at home. Sharon was just twenty-one then, with two-year-old Tommy to keep out of mischief and Cindy on the way. Bonnie, twenty-six, had three lively toddlers.

"Babies are no handicap in a home career, we're housebound most of the time anyway," said Sharon, who even took advantage of a maternity stay in a hospital two years ago to fill an order.

The two women first met through their church, where Sharon was chairman of the fund raising committee. She asked Bonnie to be on her committee, and they decided to make paper flowers to sell for church benefits and to use as decorations for a dinner-dance. Colored tissue paper turned out the most glamorous flowers. At first they followed directions that were enclosed with the package of paper, but they soon worked out their own designs.

As we talked, Sharon and Bonnie were sitting at a round table in the family room of Bonnie's house, filling an order for the Baptist Hospital Gift Shop, a regular customer, where two dozen flowers are sold each week. Working together, the two can make a dozen flowers an hour. But they seldom make the flowers together except on a small order such as this one, which provides just enough time for a nice social visit. Usually they

work at home alone, with an assembly line system that begins
at Sharon's house. She's the "cutter-outer" of petals and leaves,
which are then dropped off at Bonnie's house, a mile and a half
away, to be assembled into the finished flowers.

On the day of my visit, the few materials and tools required
to make the flowers were within easy reach on a table between
them. The colored tissue paper—which comes in forty-two
colors—costs $6.50 wholesale. Thirty-gauge spools of wire pro-
vide the means of holding the flowers together. Wire coat
hangers are cut and used for the eighteen-inch stems that hold
each bloom. Friends and family save wire hangers from the
laundry, so there's been no expense for these. (To buy them
would cost 2½ cents each.) Green florist tape is used to wind
around the flower stems, and a clear lacquer spray makes the
flowers shiny. Dressmaker scissors to cut out the petals and
wire-cutting shears are their only tools. For local deliveries, the
flowers are not boxed; they are massed in metal wastebaskets
bought at the dime store for $1.09 each. Out-of-town orders are
shipped by parcel post in cardboard boxes. One hundred dollars
buys enough materials to make four thousand flowers! Each
flower costs 9½ cents to make and is sold at $1 wholesale and
$2 retail. These are the flowers they sell in volume. A special
giant flower with curled edges is made to sell for $6 wholesale,
and during the football season, pompons in school colors are
sold for 50 cents for a man's boutonniere and 75 cents for a
woman's corsage.

Sharon was cutting out petals freehand on strips of folded
paper along the outside edge. These strips are graduated in
width since each flower has five layers of petals. Bonnie was
picking up the eleven-inch strips, inserting a metal ruler in
the fold of each strip, and shirring the paper to make the center
of the flower. The flexible wire was used to anchor the bunched
shirring, finishing one layer of petals.

"How many different types of flowers do you make?" I asked.

"We limit ourselves to three types and we don't try to be
realistic," said Bonnie. "If we had to describe the real flowers
that our most popular variety looks like, I'd say the peony."

"By the way, how do you sell your flowers?"

Bonnie made a face and said, "I couldn't sell a solid gold
Cadillac for a nickel, but Sharon just walks in and gets an order,
so that's her department."

Sharon is the extrovert. Her first sales were to local boutiques and gift shops. Her first customer was The Pineapple Shop in her neighborhood. She had massed eighteen flowers together in a white metal wastebasket and walked into the store looking like an animated cover for a flower catalog.

"Most of the time I don't have to say a word. The flowers sell themselves," she said.

Within two weeks The Pineapple Shop had reordered, and the Caprice Boutique had placed an order for six dozen. Whenever she gets an order for six dozen, Sharon gives her customer a dozen free as a bonus. Dizzy with her initial success, Sharon gathered up her courage and went to see the buyer at Jordan Marsh department store, where she sold thirty-six dozen for their six stores.

Tom Hart, a district sales manager for a margarine company in the South, has to be on the road every other week for four or five days, and Anthony Livingstone, a dentist, often takes some evening patients. These evenings when Sharon and Bonnie are home alone with their children are the most productive hours they spend making paper flowers. Sharon's business experience before she was married (at eighteen) was a brief period when she sold classified advertising for Miami and Coral Beach newspapers. Bonnie was a registered nurse who, after graduation, went right to work for her husband, whom she had met while she was still in training.

"Tom has masterminded all our business management," said Sharon. "Bonnie and I have a bank account for Bonnie Blooms, Inc., but we each file joint income tax returns with our husbands. We split our profits fifty-fifty. Bonnie keeps the books and keeps track of expenses and I do the selling, send out the bills, and bank the money.

"Our husbands don't see any of our money. My first $95 check was spent on an upholstered chair and ottoman. Bonnie spent hers on blackout shades for her bedroom so that she could sleep in the mornings. Now we each make enough to pay for a once-a-week cleaning woman, and we don't feel guilty if we have to make a second visit to the hairdresser in a week when there's a special party coming up."

Sharon takes a couple of business trips a season with her husband to get out-of-town orders. Her mother comes to stay with the children, and the trips take her away only two or three days at a time.

"Our husbands were rather amused at our project in the beginning," said Bonnie. "They offered to celebrate the sale of our first five hundred flowers by taking us out to dinner. And where do you suppose they took us? To a restaurant called the Mouse Trap. They felt very clever about choosing a place with a name that brought to mind the old saying, "If you build a better mousetrap than your neighbor, the world will make a beaten path to your door.' "

22 Pot Luck Changed Her Life

"It was just an accident of fate that I discovered I had a talent for making pottery," said Betty Neubert, the tall and slender redhead who was in her studio showing me her exquisite miniature vases, urns, weed pots, jars, and fairy tale character figures. Her skillful hands and lively imagination had shaped these figures into decorative fantasies that sell in a dozen quality gift shops throughout the Southwest.

"If my friend Kathy Holsinger hadn't persuaded me to join her in a night school course at the University of Arizona twice a week, I might never have discovered that my fingers could do any more than punch keys on an office calculator.

"That was just ten years ago, when I was no kid. I was thirty-seven years old. I had been working at Steinfeld's Department store here in Tucson, doing statistical work and bookkeeping for $150 a month. My husband Bill is now an associate engineer at Hughes Aircraft, but we both had traveled far and tried many jobs from teaching dancing at an Arthur Murray Studio in Kansas City, where we met in our twenties, to working for the Park Service in Colorado Springs, where he was a seasonal ranger and I worked in a stockbroker's office. We kept searching for a healthy and happy way of life. Bill had an acute sinus condition, which brought us to Tucson without jobs and with only $500 in savings. We've loved every minute of our lives here, and Bill has done well in electronics, his special gift. It took us six years to build our house, mostly with our own hands, on top of Swan Road, which overlooks the city. We lived in a trailer while we built enough of the house to live in."

219

Betty's and Bill's house is as much a storybook house as Betty's career at home—making ceramics. Built of redwood on three levels, the different roof lines are outlined in a vivid Mexican pink with a large double door entrance, also pink, with massive Mexican brass hinges. The entrance hall has a skylight that converts it into a greenhouse with an exotic jungle of tropical plants. The living room, with its twelve feet of glass overlooking the city, is an art gallery in which they display their collection of ceramics by local artists. Their bedroom has a king-size bed with a turquoise tile sunken bath as big as the bed in one corner.

"Why shouldn't a bathtub be beautiful and therapeutic as well as utilitarian?" said Betty, whose philosophy of life seems to be summed up in that sentence.

"Your studio and kiln are quite a production. When did you build those, Betty?" I asked as I sought to fix the date in her life when her hobby became her home career.

"The studio didn't come until I had spent nearly four years working my way through more professional training. I was hooked after that first $35 course at the university. Phil Bellomo, one of our best artists out here, had started the Ceramic Arts Studio, where the full range of pottery techniques was taught to two or three students at a time. The lessons cost $7.50 for four hours, and when I began to study more than once a week, I exchanged work in the studio to help me pay for the lessons. By then I knew this was no hobby—this was my life's work."

Betty never entered contests or exhibitions or joined crafts organizations. She says she was much too shy and insecure.

Tucson is a crafts center with really great artists," she said, "and they were an inspiration to me. I didn't have the nerve to try to compete with them when I didn't even have a studio of my own to work in."

When Betty was asked to help in the creation of a new art gallery called Studio West, she thought she had the perfect setup. She was to become the gallery manager. She would be given a studio of her own to work in and would have to go on buying trips throughout the Southwest, collecting paintings, sculptured items, and pottery. Many of the paintings that hang on the Neuberts' walls were bought on those trips, and the entire experience was invaluable to Betty. She learned a great deal about the background of the art and artists of the whole region. However, keeping her books, dealing with the public, and organizing office details consumed so much time that Betty had no time to pursue her own pottery making. She felt she needed more training, so she went back to the studio school, where she exchanged studio caretaking for lessons three times a week.

I asked Betty about her first sale.

"That's another one of those lucky breaks I never expected," laughed Betty. "I had had lunch with an artist who made jewelry, and I was going with her to the Desert House Crafts, where she was making a delivery to the owner. I happened to have some of my small pieces on the back seat of my car. When my friend examined them, she insisted I show them to Mr. Tanner. His is one of the best shops in town, and I was sure they weren't good enough to sell there. But when he saw them, he said he'd buy them all and as many more as I could make. Their miniature size, the unusual turquoise glaze, and the low price made them very salable. That's how I began to sell."

Reorders and new orders placed by gift shop buyers who have seen her products in gift shops produce the business Betty has built up in Aspen, Fort Worth, Santa Fe, Albuquerque and six more shops in Arizona. She does not have an agent nor does she take samples on the road herself, the method by which most artists build up a following. "That's why I'll never get rich!" Betty said.

"Is making pottery a very complicated and expensive craft?" I asked.

"On an amateur level it can be learned by a child. Many children start with modeling clay even in nursery school. An electric wheel and kiln can be bought inexpensively in hobby shops, or the firing can be done in an outside kiln.

"From the very beginning I was surrounded by professionals. Most of the students at the University of Arizona were art teachers, and we were put to work at once on a potter's wheel. No hand modeling or shaping was included in that course. The wheel is used only for pots, bowls, cups, ash trays, casseroles, jugs, and pitchers—any object that will be hollow. A shape that involves a figure or a head is molded by hand or shaped over a mold. Other techniques that do not involve the wheel are slab work, which is a rolling pin procedure on a flat surface, and coiling, the method used by the Indians to build up their pots with a series of coils. A professional masters them all, of course, using the wheel to produce pots in quantity.

"Throwing a pot is a skill that means centering a ball of clay very precisely on the wheel in order to achieve perfect symmetry—the true test of a professional potter."

When Betty decided she was ready for a career at home with her pottery making, her engineer husband got into the act by designing and building her a ten- by fifteen-foot studio. He lined its walls with shelves and cupboards, installed a sink with hot and cold running water, and built counters and the slab of casting plaster on which she kneads the air and water out of the clay she uses. They did not economize on the electric potting wheel or the kiln; they are the best that money can buy. The wheel cost around $450, and the new materials for the firing kiln, which her husband put together, cost $600. Had he not been competent to do this, the installed cost of this furnace would have come to $2,500. The firing kiln is just outside the studio and is an "up-draft, down-draft" type, fueled by high fire gas. It accommodates about two hundred pieces of bisque—the pottery pieces before the glaze is applied—at one time. An electric grinder is used to smooth pot bottoms after the second firing when the glaze has been added. An electric spray is used to glaze larger pieces.

Three types of clay are usually used to make ceramic pieces—earthenware, stoneware, and porcelain. Betty uses high fire stoneware, which is fired at 2,300° Fahrenheit.

Betty used to mix her clay, but now she buys it ready mixed for 8 cents a pound, including the shipping charge. The time she saves in her own labor more than offsets the slight increase in cost. She buys a thousand pounds at a time, which is enough to last her two years.

The artistry of pot making depends as much on the beauty of the glaze as on the contour of the pot. Thirty-four raw materials go into the recipes Betty uses for making her glazes, not including the oxides and carbonates used as coloring agents. She specializes in turquoise, greens, and browns, often with an iridescent cast. Betty collects glass formulas, which she mixes in gallon lots and stores on her shelves to be ready for use. Each glazed piece requires two firings, the first without the glaze and the second after the glaze has been applied.

The equipment in Betty's studio also includes "bats"—the

disks of casting plaster on which she "throws" her pots so that the whole disk can be lifted from the wheel without touching the shaped wet clay. When the pot has dried, it can be removed without altering its contour. There are also half a dozen hand tools for trimming and etching designs; a sponge; a gram scale to measure glazes; two large stainless steel bowls for mixing glazes; two screen mesh sifters for straining glazes; wooden stirring spoons; a rolling pin; and a variety of molds.

"When I first sat down at my potter's wheel, I was doing all right if I made one perfect pot in ten. Now if I lose one in ten I'm disgusted. The beginner has to be prepared for pots to warp and crack and for glazes to run. The hardest lesson to learn is how to dry pots very slowly. When clay is purchased, it is critical to know at exactly what temperature that clay must be fired. Many beginners ruin countless pieces because they don't find this out in advance. The magazine *Ceramics Monthly* is full of helpful information. Every day there is something new to learn about ceramics, and experimentation goes on forever. My next adventure will be working in porcelain."

"How many pieces would be an average order from a gift shop?" I asked.

"I would say four dozen. An order for a hundred pieces would be unusually large. My retail prices start at $3.50 and go up to $17.50. I only sell wholesale, so my share would be half of the retail price. Weed pots and jars range in size from one to six inches. I price my figures by the inch, and they stand from fifteen to eighteen inches tall. Four- to eight-inch pitchers are retail priced at from $12.50 to $20."

"How much profit can you make working alone as you do now?"

"If I didn't love it, it wouldn't be worth while. I make enough to pay the monthly installments on the money we borrowed to build and equip my studio. Later that will be clear profit. Last year I didn't clear more than about $1,200 because I sacrificed so many pots in experimenting with the kiln and different glazes. From now on I expect to clear two or three times that much as a loner. I don't want to be bothered with a payroll, workmen's compensation, or all those extra administrative details you get into when you hire outside help. I'll continue to work alone even if it means keeping my production low. I liberated myself from the tyranny of figures when I became a potter, and I don't intend to get trapped again."

23 Fashion Pays Off at Home

When the bell rang, a toddler about four years old appeared at the screen door. He had a dripping scrub brush in one hand and a gray plastic elephant clutched in the other arm. Another little boy could be seen at the foot of the stairs behind him.

"What's your name?"

"Jeffrey Martinek. My mommy's working."

"Is she home?"

"Yes, she's upstairs."

"Please come on in," floated a voice from above. "I'll be right down."

Jeffrey went back to join his pal and finish scrubbing his elephant. Adele Martinek, a small redhead, came skipping down the stairs of her roomy Hackensack, New Jersey, house. She looked more like a teenage baby-sitter than a mother of two.

"I just put Thomas, the baby, down for his nap. This afternoon is my turn to watch my neighbor's little boy.

"Take your pail and animals out to the backyard, now. Mommy's going to talk to the lady," she told the children.

Both children scampered out the back door, and we went into the kitchen and sat down at the table by the window overlooking the yard, where Adele could keep an eye on the children.

"Can you work with the distraction of small children running around the place all the time?"

"Oh, sure. When Jeffrey's little playmate is here, I can easily watch them from the window of my workroom upstairs. When he's alone, he plays in a corner of my workroom. I save scraps of fabric for him and all the children in the neighborhood. He's getting pretty good with the scissors. When I have a rush job, my neighbor takes him. In return, I do hems and other little sewing jobs for her. We have a great barter system on this block."

"When do you do your housework?"

"We all stay in bed until my husband gets off to work around eight in the morning. He makes the coffee. Then we get up, and I tend to the children, straighten the house, load the clothes in the washer, and I'm through by noon. Afternoons and three evenings a week when my husband is at night school are my times for sewing."

"Whom do you sew for?"

"I make model dresses for a pattern company, I make boutique items, I do crewelwork and smocking, and I have several private customers."

"How much do you charge?"

"I charge $2 an hour for a simple quickie dress. Last week I made two in a day and an evening. But if the job is complicated and involves handwork, I charge $3 an hour."

We went upstairs to Adele's sunny sewing room and looked over pattern books and photographs in magazines and catalogs illustrating shifts, dresses, hip-hugger shorts, slacks, smocked blouses, and embroidered linens made by Adele.

An inventory of her fifteen- by fifteen-foot workroom in-includes a three- by six-foot cutting table made by her father, an electric sewing machine, an ironing board with an overhead lamp on a swinging arm, an old-fashioned set of bookcases with see-through glass fronts (used to store fabrics), and two closets.

"My customers supply all fabrics, but when I buy for myself I look for the fabrics that say *'absolutely no ironing!'*

"The first six months of this year I made $1,000. Nobody's been sick, and I've had lots of time to work. Last year, just after my second baby was born, I took six months off. That's what's so great about working at home. I can do as much or as little as I want."

"How did you happen to get started with pattern companies?"

"Before my first baby was born, I worked as a girl Friday and typist for the art department of a pattern company. I've always made my own clothes, and some of the girls in the office asked me to make dresses for them in my spare time. When I had to quit to have the baby, I saw a chance to take in money at home by making up patterns for photographing. I got jobs with other companies, and I was recommended to a New York East Side boutique."

"If you were a typist and office assistant, how did you acquire the skill to do sewing on such a professional level?"

"My English grandmother started me off when I was six years old. She was quite a character. She used to watch wrestling on television as she sewed, and I used to sit with her and learn how to make the stitches. She'd have her embroidery materials and a glass of beer beside her on a table. The first 5 cents I earned was for threading 150 embroidery needles for her. In high school I took sewing and art as electives, and I went to Pratt Institute for two years, where I learned pattern making and construction."

"What kind of work does your husband do?"

"He works for a music licensing company, but he's been completing his college work at night school. He was just graduated from Rutgers University, and he's going for his M.A. at Seton Hall. He wants to be a college professor."

"How long have you been married?"

"Six years; I was 21, and he was 24. I made my wedding dress of the most beautiful pure silk satin and Alençon lace. The two of us went down to the bargain stalls on Delancey Street, near the Bowery, on the Lower East Side of Manhattan, where we bought the satin for $1.50 a yard. My wedding dress cost $35, but it was as beautiful as a ready-made dress that would have cost two or three times that much."

"This is a big house for young marrieds to handle—eight rooms. How big a bite does it take out of your budget?"

"It's $225 a month including fuel and utilities. Our food runs us about $25 to $30 a week, but my husband is the cook—and a gourmet too! Next to becoming a college professor, he'd like to be a chef. Coq au vin and all kinds of pastas and sauces are his specialties. I'm the dishwasher. Why, he's good enough so that he's taken on catering jobs for his boss. Both of us have always been willing to take on anything when we need extra money. We always manage to meet our bills."

"How about your social life?"

"There isn't time just now in our lives to do much except on a very simple scale. Our friends are in the same boat. Four couples who live nearby have get-togethers often, and we visit our families a lot. I teach Sunday school at the Lutheran Church in Hasbrouck Heights. During the week when I want to take a break and enjoy some adult talk, I drop in at my neighbors' with the children and some handwork."

"If you had your choice, would you rather do the work you're doing at home or work in an office, as you did before?"

"Oh, I love to sew. There's satisfaction in creating something, and I have independence and freedom. I'd have to make $150 a week to replace myself at home, and I couldn't bring up my own children. I get a break on the income tax too. I can deduct some for using my house as a place of business. All my materials are supplied by my customers, so there's no inventory or risk involved. My husband makes deliveries for me. I figure I have the best of two worlds."

And Adele's husband Warren thinks he has the best of two worlds, too.

"He's kind of proud I'm doing so well—and a little surprised!"

24 Money Grows on Easter Egg Trees

At about six o'clock on a typical weekday evening the serenity of the Alan B. Brittons' living room in Scarsdale, New York, takes on the excitement of a homecoming. Three daughters—aged fifteen, fourteen, and ten—dart in and out looking for Mom to tell her what has gone on at school, about the sick puppy at the veterinarian's down the street, or of the plans being made for next month's athletic meet.

Alan Britton, father of this group, is expected home any minute. He will have to eat an early dinner so that he can get to the evening rehearsal of a local production of *Arsenic and Old Lace,* in which he has an important part. Gabrielle, the enormous Saint Bernard puppy that weighs more than anyone in the family except Father, must be fed her pound of meat. Dot Britton, mother of the brood, moves quietly around the kitchen, joining in the girl talk while preparing the evening meal.

"We'll eat in the breakfast nook tonight so our gift exhibit won't have to be moved from the dining room table," she tells me.

A Hans Christian Andersen fairy tale display is spread like a sparkling miniature stage set on the mahogany table. Easter egg trees, from eight to sixteen inches in height, dangle "jeweled" eggs from their branches. The eggs, made of plastic in colors of turquoise, emerald, aquamarine, opal pink, and topaz, are decorated with beads, simulated pearls, golden and silvery plastic lace, and braid.

"Lightness and delicacy of color are what make these Easter trees attractive," explains Dot Britton. She is careful not to

228

overornament her eggs. The smallest of the trees sells for $4.95, and as the sizes get larger, they go up in price to $12.95. Her cookie cutter music boxes are in the shape of bunnies and cost $7.25 each; the cookie cutter can be removed and used for its original purpose.

"We are a typical suburban family," Dot says. "I have done many hours of volunteer work, and my husband is the world's best salesman of anything he believes in. Tracy is a busy fingers with great patience and dexterity. She is my partner, the vice-president of our company, Tracidot Products. Without her I couldn't have developed our business."

When Tracy, the youngest, was home alone with her mother while her older sisters were at school, she learned to help Dot, who was then making gifts to sell at church bazaars. Now Tracy gets 1 cent an egg and often earns $3 over a weekend. It was her inventive mind that conceived the idea of converting walnut-shell halves into little golden cradles for tiny dolls. They have become best sellers. She and her mother go to the New York Botanical Garden and collect seed balls that have fallen to the ground from the sweetgum trees. Tracy stuffs the seed balls into a pillowcase and brings them home to cluster together as toy trees. She sprays them with gold or silver paint.

Dot Britton's gift ideas began to make money for her five years ago. As a volunteer, she had worked for several years making articles for hospital gift shops, Girl Scout benefits, and church bazaars.

"I learned to create objects from very inexpensive materials such as seed balls, pinecones, walnutshell halves, inexpensive yarns, and remnants," Dot relates. "With a friend I developed enough ideas to collect $3,000 in a one-day Easter bazaar for Saint Paul's Methodist Church, in Hartsdale, New York. I have since sold many hundreds of dollars' worth of Easter egg trees through the Woman's Exchange and local stores.

"My little tree adapts itself to all sorts of variations. I make trees hung with lightweight toys as gifts for hospitalized or home-confined children. There's a pirate tree, a halloween tree, and—one of my most popular—a valentine tree with little red hearts cascading from white branches.

"The Woman's Exchange here and in New York can sell everything I turn out. One year I cleared almost $5,000. It would have been more if I hadn't had to turn down an order

from Neiman-Marcus for sixteen dozen decorated Easter egg
trees; they were too fragile to ship to Texas. My husband's real
estate business takes him into New York about once a week. He
loads our station wagon with my items and drops them off for
me at the Women's Exchange in Manhattan. I also sell through
a local outlet here in Scarsdale.

"This year I have added a crèche scene to my output, with the
infant Jesus nestled in a tiny walnut shell half sprayed with gold
paint, a red coverlet about Him, and a bright star glued above
His head. The little golden cradles also make charming ornaments suspended from gold cord on my Easter trees or on
Christmas trees.

"Most of my materials are imported from Hong Kong and
are inexpensive. To get them we make a three-hour trip to The
Pink Sleigh, a fabulous place in Oldwick, New Jersey, which
has litterally thousands of miniature items from which we can
choose."

Dot and Tracy made about five hundred decorated gift trees
last year, along with a couple of hundred music boxes.

Though her home business is flourishing, Dot still has time
for her favorite volunteer activity, a workshop for church bazaars.

Six weeks before a bazaar the women start getting together
four days a week to learn from Dot how to make some of the
things they will sell. By concentrating the effort into a period
of weeks instead of months, the enthusiasm is maintained at
high pitch.

Dot believes an Easter bazaar makes more sense than a Christmas church sale does. As she puts it, "The cold dull months
after Christmas need the lift of activity that preparing for a
spring bazaar provides."

After having been a homemaker for fifteen years, Dot recently
had to turn down the job of her dreams. Having had experience
in personnel work before her marriage, she was asked to serve as
a coordinator of volunteers for a large hospital in Westchester
County, New York. "But my husband did not want me to be
away from home that much," says Dot. "He felt our girls would
not have enough supervision."

So Dot has resigned herself to working at home—making
things she loves, showing a handy profit for her labors.

25 Plain Profit from Fancy Cakes

You'll find sugar and spice and everything nice—especially the price—in the cakes that Delores Fillinger bakes and sells in her home kitchen in Marion, Ohio. Considering the elaborateness of her creations, they are quite inexpensive. For example, wedding cakes are priced so that the cost comes to just 25 cents per guest portion, while a two-layer, eight-inch birthday concoction decorated to represent the personality or hobby of the honored guest goes for $4.

Walking into Delores's cake-decorating workroom—a converted family room across the hall from the kitchen—you see many of your favorite childhood storybook characters and scenes in a variety of shapes. Raggedy Ann and the Gingerbread Man hang on the walls in the shape of copper cake pans. A finished cake that looks like a fairy tale castle may be ready for delivery to a birthday girl—as one was the afternoon I arrived for the interview.

Shelves hold trays of colored sugar flowers—roses, pansies, violets, daisies—waiting to bloom on fluffy party cake mountains. Small dolls stand on other shelves; these, too, will be used on future cakes.

Just outside the "cake room," I spotted four of the five Fillinger children eating dinner at the kitchen table. They were Lori, six; Rita, seven; Linda, eight; and Randy, four. The fifth and oldest child, Denny, eleven, was out at the time. The interview was arranged at a time when their father Jack could take over so Delores would be free to talk about her home career. Jack is a factory machinist.

"Tell us about the family's own birthday cakes," I asked Delores.

"I'll start with Randy, whose birthday was most recent. I made a train with a locomotive, coal car, three boxcars, and a red caboose. I used four- and six-inch miniature loaf pans I'd bought at a dime store. I put Randy's four candles on top of the coal car. My background frosting was white, and I used red and blue for trimmings. I created a face on the front of the locomotive.

"Lori's cake was a castle made in a pan called a Bundt. It has a cylinder in the center like an angel food pan, but it has ridges on the sides. I put two smaller layers on top held up by little posts called separators, and I built the turrets out of inverted ice cream cones that I'd defrosted.

"Rita and Linda each wanted a doll cake—a cake with a hole in the middle. I inserted an eight-inch doll so that it would be covered up to the waist. The bottom of the cake became a very full skirt, which I decorated with frosting ruffles and flowers. It could have been stripes or whatever would appeal to me or the girls.

"Denny had a baseball cake for his eleventh birthday. This was a one-layer, ten-inch square cake with green icing. I drew the baseball diamond on top with cinnamon and sugar, and I placed figures of little leaguers in their proper positions.

"My husband's cake represented his favorite hobby—fishing. His was a one-layer sheet cake frosted in blue for water, with green edges to show a grassy river bank. I put a fisherman on the bank with a line from his rod into the blue frosting."

Delores explained that the mail order cake decorating supply companies have a fascinating range of decorations. "I can't resist them," she said. "Look at those shelves full of miniature thingamajigs.

"What I love most about my work," she continued, changing the subject, "is that I share everyone's happy times. Girls come to see me months before their weddings. Two of my children's teachers were married last June and ordered their wedding cakes from me; Rita's first-grade teacher had a seven-tier round cake. (Incidentally, I always give a free top tier to be put in the freezer and eaten when the couple celebrate their first wedding anniversary.) Her cake was the first I've baked that featured a tiny electrically lighted wedding bell on top, casting a glow on the bride and groom figures just beneath it.

"The second-grade teacher had her wedding cake on a base shaped like a cross. The bride and groom on this cake were not on top but on the path leading from the cross. The bride doll wore a dress made of the same material as the real bride's wedding gown.

"I assemble elaborate cakes like this after I deliver them. That way I make sure there are no accidents. Some wedding cakes are four feet high, and carrying them already assembled would be impossible."

I hadn't talked about making the cake layers themselves.

"White cakes seem to be the big favorites, especially for weddings," Delores said. "In the beginning I used my own recipes, but later I discovered I got just as many compliments when I used a mix. Now I use mixes exclusively unless I'm requested not to. I always ask if there's a favorite family recipe the bride would like me to use. Two of my specialties are hazelnut and lemon batter recipes, which cost a little more than mixes.

"A wedding cake generally takes me half a day to bake and a full day to decorate. On the other hand, I can complete birthday cakes in just a couple of hours. I bake in the afternoon and decorate in the evening."

I asked Delores to tell me about her ovens, pans, and decorating tools.

"What do you mean, 'ovens'?" she replied. "I have only one. My electric range is standard-size, and the oven takes a sixteen-inch pan. I have two complete sets of cake pans—one round and one square. Each set has five pans gradated in size from six to fourteen inches. I also own pans in special shapes—a guitar, piano, book, and the Raggedy Ann and Gingerbread Man figures. I have a set of tubes for squeezing the icing and cloth bags for holding colored icings. I make my flowers with a metal disk. I use eight basic colors, plus orange and purple for frosting. I like paste colors better than liquids or those that come in tubes."

"How did you learn such professional techniques?"

"I was a service wife until two years ago; my husband was in the Air Force. A neighbor in Spokane, Washington, who was also an Air Force wife, gave lessons at the base. She did the baking for the officers' club. I joined her class one night a week for ten weeks. When I finished the course, my friend moved away, and I took over her job at the club.

"When we moved here to Marion two years ago, my oldest girl joined the Brownies, and her leader asked me to teach the girls how to decorate cakes. The word got around, and the local newspaper wrote a story about me. Soon my telephone began ringing with orders for special cakes. That's how I got started.

"Now I also teach classes once a week at the YWCA. Around a dozen women pay $3 a lesson for a two-hour class. Besides that I hold classes here at home. My gross income is now about $1,600.

"Cake decorating is the best cure for the blues," Delores philosophized. "I know! Giving birth to so many children so close together in addition to suffering a frightful automobile accident had made me subject to depression. With my home career I hardly ever get depressed. My cakes have made friends for me, and that's the greatest satisfaction of all."

26 She Had 78 Babies in 30 Years

We talked in Frances and Gerald McLane's attractive living room. They are "mom" and "dad" to their two grown foster children Freddie and Irene, who had joined us to reminisce about the seventy-six other foster babies who, in this very house in Bayside, New York, had been given a start in life.

The unusual thing about Irene and Freddie is that they were among the first babies that Frances brought home. They stayed on to adulthood, but this was far from the original plan.

"If we hadn't had them, I couldn't have endured parting with my other babies when the time came for them to leave at the end of a year or two, when they were placed for adoption or returned to their own parents," said Frances McLane, a lovely woman with crisp, curly gray hair.

Freddie is now thirty-four. He is married and has four children of his own.

"I had plenty of practice with all those babies when I was a kid," he said, grinning as he remembered.

"I seem to remember you spent more time making French toast and smoking up the house than you did changing diapers," laughed Frances.

Irene, a thirty-year-old career girl with snapping black eyes, said, "All the children in the neighborhood used to come and help take care of the babies and do the things I was supposed to do."

Irene, though financially independent, still makes her home with her foster parents. Her sewing machine stands in the dining room. She makes all of her own and her mother's clothes.

She graduated from Hofstra College, and from her work she has
saved enough money to vacation abroad. But she always comes
home to the McLanes.

"No two children ever had more loving parents," she says,
and her happiness in continuing to live with them is reflected
in the warm affection with which she speaks.

Frances had worked for ten years in New York City, selling
and doing office work. She did not marry until she was thirty
years old. She had had a lonely childhood, having been brought
to the United States by her parents as an infant from Scotland.
Within a short time her father died, and she grew up the child
of a working mother. Her schooling was in North Andover,
Massachusetts. It was interrupted by frequent stays with relatives in Scotland, who seemed more like strangers.

"I knew what it was to be a child in need of love."

Her husband Gerald was thirty-three years old when they
were married. They met at a dance, and he took her home early
because he had to get up the next day to serve on the altar of
the Episcopal Church. His daily job was working as a letter
carrier for the post office. In six months they were married.

"Without a doubt my husband has the best disposition in the
world," says Frances. "He lives by what religion has taught
him."

Gerald's present of a dozen red roses to Frances's mother the
first time he called showed he also knew how to charm the
ladies.

After their marriage, when Frances learned she would be
unable to bear children because of peritonitis after an appendix
operation, Frances's loneliness in their eight-room house was so
intense that she asked her husband to permit her to take a foster
child. With his consent she made her first personal visit to the
Sheltering Arms Children's Service at 122 East 29th Street in
New York City, the Protestant foster care agency established in
1864 "to furnish a home for various classes of children who
could not be admitted by any existing institution."

"Why do you really want to do this?" the social worker asked.

"My husband is a mailman, so of course we're not rich. But
we have everything we need and want—good friends and neighbors and an eight-room house—everything except children."

"You realize that foster care is temporary care, don't you?
Are you prepared to give up a child for whom you have cared
for a year or more?"

Frances recalled this conversation and admitted she didn't dream there would be times when it would seem so hard. She said yes to the social worker, and arrangements were made for interviews in their home with her husband, their friends, their doctor, and their minister. The Board of Health Inspector examined their house, measured the rooms, and gave sanitary approval to the bathroom and kitchen.

Frances waited for six months for a caseworker to telephone. One morning she was told that a little two-year-old named Freddie would be coming to live with them. In those days (1938) an allowance of $20 a month was paid to foster parents to contribute to the support of a foster child. Medical care and clothing were paid for separately. Gerald's pay was then $42 a week, but they knew they could manage somehow. With the advent of Social Security the financial support for foster children has increased steadily over the years. Today a monthly allowance of at least $130 (exclusive of medical and clothing requirements) is given for each foster child under twelve. If the child is over the age of thirteen, the rate goes up to $140 a month.

"The day I was to bring Freddie home I called for Gerald at the post office so that the two of us could bring him home together. Neither of us seemed to worry about whether we could handle a two-year-old child. We just wanted a child to love. This little boy had been in several homes before he came to us, so I was prepared to be patient. It took me a year to get him to call me "mommy" and to kiss me. He was hard to toilet-train. I had to do the disciplining. My husband couldn't discipline a mosquito. But Freddie is the boy who stayed with us all through the years, who was so homesick when he went to camp that we had to bring him home, of whom we were so proud when he won the YMCA swimming meets, who never missed Sunday School. Wherever Freddie goes he has friends. He wasn't easy to rear, but he's thanked me over and over again because I was strict."

Listening to these accolades Freddie made a face, but he was pleased with his parents' approval.

"Irene was our third foster child. The second one stayed a very short time before being taken for adoption. Most of my children have been the children of unwed mothers, but Irene's didn't want to give her out for adoption. She came to us the day she left the hospital. She was a real crybaby, but she was bright and cute. We loved her very much. By the time she was a teenager and might have returned to her own mother, it was too late, she didn't want to leave us."

Only one child taken into the McLane home had to be transferred to another home. The little boy was Freddie's age.

"Freddie became so jealous of him he raised Cain. He would hide his toys and fight with him until we couldn't stand it. We asked to have him transferred and took only baby girls for the next ten years."

Because the babies came to them as infants, their cribs had to be placed in the master bedroom. Gerald had to get up for work at 5:30 A.M., so when the babies cried, Frances took them downstairs and walked the floor so as not to disturb her husband.

"But Gerald became better than I at quieting them. He didn't seem to mind rocking them and patting them and saying soothing things. He learned to change diapers as well as I did."

Those were the days when there were no automatic washing machines or diaper services. Frances would at times wash an average of forty diapers a day and do three loads of wash a day. She kept eighteen bottles of formula going, but she recalls with amazement that she didn't feel overworked. Often she would take two babies at the same time, and once she had two babies plus twins—four cribs in their bedroom over Christmas.

"When these babies left you, did you know where they were sent or ever hear from them again?"

"No. I was not even supposed to meet the new parents. This was the hardest part because the babies were ours for many months—sometimes several years."

"Mom and Freddie and Daddy would cry at the drop of a hat," said Irene, "and I'll admit I felt pretty bad myself when some of our babies left us."

I turned to Freddie to ask if he had special memories about some of the babies who came into their home.

"Who could forget little Diana? She was abandoned in a subway station. All the papers had stories about her, so of course I can't help remembering her—and she was so pretty."

That was in 1948, and the Sheltering Arms placed her for adoption within the year. Freddie and Irene were twelve and eight years old, respectively, when Diana came. At the time twin boys fifteen months old were being cared for by Mrs. McLane, but there was always room for one more. The twins were ultimately adopted together, which made everybody happy.

"What pushed your endurance to the point where you weren't sure you could cope?" I asked, knowing that in those years there had to be at least one situation so trying that Frances was ready to surrender.

"I think the child that had casts on both feet was the most exhausting because he had to be taken twice a week to the orthopedic clinic. Even giving him his bath every day was a real ordeal. He was born with his feet turned in, but by the time he went to his new parents his feet were normal, and I was glad that I had been able to hold up. To see him normal and happy was a real triumph!"

In the course of the thirty years Frances has had one baby that was tested as having a genius IQ and one that was mentally defective.

At the age of three months the babies are tested by the agency psychologist to determine their IQ. Frances didn't think the genius was very different from any of the other babies she had taken care of, and she will never know if he grew up to receive a Nobel prize. She does remember that he was very easy to handle. He wasn't frustrated, and he was responsive and curious. He could say a word or two at the age of ten months. The most touching story was about the little blind baby that was adopted into a lovely home very early in his life—as if the parents wanted to give extra love to a child that was handicapped.

When infants under one year are placed in a foster home, a visiting nurse is assigned to make as many calls to help the foster mother as are necessary. After the adjustment is made, their visits are arranged at regular intervals of two weeks at first and then once a month. The agency assigns a caseworker to each family. Sometimes the same caseworker stays with one family for years, as did Mrs. Marjorie Edwards, who was with the McLanes for twelve years. When she was transferred to the adoption service, the McLanes felt so grateful to her that they presented her with a string of pearls.

"Mrs. McLane always kept her children beautifully," said Mrs. Edwards when I talked to her. "She'd take babies that weren't much to look at, but within months they'd look like picture book babies."

"Infants are not nearly as prone to sickness as are young children," said Mrs. McLane when we asked her about health emergencies. "In case of accidents or critical illness the Sheltering Arms takes over at once and provides the best medical care

money can buy. My babies had very little sickness. Freddie and
Irene went through the usual measles, mumps, chicken pox, and
other childhood diseases, but the babies never became infected.
When Irene and Freddie needed dental care they were given the
best."

As we looked over scrapbooks and talked about graduations,
confirmations, and vacations, the story of Freddie's own wedding
ten years ago was described. He was twenty-four years old, and
he paid for the big wedding himself. He saved $20 a week until
he had enough money to invite two hundred guests and to take
his bride to the Poconos for their honeymoon. He worked in a
printing and bookbinding shop then, and he still works for the
same company and supports his wife and family of three girls
and one boy.

The hours that Gerald spent at the dining room table helping
Freddie with his homework have paid off in lasting closeness
between them. Irene never needed much help. Getting into college was a cinch for her. Freddie never made it. Both were loved
equally, and they have been a source of comfort and satisfaction
to the McLanes.

A heart attack put an end to any more foster babies for
Frances. But if she and Gerald could do it over again they would
still have seventy-eight babies in thirty years.

Part III
Information Center

1 Where to Learn

Classes and counseling in many crafts, services, and small business enterprises prepare interested people for careers at home. Write or phone those in your area for catalogs and information about workshop programs. A state-by-state listing follows. In contacting colleges and universities, write to the Admissions Office. For a list of the names of correspondence schools accredited by the National Home Study Council, write to National Home Study Council, 1601 18th Street, N. W., Washington, D. C. 20009.

ALABAMA
Birmingham Small Business Adm.
908 S. 20th St. (35205)
Mobile U. of South Alabama
Montevallo U. of Montevallo
Troy Troy State U.
Tuscaloosa U. of Alabama

ALASKA
Anchorage Small Business Adm.
Suite 200
1016 W. Sixth Ave. (99501)
Fairbanks Small Business Adm.
510 Second Ave. (99701)
Juneau Alaska Native Arts &
Crafts Div.
Alaska Native Service (99801)
Dept. of Education
Off. of Vocational Rehabilitation
P.O. Box 2568 (99801)

ARIZONA
Flagstaff Northern Arizona U.
Phoenix Small Business Adm.
2727 N. Central Ave. (85004)
Tempe Arizona State U.
Tucson Small Business Adm.
155 E. Alameda (85701)
U. of Arizona

ARKANSAS
Conway State College of Arkansas
P.O. Box 966 (72032)
Little Rock Small Business Adm.
600 W. Capitol Ave. (72201)
Arkansas State U.

CALIFORNIA
Beverly Hills Roxbury Park
Roxbury Drive
Arts and Crafts Cooperative
1652 Shattuck (94709)

Berkeley U. of California

Campbell Hopper Glassblowing School
3495 S. Bascom Ave. (95008)

Claremont Scripps College
9th & Columbia St.

Cupertino De Anza College
21250 Stevens Creek Blvd.

Davenport Big Creek Pottery
(95017)

Davis U. of California

El Cajon Grossmont College
8800 Grossmont College Dr.

El Monte El Calvario Community Ctr.
P.O. Box 303 (91734)

Fresno Fresno State College
Shaw & Cedar Sts. (93726)

North Ave. Community Ctr.
135 W. North Ave. (93706)

Small Business Adm.
Room 4015, Federal Bldg.
1130 O St. (93721)

Granada Hills North Valley Jewish Community Ctr.
16601 Rinaldi (91344)

Idyllwild Idyllwild School of Music and the Arts
U. of Southern Calif. (92349)

Irvine U. of California

Kentfield Art Dept., College of Marin (94904)

La Jolla La Jolla Museum of Art
700 Prospect St. (92037)

Long Beach California State Col.
6101 E. 7th St.

Los Angeles All Nations Neighborhood Ctr.
2317 Michigan Ave. (90033)

All Peoples Christian Ctr.
806 E. 20th St. (90011)

Avalon-Carver Community Ctr.
3517 S. Avalon Blvd. (90011)

Barnsdall Arts and Crafts Ctr.
4800 Hollywood Blvd. (90027)

Calif. State College at Los Angeles
5151 State College Dr.

Catholic Youth Organization
1400 W. Ninth St. (90015)

Immaculate Heart College
2021 N. Western Ave. (90027)

Otis Art Inst. of Los Angeles County
2401 Wilshire Blvd.

Small Business Adm.
849 S. Broadway (90014)

UCLA Dept. of Art
405 Hilgard Ave.

Westminster Neighborhood Assn.
10125 Beach St. (90002)

Mendocino Mendocino Art Center

Northridge San Fernando Valley State College
18111 Nordhoff St.

Oakland Calif. College of Arts & Crafts
5212 Broadway

Mills College

Pasadena Pasadena City Col.
1570 E. Colorado Blvd.

Redlands U. of Redlands

Richmond Richmond Art Ctr.
Civic Center Plaza (94804)

Riverside Community Settlement Assn.
4366 Bermuda Ave. (92507)

Rohnert Park Sonoma State College
1801 E. Cotati Ave.

Sacramento Sacramento State College
6000 Jay St.

San Diego Neighborhood House Assn.
1809 National Ave. (92113)

Potter's Guild
Studio 29, Spanish Village
Balboa Park 92101

San Diego State College

Small Business Adm.
110 W. C St. (92101)

San Francisco San Fran. Art Inst.
800 Chestnut St.

San Francisco State Col.
1600 Holloway Ave.

Small Business Adm.
450 Golden Gate Ave.
Box 36044 (94102)

Telegraph Hill Neighborhood
Assn.
660 Lombard St. (94133)

Visitacion Valley Community Ctr.
50-66 Raymond Ave. (94134)

Booker T. Washington
Community Service Ctr.
800 Presidio Ave. (94115)

San Jose San José State College

San Luis Obispo Calif. State
Polytechnic College Art Dept.
(93401)

San Rafael Dominican College

Santa Barbara Brooks Inst. School
of Fine Arts
2020 Alameda Padre Serra

Sausalito Sausalito Arts Ctr.
Nevada St.

Stockton U. of the Pacific

Torrance El Camino College

Vallejo Solano College
100 Whitney Ave.

Van Nuys Everywoman's Village
5650 Sepulveda Blvd.

Walnut Mt. San Antonio Jr. College
1100 N. Grand Ave.

COLORADO

Alamosa Adams State College

Boulder U. of Colorado

Denver Small Business Adm.
1961 Stout St. (80202)

Southwest Community Ctr.
1000 S. Lowell Blvd. (80219)

Steele Community Ctr.
3341 W. 30th Ave. (80211)

U. of Denver

Fort Collins Colorado State U.

Greeley Colorado State College

Gunnison Western State College of
Colorado   .

Pueblo Southern Colorado State
College

CONNECTICUT

Bridgeport U. of Bridgeport

Brookfield Brookfield Craft Ctr.
Route 25 (06804)

Hartford Hartford Neighborhood
Ctrs.
38 Lawrence St. (06106)

Hartford Art School
U. of Hartford
200 Bloomfield Ave.

Small Business Adm.
450 Maine St. (06103)

Middletown Wesleyan Potters, Inc.
75 Pease Ave. (06457)

Wesleyan U.

New Britain Central Conn. State
College

New Haven Creative Arts Workshop
55Audubon St.

Southern Conn. State College
501 Crescent St. (06515)

YWCA, 48 Howe St. (06511)

Willimantic Eastern Conn. State
College

DELAWARE

Newark University of Delaware

DISTRICT OF COLUMBIA

Washington Corcoran School,
Corcoran Gallery of Art
17th St. & New York Ave.

Small Business Adm.
1405 I St., N. W. (20417)

George Washington U.

FLORIDA

Clearwater Florida Gulf Coast Art
Ctr., Inc.
111 Mantee Rd., Belleair 33516

Coconut Grove Grove House
3496 Main Highway

Deland Stetson U. (32720)

Gainesville U. of Florida

Jacksonville Jacksonville Art
Museum
4160 Boulevard Center Dr. (32207)

Jacksonville U.

Small Business Adm.
400 W. Bay St., P. O. Box 35067
(32202)

Miami Miami Dade Junior College
11380 N. W. 27th Ave. (33167)

Small Business Adm.
Rm. 912, 51 S. W. 1st Ave. (33130)
Sarasota Colson School of Art
1666 Hillview
Tampa Small Business Adm.
Rm. 308, Federal Off. Bldg.
500 Zack St. (33602)
Tampa United Methodist Ctrs.
3305 15th St. (33605)
West Palm Beach Norton Gallery &
School of Art
P. O. Box 2309
Pioneer Park (33405)

GEORGIA
Athens U. of Georgia
Atlanta Small Business Adm.
100 Edgewood Ave. N. E. (30303)
Wesley Community Ctrs.
P. O. Box 6802
9 McDonough Blvd. S. E. (30315)
Macon Wesleyan College
Mt. Berry Berry College
Rising Fawn Rising Fawn Crafts
The Pottery Shop, Rte. 2 (30738)
Statesboro Georgia Southern
College
(30458)

HAWAII
Honolulu Small Business Adm.
Rm. 402, 1149 Bethel St. (96813)
U. of Hawaii
2560 Campus Rd.

IDAHO
Boise Small Business Adm.
Rm. 408, 216 N. 8th St. (83702)
Moscow U. of Idaho
Pocatello Idaho State U.

ILLINOIS
Bloomington School of Art
Illinois Wesleyan U. (61701)
Carbondale Southern Illinois U.
Champaign U. of Illinois
Charleston Eastern Illinois U.
Chicago School of the Art Institute
of Chicago
Michigan Ave. at Adams St. (60604)

Chicago Commons Assn.
915 N. Wolcott Ave. (60622)
Gads Hill Ctr.
1919 W. Cullerton St. (60608)
Hull House Assn.
3179 N. Broadway (60657)
Hyde Park Neighborhood Club
5480 S. Kenwood Ave. (60615)
Northwestern U. Settlement
1400 Augusta Blvd. (60622)
Roosevelt U.
430 S. Michigan
Small Business Adm.
219 S. Dearborn St. (60604)
DeKalb Northern Illinois U.
Elgin Elgin Community College
373 E. Chicago St.
Macomb Western Illinois U.
Peoria YWCA, Downtown-
Lakeview
301 N. E. Jefferson St. (61602)
YWCA, Lakeview Park
1013 W. Lake (60614)
Rockford Rockford College
5050 E. State St.
Rock Island Augustana College
Bergendorff Bldg.

INDIANA
Anderson Alford House
Anderson Fine Arts Ctr.
226 W. 8th St.
Bloomington Indiana U.
Fort Wayne Fort Wayne School of
Fine Arts
1026 W. Berry St.
Greencastle DePauw U.
Indianapolis Christamore House
502 N. Tremont St. (46222)
Hawthorne Social Service Assn.
2440 W. Ohio St. (46222)
Herron School of Art
Indiana U.
1701 N. Pennsylvania St. (46202)
Indiana Central College
4001 S. Otterbein Ave.
Small Business Adm.
36 S. Pennsylvania St. (46204)
Lafayette Purdue U.

Muncie Ball State U.
Notre Dame St. Mary's College
Terre Haute Indiana State U.

IOWA
Ames Iowa State U.
  The Octagon
  Ames Society for the Arts
  232½ Main St.
Cedar Falls U. of Northern Iowa
Cedar Rapids Jane Boyd
    Community House
  943 14th Ave., S.E. (52401)
Clinton YWCA, 317 7th Ave. S.
  (52732)
Davenport Friendly House
  303 Taylor St. (52802)
Des Moines Des Moines Art Ctr.
  Greenwood Park
  Art Education Dept.
  Drake U.
  25th & University Ave.
  Small Business Adm.
  Rm. 749, 210 Walnut St. (50309)
Iowa City School of Art, U. of Iowa
  (52240)
Iowa Falls Ellsworth College
  1100 College Ave.
Lamoni Graceland College
Pella Central College
Sioux City Mary J. Treglia
    Community House
  900 Jennings St. (51101)

KANSAS
Emporia Kansas State Teachers'
    College
Hays Fort Hays Kansas State
    College
Lawrence U. of Kansas
Lindsborg Bethany College
Manhattan Kansas State U.
Pittsburg Kansas State College
Sterling Sterling College
Topeka Art Dept., Washburn U.
  (66621)
Wichita Small Business Adm.
  Rm. 302, 120 S. Market St. (67202)

Wichita Art Assn.
9112 E. Central
Wichita State U.

KENTUCKY
Anchorage Louisville School of Art
  100 Park Rd.
Berea Berea College
Bowling Green West Kentucky U.
Lexington U. of Kentucky
Louisville Market St. Neighborhood
    House
  1021 W. Market St. (40202)
  Neighborhood House
  225 N. 25th St. (40212)
  Presbyterian Community Ctr.
  760 S. Hancock St. (40203)
  Wesley Community House
  801-09 E. Washington St. (40206)
  Bellarmine-Ursuline College
  2000 Norris Pl.
  Small Business Adm.
  Rm. 1900, 4th & Broadway (40202)
Richmond Eastern Kentucky U.

LOUISIANA
Baton Rouge Louisiana State U.
Monroe Northeast Louisiana State
    College
New Orleans Louisiana Crafts
    Council
  139 Broadway (70125)
  Small Business Adm.
  124 Camp St. (70130)

MAINE
Augusta Small Business Adm.
  40 Western Ave. (04330)
Deer Isle Haystack Mountain
    School of Crafts (04627)
Hinckley The Hinckley School
  (04944)
Kennebunk Maine Arts and Craft
    Council, Inc.
  P.O. Box 63 (04043)
Orono U. of Maine
Portland YWCA, 87 Spring St.
Tenants Harbour Plymouth Hoe
    Hand Craft Workshop (04860)

MARYLAND

Baltimore Baltimore Museum
of Art
Art Museum Drive (21218)
College of Art
Maryland Institute
1300 Mt. Royal
Jewish Community Ctr.
5700 Park Heights Ave. (21233)
Small Business Adm.
Rm. 1113, 31 Hopkins Plaza
(21201)

Bowie Bowie State College
Department of Art (20715)

College Park U. of Maryland

Towson Towson State College

MASSACHUSETTS

Amherst U. of Massachusetts

Boston Dept. of Adult Education
Boston Public Schools
15 Beacon St.

Boston U.
855 Commonwealth Ave.

Emmanel College
400 The Fenway (02115)

Federated Dorchester Neighborhood Houses
1353 Dorchester Ave. (02122)

Massachusetts College of Art
364 Brookline Ave.

School of the Museum of
Fine Arts
230 The Fenway

Small Business Adm.
Kennedy Federal Bldg. (02213)

South Boston Neighborhood
House
521 E. Seventh St. (02127)

United South End Settlements
48 Rutland St. (02118)

YWCA, 140 Clarendon St. (02116)

Cambridge Alliance of Cambridge
Settlement Houses
99 Austin St. (02139)

Cambridge Ctr. for Adult
Education, 42 Brattle St.

Lincoln DeCordova Museum

North Dartmouth Southeastern
Massachusetts U.

Peabody Endicott Junior College

South Lancaster Atlantic Union
College

Worcester Craft Ctr.
25 Sagamore Rd.

MICHIGAN

Adrian Adrian College
Studio Angelico of Siena Heights
College
Siena Heights Drive (49221)

Albion Albion College

Ann Arbor U. of Michigan

Birmingham Bloomfield Art Assn.
1516 S. Cranbrook Rd.

Bloomfield Hills Cranbrook
Academy of Art
500 Lone Pine Rd.

Chassell Buellwood Weavers
Rte. 1

Dearborn Henry Ford Community
College
5101 Evergreen Rd.

Detroit Art School, Society of
Arts & Crafts
245 E. Kirby St.

Brightmoor Community Ctr.
14451 Burt Rd. (48223)

Michigan State U.
Pewabic Pottery
10125 E. Jefferson (48214)

Wayne State U.

East Lansing Michigan State U.

Flint Flint Community Junior
College

Flint Institute of Arts
DeWaters Art Ctr.
1120 E. Kearsley St.

Interlochen Arts Academy
National Music Camp (49643)

Kalamazoo Kalamazoo Inst. of
the Arts
314 S. Park St.

Western Michigan U.

Marquette Northern Michigan U.
Small Business Adm.
502 W. Kaye St. (49885)

Mount Pleasant Central Mich. U.
Trout Lake Ruth M. Scherer
P.O. Box 96
Ypsilanti Eastern Mich. U.

MINNESOTA
Crystal Bay Minnetonka Ctr. of
Arts & Education
2180 North Shore Dr.
Duluth U. of Minnesota
Mankato Mankato State College
Meridan Meridan Junior College
Minneapolis East Side Neighbor-
hood Service
1929 2nd St., N. W. (55418)
Northside Settlement Services
614 W. Broadway (55411)
Small Business Adm.
816 2nd Ave., S. (55402)
Phyllis Wheatley Community
809 Aldrich Ave., N. (55411)
YWCA, 1130 Nicollet Ave. (55403)
Moorhead Moorhead State College
St. Paul Hamline U.
Macalester College
Summit & Grand Sts. (55105)
Merriam Park Community Ctr.
Wilder at St. Anthony (55104)
Merrick Community Ctr.
715 Edgerton St. (55101)
St. Paul School of Art
Minnesota Museum of Art
30 E. Tenth St.
School of the Associates in Arts
344 Summit Ave.
YWCA, 65 E. Kellogg Blvd. (55101)

MISSISSIPPI
Columbus Mississippi State College
for Women
Jackson Small Business Adm.
P.O. Box 2351
245 E. Capitol St. (39205)
University U. of Mississippi

MISSOURI
Cape Girardeau Southeast Missouri
State College
Columbia U. of Missouri

Hillsboro Jefferson College
Kansas City Guadalupe Ctr.
1015 W. 23rd St. (64108)
Kansas City Art Inst.
4415 Warwick Blvd.
Minute Circle Friendly House
2405 Elmwood (64127)
Small Business Adm.
911 Walnut St. (64106)
Whatsoever Circle Community
House
6801 E. 12th St. (64126)
Kirksville Northeast Missouri State
College
Kirkwood Libbie Crawford Studio
140 Sweetbriar Lane
Maryville Northwest Missouri State
College
Raytown Suburban Jackson County
YWCA
9110 E. 63rd St. (64133)
St. Louis Kingdom House
1321 S. 11th St. (63104)
Small Business Adm.
208 N. Broadway (63102)
United Church of Christ
Neighborhood Houses
P.O. Box 1221 (63188)
Washington U.
Webster College
470 E. Lockwood Ave.
Springfield Southwest Missouri
State College
Warrensburg Central Missouri State
College

MONTANA
Billings Yellowstone Art Ctr.
401 N. 27th St.
Bozeman Montana State U.
Havre Northern Montana College
Helena Archie Bray Foundation
Small Business Adm.
P.O. Box 1690
205 Power Block (59601)
Missoula U. of Montana

NEBRASKA
Chadron Chadron State College

Omaha Small Business Adm.
Rm. 7425, 215 N. 17th St. (68102)
United Methodist Community
Ctrs.
2001 N. 35th St. (46201)
U. of Nebraska

Peru Peru State College (68421)

Wayne Wayne State College

NEVADA

Las Vegas Small Business Adm.
Rm. 4-104
300 Las Vegas Blvd., South (89101)

NEW HAMPSHIRE

Concord League of New Hampshire
Craftsmen
205 N. Main St.

Small Business Adm.
55 Pleasant St. (03301)

Manchester Manchester Inst. of
Arts & Sciences
148 Concord St.

Nashua The Arts & Sciences Ctr.
41 E. Pearl St.

Peterborough Sharon Arts Ctr.
RFD 2

NEW JERSEY

Basking Ridge Weiss Studio
161 Culberson Rd.

Clinton Hunterdon Art Ctr.
Old Stone Mill, Center St. (07011)

Cranford Artist & Craftsman Guild
17 Eastman St.

Denville Denbrook House Stitch
Witchery
Rte. 10, P.O. Box N (07834)

Jersey City Jersey City State College

Lakewood Georgian Court College

Montclair Montclair Art Museum
School, 3 South Mountain Ave.

Morristown Neighborhood House
12 Flagler St. (07960)

Newark Fuld Neighborhood House
71 Boyd St. (07103)

Newark Museum Arts Workshop
43-49 Washington St.

Small Business Adm.
Rm. 1636, 970 Broad St. (07102)

New Brunswick The Neighborhood
House, Inc.
184 Commercial Ave. (08901)
Douglas College
Rutgers U.

Northvale Staned Glass Club
482 Tappan Rd.

Orange YWCA, Holly House
19 High St.

Penns Grove Salem County
Technical Inst.
P.O. Box 551

Tenafly Art Ctr. of Northern New
Jersey, 10 Jay St.

Trenton Trenton State College
Pennington Rd.

Union Newark State College

Wayne Paterson State College
300 Pompton Rd. (07470)

West Long Branch Monmouth
College
Cedar and Norwood Aves.

NEW MEXICO

Albuquerque Small Business Adm.
500 Gold Ave., S.W. (87101)
U. of New Mexico

Las Cruces New Mexico State U.

Las Vegas New Mexico Highlands
U.

Santa Fe Espiritu Libre-Cross
Cultural Ctr.
P.O. Box 231, Rte. 1

Inst. of American Indian Arts
Cerrillos Rd.

Rumpel Art Studio
320 Cadiz Rd.

Ruidoso Carizo Lodge, Inc.
P.O. Box Drawer A (88345)

NEW YORK

Albany Small Business Adm.
91 State St. (12207)

Alfred Alfred U.
College of Ceramics

Brockport State U. of New York

Buffalo Small Business Adm.
Rm. 9, 121 Ellicott St. (14203)
YWCA, 190 Franklin St. (14202)

Chautauqua Chautauqua Inst.
Summer School (14722)

Clayton Thousand Islands Museum
Craft School
314 John St.

Cortland State U. of New York

Croton-on-Hudson The Niddy
Noddy
1 Croton Point Ave.

Elmira Elmira Neighborhood
House
671 Dickinson St. (14901)

Garrison Garrison Art Ctr.

Genesco State U. College of Arts &
Science

Glen Cove Phebe Allen Blake
68 Frost Pond Rd.

Great Neck Adult Program
Great Neck Public School
10 Arrandale Ave.

Huntington Huntington Historical
Society, 2 High St. (11743)

Ithaca Cornell U.
3-12 Van Rensselaer Hall

New Paltz State U. of New York

New Rochelle College of New
Rochelle

New York City Art Students League
215 W. 57th St. (10019)

Brooklyn Museum Art School
Eastern Parkway, Brooklyn

Fashion Inst. of Technology
227 W. 27th St.

Goddard-Riverside Community
Ctr.
161 W. 87th St. (10024)

Greenwich House Pottery
16 Jones St.

Grosvenor Neighborhood House
176 W. 105th St. (10025)

Henry Street Settlement
265 Henry St. (10002)

Hudson Guild
441 W. 26th St. (10001)

Hunter College
695 Park Ave.

Stanley M. Isaacs Neighborhood
Ctr.
415 E. 93rd St. (10028)

The Jewish Museum
Tobe Pascher Workshop
1109 Fifth Ave.

James Weldon Johnson
Community Ctr.
2205 First Ave. (10029)

LaGuardia Memorial House
311 E. 116th St. (10029)

Lenox Hill Neighborhood Assn.
331 E. 70th St. (10021)

Manhattanville Community Ctr.
530 W. 133rd St. (10027)

The New School
66 W. 12th St.

New York Inst. of Arts & Crafts
37 E. 7th St.

New York U. School of Education
Educational Craft Shop
10 Washington Place
Washington Square East

Pratt Inst.
215 Ryerson St., Brooklyn

Pratt Graphics Ctr.
831 Broadway (10003)

Riverside Church
490 Riverside Dr.

Riverdale Neighborhood House
5521 Mosholu Ave., Bronx (10471)

Small Business Adm.
Rm. 3108, 26 Federal Plaza (10007)

Teachers College
Columbia U.
525 W. 120th St.

Union Settlement
237 E. 104th St. (10029)

YWCA, Central Branch
610 Lexington Ave. (10022)

YWCA, Craft Students League
51st St. & 8th Ave.

Port Chester Clay Art Ctr.
40 Beech St.

Poughkeepsie Dutchess Community
College
Pendell Rd.

Purchase Manhattanville College

Rochester Genesee Settlement
House
10 Dake St. (14605)

Lewis Street Ctr.
57 Lewis St. (14605)

Memorial Gallery, U. of Rochester
490 University Ave. (14607)

Montgomery Neighborhood Ctr.
10 Cady St. (14608)

Rochester Inst. of Technology
School of American Craftsmen
1 Lomb Memorial Drive

YWCA, Rochester & Monroe Co.
175 Clinton Ave. N. (14604)

Saratoga Springs Skidmore College

Scarsdale Studio Workshop for Art
2 Dolma Rd. (10583)

Southampton Southampton College
Long Island U.

Staten Island Wagner College
Grymes Hill (01301)

Syracuse Small Business Adm.
Fayette & Salina Sts. (13202)
Syracuse U.
309 University Plaza

Utica Cosmopolitan Ctr., Inc.
470 Whitesboro St. (13502)
Munson-Williams-Proctor Inst.
School of Art
310 Genesee St.

West Nyack Rockland Foundation, Inc.
27 Old Greenbush Rd.

White Plains Westchester Art
Workshop, County Ctr.
YWCA, 515 North St. (10605)

Woodstock Woodstock Guild of
Craftsmen, 34 Tinker St.

NORTH CAROLINA

Asheville Southern Highland
Handicraft Guild
15 Reddick Rd. (28805)

Brasstown John C. Campbell Fold
School

Charlotte Small Business Adm.
222 S. Church St. (28202)

Cullowhee Western Carolina U.

Durham U. of North Carolina

Greensboro North Carolina A & T
State U.

Greenville East Carolina U.
P.O. Box 2704

Penland Penland School of Crafts
(28765)

Raleigh North Carolina State U.
(27607)

Winston-Salem Arts & Crafts Assn.
610 Coliseum Drive

NORTH DAKOTA
Fargo Small Business Adm.

OHIO
Akron East Akron Community
House
1259 Third Ave. (44306)

Athens Ohio U.

Bowling Green Bowling Green
State U.

Cincinnati Cincinnati Union Bethel
Neighborhood Services
1826 Baltimore Ave. (45225)
Emanuel Community Ctr.
1308 Race St. (45210)
Small Business Adm.
5026 Federal Bldg. (45202)

Cleveland Alta Social Settlement
12510 Mayfield Rd. (44106)
Cleveland Inst. of Art
11141 East Blvd.
Cleveland Music School
Settlement
11125 Magnolia Drive (44106)
Collingwood Community Services
Ctr.
14906 Aspinwall Ave. (44110)
Community Services Ctr. of Mt.
Pleasant
12714 Union Ave. (44105)
Friendly Inn
2382 Unwin Rd. (44104)
Karamu House
2355 E. 89th St. (44106)
League Park Ctr.
6601 Lexington Ave. (44103)
Merrick House
1050 Starkweather Ave. (44113)
Small Business Adm.
Rm. 317, 1240 E. 9th St. (44199)

West Side Community House
3000 Bridge Ave. (44113)

The Phillis Wheatley Assn.
4450 Cedar Ave. (44103)

Columbus Gladden Community House
183 Hawkes Ave. (43223)

Neighborhood House
800 Leonard Ave. (43203)

Ohio State U.
128 North Oval Drive

Small Business Adm.
50 W. Gay St. (43215)

Dayton School of Dayton Art Inst.
P.O. Box 941

Riverbend Art Ctr.
142 Riverbend Drive

Granville Denison U.

Kent Kent State U.

Lorain Neighborhood House Assn.
1536 E. 30th St. (44055)

Massillon Massillon Museum
212 Lincoln Way East

Painesville Lake Erie College

Springfield Union Settlement House
222 E. Mulberry St. (45505)

Toledo Toledo Museum of Art School of Design

Small Business Adm.
234 Summit St. (43602)

Warren Rebecca Williams Community House
760 Main Ave., S. W. (44483)

Yellow Springs Antioch College

Youngstown Associates Neighborhood Ctrs.
755 Lexington Ave. (44510)

OKLAHOMA

Edmond Central State College

Norman U. of Oklahoma
840 Asp

Oklahoma City Small Business Adm.
Rm. 501, 30 N. Hudson (73102)

Stillwater Oklahoma State U.

Tahlequah Northeastern State College

Tulsa Philbrook Art Ctr.
2727 S. Rockford (74114)

U. of Tulsa
600 South College

OREGON

Corvallis Oregon State U.

Eugene Maude I. Kerns Art Ctr.
1910 E. 15th Ave.

U. of Oregon

Monmouth Oregon College of Education

Portland Arts & Crafts Society
616 N. W. 18th

Friendly House, Inc.
2617 N. W. Savier (97210)

Lewis and Clark College
0615 S. W. Palatine Hill Rd.

Linnton Community Ctr.
10614 N. W. St. Helens Rd. (97231)

Museum Art School
S.W. Park at Madison

Small Business Adm.
Rm. 700
921 S. W. Washington St. (97205)

PENNSYLVANIA

Dalton The Village Craftcenter & Gift Shop, 106 Main St.

Greensburg Seton Hill College

Huntingdon Juniata College (16652)

Indiana U. of Pennsylvania

Kutztown Kutztown State College

Meadville Allegheny College

Millersville Millersville State College

Philadelphia Diversified Community Services
2601 Lombard St. (19146)

Friends Neighborhood Guild
703 N. Eighth St. (19123)

The Lighthouse
152 W. Lehigh Ave. (19133)

Lutheran Social Mission Society
1340 Frankford Ave. (19125)

Moore College of Art
20th & Race Sts.

Philadelphia College of Art
Broad & Pine Sts.

College of Textiles & Science
Schoolhouse Lane & Henry Ave.

Philadelphia Guild of
Handweavers
Woodmore Art Gallery
9201 Germantown Ave.

Small Business Adm.
1317 Filbert St. (19107)

Tyler School of Art, Temple U.
Beech & Penrose Aves.

Willet Stained Glass Studios
10 E. Moreland Ave.

Pittsburgh Arts & Crafts Ctr.
Fifth & Shady Ave.

Brashear Assn., Inc.
2005 Sarah St. (15203)

Carnegie-Mellon U.

Chatham College

Hill House Assn.
2358 Fifth Ave., P.O. Box 7465
Oakland Station (15213)

YWCA, Fourth & Wood Sts.

Scranton Progressive-Bellevue
Community Ctrs.
414 Olive St. (18509)

University Park Penn. State U.

RHODE ISLAND

Newport Martin Luther King Ctr.
20 W. Broadway (02840)

Providence Nadeau Inst. of
Weaving Technology
725 Branch Ave.

Nickerson House
133 Delaine St. (02909)

Rhode Island College
Mt. Pleasant Ave.

Rhode Island School of Design

Small Business Adm.
Rm. 702, 57 Eddy St. (02903)

SOUTH CAROLINA

Columbia Small Business Adm.
1801 Assembly St. (29201)

Greenville Bob Jones U.
Furman U.

SOUTH DAKOTA

Aberdeen Northern State College

Brookings South Dakota State U.

Sioux Falls Small Business Adm.
Rm. 402, 8th & Main Ave. (57102)

Vermillion U. of South Dakota
(57069)

TENNESSEE

Clarksville Austin Peay State U.

Gatlinburg Arrowmont School of
Arts & Crafts
P.O. Box 567 (37738)

Jefferson City Carson-Newman
College

Johnson City East Tennessee State
U.

Knoxville Small Business Adm.
Rm. 307, 502 Gay St. (37902)

U. of Tennessee

Murfreesboro Middle Tennessee
State U. (37130)

Nashville Eighteenth Ave.
Community Ctr.
1811 Osage St. (37208)

George Peabody College for
Teachers, 21st Ave., S.

Small Business Adm.
500 Union St. (37219)

United Methodist Neighborhood
Ctrs.
P.O. Box 5641

Overton Park Memphis Academy of
Arts

TEXAS

Abilene Hardin-Simmons U.

McMurry College
South 14th St. & Sayles Blvd.

Austin U. of Texas

Belton Mardy Hardin Baylor
College

Canyon West Texas State U.

Corpus Christi Neighborhood Ctrs.
614 Horne Rd. (78416)

Dallas Craft Guild of Dallas
Dallas Museum of Fine Arts

Small Business Adm.
411 N. Akard St. (75201)

Southern Methodist U.

Denton North Texas State U.

Texas Women's U.
University Station

El Paso The U. of Texas at El Paso

Fort Worth Bethlehem Community
Ctr.
970 Humbolt St., E. (76104)

Fort Worth Art Ctr. Museum
School, 1309 Montgomery

Texas Christian U.

Harlingen Small Business Adm.
219 E. Jackson St. (78550)

Houston Museum of Fine Arts
School, 1001 Bissonnet

Small Business Adm.
808 Travis St. (77002)

Texas Southern U.
3201 Wheeler Ave. (77004)

YWCA, 1521 Texas Ave. (77002)

Irving U. of Dallas Station
U. of Dallas

Lubbock Small Business Adm.
Rm. 204, 1616 19th St. (79401)

Texas Technological College

Marshall Small Business Adm.
Rm. 201, P.O. Box 1349
505 E. Travis St. (75670)

San Antonio House of Neighborly
Service
407 N. Calaveras St. (78207)

Small Business Adm.
Rm. 300, 301 Broadway (78205)

Southwest Craft Ctr. Workshop
420 Villita St. (78205)

UTAH

Cedar City College of Southern
Utah
Southern Utah State College
(84720)

Logan Utah State U.

Ogden Weber State College

Provo Brigham Young U.

St. George Dixie College

Salt Lake City Small Business Adm.
Rm. 2237, 125 State St. (84111)
U. of Utah

VERMONT

Bennington Bennington College

Montpelier Small Business Adm.
87 State St. (05601)

Plainfield Goddard College

VIRGINIA

Alexandria Potomac Stoneware
417 N. Union St.

Bristol The Kiln Room
918 Moore St. (24201)

Farmville Longwood College

Hampton Hampton Inst.

Petersburg Virginia State College

Williamsburg College of William
and Mary (23185)

WASHINGTON

Bellevue Bellevue Community
College

Bellingham Western Washington
State College

Cheney Eastern Washington State
College

Ellensburg Central Washington
State College

Pullman Washington State U.

Seattle Factory of Visual Arts
5040 9th Ave., N. E. (98105)

Neighborhood House Service Ctr.
3004 S. Alaska (98108)

Pottery Northwest
305 Harrison St. (98109)

Small Business Adm.
Rm. 1206, 506 Second Ave. (98104)

U. of Washington

Spokane Small Business Adm.
Rm. 651, P.O. Box 2167 (99210)

YWCA, W. 829 Broadway Ave.
(99201)

Tacoma U. of Puget Sound

WEST VIRGINIA

Charleston Small Business Adm.
Rm. 3410, 500 Quarrier St. (25301)

Clarksburg Small Business Adm.
119 N. 3rd St. (26301)

Fairmont Fairmont State College

Glenville Glenville State College

Huntington Huntington Galleries
Park Hills

Institute West Virginia State
College

Shepherdstown Shepherd College

Wheeling Oglebay Inst.
841½ National Rd.

WISCONSIN

Appleton Lawrence U.

Eau Claire Wisconsin State U.

Kenosha Kenosha Public Museum
Civic Center

Wisconsin State U.

La Crosse Viterbo College
815 S. 9th St.

Wisconsin State U.

Madison Edgewood College
855 Woodrow St.

Madison Neighborhood Ctrs.
29 S. Mills St. (53715)

Small Business Adm.
25 W. Main St. (53703)

U. of Wisconsin

Menomonie Stout State U.

Milwaukee Alverno College
3401 S. 39th St.

Milwaukee Area Technological
College
1015 N. 6th St.

Milwaukee Christian Ctr.
2137 W. Greenfield Ave. (53204)

Mount Mary College

Potter's Wheel
1022B N. Third St.

Small Business Adm.
238 W. Wisconsin Ave. (53203)

Cardinal Stritch College
6801 N. Yates Rd.

U. of Wisconsin at Milwaukee

YWCA, 610 N. Jackson St. (53202)

River Falls Wisconsin State U.

Whitewater Wisconsin State U.

WYOMING

Casper Small Business Adm.
300 N. Center St. (82601)

Powell Northwest Community
College

2 Where to Display and Sell

The following is a guide to state, county, and local fairs, woman's exchanges, and crafts organizations in which a careerist at home may display and/or sell her work. Included also are individual shops that may be contacted by interested craftsmen.

ALABAMA

Alberta Freedom Quilters Bee
Rte. 1, P.O. Box 72 (36720)

Birmingham Alabama State Fair
P.O. Box 3800B (35208)

Handmakers
2007 11th Ave., S.

Boaz Marshall County Fair
PO. Box 74 (35957)

Cullman Cullman County Fair
P.O. Box 103 (35055)

Florence North Alabama State Fair
P.O. Box 165 (35630)

Jasper Northwest Alabama State
Fair
1707 Second Ave. (35501)

Mobile Greater Gulf State Fair
751 Government St. (36602)

Montgomery The Alabama
Craftsmen's Council
437 S. Perry St. (36104)

South Alabama State Fair
P.O. Box 3304 (36109)

ALASKA

Anchorage Annual Alaska Festival
of Native Arts in June
338 Denali St.

Bootlegger's Cove Pottery
P.O. Box 1038

Painting and Pottery by Park
P.O. Box 6285

Pottery by Alcie & Pauline
2107 Lincoln

Susitna Ceramics
1073 W. 23rd St.

Fairbanks Mrs. Janet Baird
Tanana Valley State Fair
P.O. Box 188 (99701)

Palmer Lowell Sutton
Alaska State Fair
P.O. Box 576 (99645)

Petersburg Lee's Pottery
P.O. Box 251

Spenard Tundra Pottery
4613 South Shore Drive

ARIZONA

Phoenix James G. Jones
Arizona State Fair
P.O. 6715 (85005)

Heard Museum Shop
22 E. Monte Vista

Scottsdale Alexander—the
continental jewelsmith
Studio 6, 75 W. Fifth Ave.

Arizona Handcrafts
114 W. Fifth Ave.

Gra Wun
64 W. 5th Ave.

Dick Seeger Design Gallery
75 W. 5th Ave

Sedona The Pendleton Shop
Jordan Rd.

Tucson Desert House Crafts
2841 N. Campbell Ave.

Tucson Art Ctr. Craft Sales Gallery
325 W. Franklin St.

Wright Designs & Associates
1736 E. Speedway

Yuma Yuma Fine Arts Assn.
248 Madison Ave.

ARKANSAS

Augusta Thomas Montgomery
Woodruff County Fair
P.O. Box 474 (72006)

Blytheville Raleigh Sylvester
Northwest Arkansas District Fair
P.O. Box 183 (72833)

Danville James C. Pledger
Yell County Free Fair
P.O. Box 87 (72833)

El Dorado Victor Dumas
Union County Fair
504 Northwest Ave. (71730)

Fort Smith Emporium Gift Shop
Fort Smith Art Ctr.
423 N. 6th St.

Hindsville War Eagle Crafts Fair
Rte. 1 (72738)

Jonesboro John H. Miller
Craighead County Fair
1807 Alonzo St. (72401)

Little Rock Arkansas Arts Ctr. Gift
Shop, MacArthur Park

Prairie Grove Labor Day
Celebration
Clothesline Art & Craft Fair

Rogers Wool-Art
422 E. Locust

Salem Pilot Knob Craft Shop
The Ozark Foothills Handicraft
Guild

Searcy Charles R. Smith
White County Fair
P.O. Box 756 (72143)

CALIFORNIA

Berkeley Artifactorie
2121 Vine St.

Arts & Crafts Co-op, Inc.
1652 Shattuck Ave. (94709)

Big Sur Phoenix Shop at Napenthe

Carmel Doris Ormsby
Carmel Crafts Guild
P.O. Box 4333 (93921)

Carmel-by-the-Sea Origins
Del Dono Court
Dolores & Fifth

Cayucos Young Ideas
146 Ocean Ave.

Del Mar Richard J. O'Connor
Southern Calif. Exposition
(92014)

El Segundo Tom McMillan
Southern Calif. Designer-
Craftsmen
P.O. Box 157 (90245)
Martin K. Weber, Pres.

Fontana K. Olsen
Slover Special School,
Crafts Auxiliary
14860 Slover Ave. (92335)

Glen Ellen Metal Arts Guild
1701 Warm Springs Rd. (95442)

Hillsborough M. Epstein, Pres.
Bay Area Arts & Crafts Guild
180 Bella-Vista Drive (94010)

LaJolla K. Whitcomb
Allied Craftsmen of San Diego
1631 Mimulus Way (92037)

Los Altos From the Mountains
346 Main St.

Los Angeles Canyon Gallery Two
8155 Melrose Ave.

Oakland Art Division
The Oakland Museum

Palo Alto House of Today
550 University Ave.

Petaluma The Glass Owl
113 Washington St.

Pomona Phil D. Shepherd
Los Angeles County Fair
P.O. Box 2250 (91766)

Sacramento Artists Cooperative
Gallery
2824 35th St.

Creative Arts League
73 Starlit Circle (95818)

Christine Daves
Sacramento Weavers Guild
2464 Portola Way (95818)

San Diego Gallery Store
Fine Arts Gallery of San Diego

Gallery Store
Potters Guild of San Diego
Spanish Village
Studio 29, Balboa Park (92101)

San Francisco American Craft Ctr.
900 North Point Rd.

Robert Fritz
Assn. of San Francisco Potters
255 Monticello St. (94132)

Marcia Chamberlain, Pres.
California Designer Craftsmen
433 Collingwood St. (94114)

Design Research
Ghirardelli Square

Exhibit Three
434 Clement St.

House of Today
2801 Leavenworth St.

A. D. Gravin
Loom & Shuttle
2691 38th Ave. (94116)

Igor Mead Gallery
2801 Leavenworth

The Sandal Shop
900 North Point Rd.

San Jose Sal Millan
Santa Clara County Fair
P.O. Box 1027 (94403)

San Rafael Tamalpais Weavers
Guild, 258 Etta Court (94903)

Santa Barbara Galeria Del Sol
516 San Ysidro Rd.

Karin Melander
Santa Barbara Handweavers'
Guild, 127 Vernal Ave. (93105)

Sausalito Upper Echelon
777 Bridgeway

Stinson Beach Sunshine Gallery
P.O. Box 283

Stockton San Joaquin County Fair
P.O. Box 2154 (95201)

Topanga Canyon Gallery One
137 S. Topanga Canyon Blvd.

Tujunga Pat Baldwin, Pres.
Tapestry West
9530 Haines Canyon Ave. (91042)

Walnut Creek Vester Vetter
Golden Gate Weavers
64 Alder Ave. (94529)

Yosemite Natl. Park Best's
Studio, Inc., P.O. Box 455

COLORADO

Aspen The Tom Thumb and
Gallery, P.O. Box 57

Colorado Springs Pike's Peak
Weavers Guild
1970 Mesa Rd. (80904)

Whickerbill Contemporary Gifts
212 N. Tejon

Denver Artisans Ctr.
315 Columbine St.

Colorado Artist Craftsmen's
Annual Exhibition
Temple Buell College

M. D. Johnson
Colorado Potters Guild
1541 S. Pearl (80210)

Denver Art Museum Bookshop
1343 Acoma

Littleton Forrest F. Hammes
Arapahoe County Fair
P.O. Box 651 (80120)

Colorado Artist Craftsmen
4228 E. Easter Pl. (80120)

M. L. Hosford
Intl. Guild of Candle Artisans
4228 E. Easter Pl. (80120)

Pueblo Thomas Knight
Colorado State Fair (81005)

Vail The Tom Thumb and Gallery

CONNECTICUT

Berlin The Heritage Guild Craft Shop, 1897 Wilbur Cross Highway

Clinton The Craft Shop 69 E. Main St.

Danbury John W. Leahy, Pres. Danbury State Fair 130 White St. (06810)

Darien E. Tuttle, Pres. Handweavers Guild of Conn. 12 Christie Hill Rd. (06820)

Glastonbury The Country Mouse 2722 Main St.

Greenwich Greenwich Exchange for Woman's Work, Inc. 28 Sherwood Pl. (06833)

Guilford Guilford Handcrafts Exposition P.O. Box 221 (06437)

Hartford The Woman's Exchange 993A Farmington Ave. (06107)

Litchfield Litchfield Exchange for Woman's Work Cobble Court (06759)

Middletown The Wesleyan Potters, Inc., 75 Pease Ave. (06457)

Mt. Carmel Current Crafts 3208 Whitney Ave.

New Milford Paul Voltaire's Contemporary Shop U.S. 7 at Rte. 37

North Haven Norvin Stephens North Haven Fair P.O. Box 14 (06473)

Old Lyme Country Crafts

Portland Mrs. John W. Sease, Pres. Society of Conn. Craftsmen, Inc. 3 Woodland Rd. (06480)

Ridgefield A House for Handcrafts 94 Main St.

Southport Fairfield Woman's Exchange, Inc. 332 Pequot St. (06490)

West Hartford The Pascos 17 S. Main St.

Westport Optimums, Inc. 47 Riverside Ave.

Wethersfield Mrs. L. Davenport New England Weavers Seminar 113 Mapleside Drive (06109)

Woodbridge A. Greenfield Guild of Book Workers Perkins Rd. (06525)

Woodbury Country Bazaar Main St.

DELAWARE

Newark The Newark Gallery 64 E. Main St.

Art Dept., U. of Delaware (19711)

DISTRICT OF COLUMBIA

Washington American Hand 1214 31st St., N.W.

Craft House 1669 Wisconsin Ave.

E. F. Mueller, Treas. Potomac Craftsmen, Inc. 3914 Huntington, N.W. (20015)

The Silver Shuttle 1301 35th St., N.W.

Ursell's, Inc. 3242 Que St., N.W.

FLORIDA

Clearwater G. Reese Tropical Weavers Guild of Florida 5 Rosery Lane (33516)

Eustis Jack E. Pae Lake County Fair P.O. Box 1006, Tavares (32778)

Fort Myers Lyle A. Payne Southwest Florida Fair 2010 Hanson St. (33901)

Jacksonville P. C. Holler, Treas. Florida Craftsmen Rte. 6, P.O. Box 120 (32223)

Greater Jacksonville Fair P.O. Box 2545 (32203)

The Museum Shop Jacksonville Art Museum 4160 Boulevard Ctr.

Marianna Louie W. Seay Jackson County Fair P.O. Box 917 (32446)

Miami M. R. Grant, Librarian
Ceramic League
7867 N. Kendall Dr. (33156)

E. Darwin Fuchs
Dade County Youth Fair
2728 N. W. 7th Ave. (33127)

Ocala Bertha C. Lindstrom, Secy.
Tropical Weavers Guild of
Orlando
1126 N. E. 7th St. (32670)

Orlando H. H. Parrish
Central Florida Fair (32801)

Palatka E. A. Loving
Putnam County Fair
P.O. Box 918 (32077)

Panama City Sanford D. Hendricks
Bay County Fair
P.O. Box 68 (32401)

Pensacola John E. Frenkel
Pensacola Interstate Fair
P.O. Box 255 (32502)

St. Augustine Tom Rahner, Pres.
Saint Augustine Arts & Crafts
Council
P.O. Box 767 (32084)

Sanibel Artisan Shop
Golf Dr., P.O. Box 638

Sarasota The Craft Shop
14 N. Blvd. of the Presidents

Ru and Ann's Studio
8854 Tamiami Trail

Kenneth A. Clark
Sarasota County Fair
2900 Ringling Blvd. (33580)

Tallahassee Lloyd Rhoden
North Florida Fair
615 Paul Russell Rd. (32301)

West Palm Beach William C. Ochs
South Florida Fair & Exposition
P.O. Box 15915 (33402)

Winter Park Karyanna Gallery, Inc.
342 Park Ave.

GEORGIA

Albany Marvin C. Lorig
Exchange Club Fair of Southwest
Georgia
P.O. Box 507 (31702)

Atlanta Maurice C. Coleman
Southeastern Fair
P.O. Box 6826 Lakewood Station
(30315)

Georgia Designer Craftsman
441 W. Peachtree St., N.E. (30308)

Signature Shop and Galleries, Inc.
3267 Roswell Rd., N.W.

Augusta Ray W. Locke, Pres.
Exchange Club Fair
P.O. Box 3884 (30904)

Clarkesville Mark of the Potter
Rte. 3

Columbus Arthur G. Springer, Jr.
Chattahoochee Valley Fair
P.O. Box 1358 (31902)

Macon Robert M. Wade
Georgia State Fair
P.O. Box 5260 (31208)

Rising Fawn Rising Fawn Craft Ctr.
Rte. 2

Rome Robert S. Walther
Coosa Valley Fair
P.O. Box 1224 (30161)

Savannah Dess R. Coleman
Coastal Empire Fair
P.O. Box 9025 (31402)

HAWAII

Honolulu Mrs. Kenneth Pratt, Secy.
Boyer's
824 Keeaumoku St.

Hawaii Handweavers Hui
4817 Au Kai Ave. (96815)

Joji's
1259 S. Beretania St.

The Little Gallery, Inc.
1943 S. King St.

Loom Originals
3098 Wailani Rd.

Maui Dick's Hawaiian Crafts
P.O. Box 395

Kaneohe (Oahu) Jean J. Williams
Hawaii Craftsmen
45-023 Mahalani Circle (96744)

IDAHO

Blackfoot J. LeRoy Howell
Eastern Idaho State Fair
P.O. Box 228 (83221)

Boise Julia Davis Park
Boise Gallery of Art
Joseph P. Church
Western Idaho Fair
5610 Glenwood St. (83702)

Moscow Mrs. Ronald A. Robinson
Palouse Hills Weavers Guild
727 E. 3rd St. (83843)

Sun Valley America House

ILLINOIS

Aledo Ken Liggett, Pres.
Mercer County Fair (61231)

Bloomington Roger L. Seeger
McLean County Fair
202 E. Locust St. (61701)

Champaign The Art Mart
614 E. Green St.

Chicago Accent, Inc.
1437 E. 53rd St.

Edward Sherbyn Gallery
2952 N. Clark St.

Sticks & Stones
5210 S. Harper Ave.

Decatur Kenneth J. Maltus
Decatur-Macon County Fair
225 Cobb Ave. (62526)

DuQuoin William R. Hayes
DuQuoin State Fair
P.O. Box 182 (62832)

East Moline Rock Island County
Fair (61244)

Evanston 4 Arts Gallery
1629 Oak Ave.

Griggsville J. R. Skinner
Western Illinois Fair
P.O. Box 248 (62340)

Kankakee Herbert J. Hess
Kankakee County Fair
P.O. Box 614 (60901)

Knoxville Wendell L. Farris
Knox County Fair
748 Bateman Bldg.
Galesburg (61401)

Lincoln Wilbur E. Layman
Logan County Fair
Woodlawn Rd. (62656)

Mazon W. F. Carter
Grundy County Fair (60444)

Mendota Hubert B. Crow
Mendota Tri-County Fair
P.O. Box 13 (61342)

Morrison Keith E. Glazier
Whiteside County Fair
603 Genesee Ave. (61270)

New Berlin Robert Pfeffer, Pres.
Sangamon County Fair (62670)

Oak Park The Elm Shop
1132 Chicago Ave.

St. Charles Reba Keeler
Kane County Fair
P.O. Box 521 (61414)

Sandwich Louis P. Brady
DeKalb County Fair
113 S. Main (60548)

Springfield Illinois State Fair
P.O. Box 576 (62705)

Urbana Keith C. Kesler
Champaign County Fair
P.O. Box 105 (61801)

Wheaton Don C. Miller
DuPage County Fair
P.O. Box 607 (60187)

INDIANA

Anderson Frank Nealis
Anderson Fair
223 West Third St.

Bloomington The Prism
State Rd., 46 East

Brownstown Malcolm Browning
Jackson County Fair
1250 W. 2nd St. (47274)

Crown Point Don S. Powers
Lake County Fair
P.O. Box 327 (46307)

Fort Wayne Mrs. Kenneth D. Cole
Designer Craftsmen Guild of
Fort Wayne
1321 Maple Ave. (46807)

Indianapolis Charles C. Davis
Indiana State Fair (46205)

LaPorte Robert M. Morse
LaPorte County Fair
Rte. 2, P.O. Box 244 (46350)

Muncie Nichols Associates
402 N. Calvert St.

IOWA

Ames Iowa Designer Craftsmen
2823 West St. (50010)

Cedar Rapids All-Iowa Fair
127 Third St., N.E. (52401)

Davenport Great Mississippi Valley
Fair
2815 W. Locust St. (52804)

Des Moines Des Moines Art Ctr.
Museum Shop
Greenwood Park
Iowa State Fair
State House (50319)

Eldon Wapello County Fair
P.O. Box 606 (52554)

Mason City North Iowa Fair
Parker Pl. (50401)

Monticello Great Jones County Fair
P.O. Box 309 (52310)

Spencer Clay County Fair
P.O. Box 951 (51301)

West Liberty West Liberty Fair
P.O. Box 261 (52776)

West Union Fayette County Fair
P.O. Box 266 (52175)

KANSAS

Belleville North Central Kansas
Free Fair (99659)

Hutchison Kansas State Fair (67501)

Smith Center Topeka Handweavers
213 W. 4th St. (66967)

Topeka Mid-America Fair
P.O. Box 945 (66601)
Kansas Artists-Craftsmen Assn.
Art Dept., Washburn U. (66601)

KENTUCKY

Berea Kentucky Guild of Artists &
Craftsmen
P.O. Box 291 (40403)

Lexington Kentuckian Gifts
166 New Circle Rd., N.E.
Lions Blue Grass Fair
P.O. Box 8263 (40503)

Louisville Art Ctr. Assn.
2111 S. 1st St. (40208)
Kentucky State Fair
P.O. Box 21179 (40221)

Louisville Craftsmen's Guild
9403 Broad Run Rd. (40291)

LOUISIANA

Baton Rouge Greater Baton Rouge
State Fair
P.O. Box 1854 (70821)

Covington St. Tammany Art Assn.
P.O. Box 779 (70433)

New Orleans Circle
1072 St. Charles St.
Louisiana Crafts Council Gallery
1114 South Carolina St.

Shreveport Joseph T. Monsour
Louisiana State Fair
P.O. Box 9100 (71109)

MAINE

Bremen Muscongus Pottery
Rte. 32

Camden Stell & Shevis Handicrafts
82 Elm St.

Kennebunk United Maine
Craftsmen
P.O. Box 63 (04043)

Kennebunkport Kilburn-Fisher
Studio

Ogunquit The Weaver & the
Silversmith
Perkins Cove

Portland Craft House Downtown
17 Exchange St.

Presque Isle Northern Maine Fair
23 Barton St. (05769)

Skowhegan Skowhegan State Fair
P.O. Box 39 (04976)

South Thomaston The Old
Spaulding House

Springvale Number Ten Oak St.
10 Oak St.

Stonington Green Head Forge
Green Head

Topsham Harpswell House Annex
49 Winter St.

Waterville Terry's Rug Shop
95 Pleasant St.

Windsor Windsor Fair
P.O. Box 47 (04363)

Wiscasset New Cargos at the Old
Custom House, Water St.

Yarmouth Society of Southern Maine Craftsmen (Maine Chapter)
28 Spring St. (04096)

MARYLAND

Baltimore Calico Cat
2133 Gwynn Oak Ave.

The H. Chambers Co.
1010 N. Charles St.

Maryland Craft Council
702 Walker Ave. (21212)

Potters Guild
Green Lea Dr. (21208)

The Store, Ltd.
Village of the Cross Keys

Woman's Industrial Exchange
333 N. Charles St. (21201)

College Park Robert Schmitz
The Crafts Guild of the University
Dept. of Housing & Applied Design
U. of Maryland (20740)

Cumberland Greater Cumberland Fair, P.O. Box 457 (21502)

Gaithersburg Montgomery County Fair, 16 Chestnut St. (20760)

Pikesville Gallery 1330
1330 Reistertown Rd.

Silver Spring Creative Crafts Council
8904 Fairview Rd. (20910)

The Twenty Weavers
412 Southwest Dr. (20901)

Stevenson Galleries Grief

Timonium Maryland State Fair
P.O. Box 188 (21093)

MASSACHUSETTS

Arlington The Weather Glass Gallery & Workshop
1189 B Massachusetts Ave.

Auburndale From the Ends of the Earth, 271 Auburn St.

Boston Janiye
551 Boylston St.

Women's Educational & Industrial Union
264 Boylston St. (02116)

Brookline Mass. Assn. of Craftsmen
756 Washington St. (02146)

Dedham Dedham's Woman's Exchange, Inc.
445 Washington St. (02026)

Great Barrington Barrington Fair
Riverside Park, Agawam (01001)

Hingham The Weavers Guild of Boston
361 Main St. (02043)

Hyannis The Society of Cape Cod Craftsmen, Inc.
92 Gosnold St. (02601)

Lincoln Center Old Town Hall Exhibition

Marshfield Marshfield Fair
Main St. (02050)

Northampton Three County Fair
P.O. Box 429 (01060)

North Andover Center The Hay Scales Exchange, Inc.
2 Johnson St. (01845)

Old Sturbridge Horn of Plenty at Entrance to Old Sturbridge Village

Plymouth Plymouth Pottery Guild
Sparrow House (02360)

Springfield Eastern States Exposition
P.O. Box 191 (01089)

Stockbridge Cat and Drum

Sudbury Craft Ctr. at Wayside Inn
Gallery III
324 Boston Post Rd.

Swampscott Collage
134 Humphrey St.

Topsfield Topsfield Fair
Rte. 1, P.O. Box 134 (01983)

Wellfleet D. E. Kendall Art Galleries

Woburn Abbot Arts
8 Cedar St.

MICHIGAN

Adrian Lenawee County Fair
202 N. Dean St. (49221)

Allegan Allegan County Fair
P.O. Box 119 (49010)

Ann Arbor John Leidy Shop
601 & 607 E. Liberty St.
Potters' Guild of Ann Arbor
1613-2 Beal St. (48105)

Baldwin Norwood Weaving Shop

Birmingham America House
555 E. Maple St.
Galerie De Boicourt
725 S. Adams Rd.
Little Gallery
915 E. Maple St.

Caro Tuscalo County Fair
3212 W. Dixon Rd. (48723)

Centreville St. Joseph County Fair
P.O. Box 578 (49032)

Corunna Shiawassee County Fair
Road Commission Bldg. (48817)

Detroit Detroit Handweavers Guild
14044 Strathmoor Ave. (48227)
Michigan Potters Assn.
19310 Harned Ave. (48234)
Michigan State Fair
1120 West State Fair Ave. (48203)

Eagle Harbor The Hobby Shop

Escanaba Upper Peninsula State
Fair, P.O. Box 335 (49829)

Glen Arbor Schimpff Studio

Grand Ledge The Gampers—Textile
Explorers
1238 Jenne, P.O. Box 63 (46537)

Grand Rapids Grand Rapids Art
Museum, 230 E. Fulton

Grosse Pointe Shore Michigan
Silversmiths Guild
65 Shoreham Rd. (48236)

Harrison Clare County Fair
105 W. State St. (48617)

Hartland Michigan League of
Handweavers
P.O. Box 53 (48029)

Hillsdale Hillsdale County Fair
P.O. Box 289 (49242)

Imlay City Eastern Michigan Fair
8394 Bowers Rd. (48444)

Ionia Ionia Free Fair
P.O. Box 96 (48846)

Jackson Jackson County Fair
200 W. Ganson St. (49201)

Kalamazoo The Giftloft
1517 S. Park St.
Kalamazoo County Fair
5121 N. Third St. (49001)

Lambertville The Toledo Area
Weavers' Guild
3487 Section Rd. (48144)

Mason Ingam County Fair
P.O. Box 55 (48854)

Midland Midland County Fair
Courthouse (48640)

Monroe Monroe County Fair
3775 S. Custer Rd. (48161)

Mt. Pleasant Michigan Craftsmen's
Council
1119 S. Mission St. (48858)

Saginaw Saginaw Fair
2701 E. Genesee St. (48601)

Stevensville The Gallery
3824 Peach St.

Southfield Raven Gallery
29101 Greenfield Rd.

Suttons Bay Inter Arts Studio & The
Bay Window

Trout Lake Upper Peninsula Crafts
Council, P.O. Box 96 (49793)

MINNESOTA

Albert Lea Freeborn County Fair
Bridge St. (56007)

Austin Mower County Fair
P.O. Box 426 (55912)

Brainerd Crow Wing County Fair

Faribault Rice County Fair
124 5th Ave., N.W. (55021)

Hutchinson McLeod County Fair

Jackson Jackson County Fair
P.O. Box 27 (56143)

Minneapolis Manamore
4536 France Ave., S.
Thomas Designs
2941 Hennepin

Minnetonka Minnesota Craftsmen
3916 Thomas Ave. (55343)

New Ulm Brown County Fair (56073)

Owatonna Steele County Free Fair
P.O. Box 506 (55060)

St. Paul Minn. State Fair (55108)

Waconia Carver County Fair (55387)

Willmar Kandiyohi County Fair P.O. Box 490 (56201)

MISSISSIPPI

Jackson Liberty House P.O. Box 3468 (39207)

Mississippi State Fair P.O. Box 892 (39205)

Tupelo Mississippi Alabama Fair P.O. Box 560 (38801)

MISSOURI

Cape Girardeau Southeast Missouri District Fair 701 Good Hope (63701)

Columbia Missouri Craftsmen's Council 1213 Parkridge (65201)

Kennett Delta Fair P.O. Box 567 (63857)

Lee's Summit Jackson County Ext. Homemakers' Handcraft Co. Rte. 22, Lake LoTawanna (64063)

St. Louis Art Mart, Inc. 9983 Manchester

Craft Alliance Gallery 6640 Delmar, University City (63130)

The Woman's Exchange 300 N. Euclid Ave.

Kansas City Fantastic Arts, Inc. 212 Nichols Rd.

Sedalia Missouri State Fair P.O. Box 111 (65301)

Springfield Ozark Empire Fair P.O. Box 630 (65801)

Broadstreets, Inc. 315 E. McDaniel

Greene County Home Economics Extension Council Suite 900, 3003 E. Trafficway (65802)

Roger Thomason 1110 S. Main St. (65804)

MONTANA

Baker Fallon County Fair P.O. Box 477 (59313)

Bigfork Flathead Lake Galleries P.O. Box 426

Billings Midland Empire State Fair P.O. Box 1302 (59103)

Great Falls Spencer's 405 Central Ave.

State Fair P.O. Box 1524 (59401)

Havre Hill County Fair P.O. Box 906 (59501)

Kalispell Northwest Montana Fair Rte. 3 (59901)

Shelby Marias Fair P.O. Box 488 (59474)

NEBRASKA

Lincoln Nebraska State Fair P.O. Box 1966 (68501)

Omaha Ak Sar Ben Rodeo & Livestock Show 63rd & Shirley (68106)

NEW HAMPSHIRE

Bristol League of New Hampshire Craftsmen, Rte. 3A

Center Sandwich Ayottes Designery Sandwich Home Industries Main St.

Concord Concord Arts & Crafts 205 N. Main St. (03301)

League of New Hampshire Craftsmen 205 N. Main St. (03301)

Contoocook Hopkinton Fair P.O. Box 146 (03229)

Deerfield Deerfield Fair P.O. Box 62 (93937)

Durham Potpourri 29 Main St.

Exeter Exeter Craft Ctr. 61 Water St.

Rockingham Craftsman Organization County Bldg., Hampton Rd. (03833)

Franconia Notch League of New Hampshire Craftsmen

Henniker Discovery

Lancaster Lancaster Fair 77 Bunker Hill (03584)

Manchester League of New
Hampshire Craftsmen
157 Eddy Rd.

Meredith Meredith-Laconia Arts &
Crafts
Rte. 3.

Newfields New Hampshire Weavers
Guild, P.O. Box 112 (03856)

North Conway League of New
Hampshire Craftsmen
Main St.

Rochester Rochester Fair
45 Hanson St. (03867)

South Wolfeboro Wolfeboro Arts &
Crafts, Rte. 28

NEW JERSEY

Andover Yankee Schoolhouse
Lenape Rd., Rte. 517

Bridgeton Cumberland County Fair
104 West Ave. (08302)

Branchville Sussex County Farm &
Horse Show
P.O. Box 156, Newton (07826)

Cape May The Circle
303 Washington St.

The Sea Chest
305-7-9 Washington St.

Englewood Englewood Woman's
Exchange
43 Park Pl. (07631)

Flemington Flemington Fair
P.O. Box 293 (08822)

Hackettstown Westfield Weavers
Guild
House of the Good Shepherd
Mtd. Rte. (07840)

Ho-Ho-Kus Depot
217 First St.

Leonia The Moon Shop
442 Broad Ave.

Little Silver Woman's Exchange of
Monmouth County
32 Church St. (07739)

Mendham The Peddler's Cellar
6 Hilltop Rd.

Millburn House of Bernard
353 Millburn Ave.

Montclair Contemporary Crafts
438 Bloomfield Ave.

Newark Newark Exchange for
Woman's Work
32 Halsey St. (07013)

Oldwick The Oldwick Design Shop
Old Turnpike Rd.

Park Ridge New York Guild of
Handweavers
138 Fremont Ave. (07656)

Pine Hill Penn. Guild of Valley
21 E. 6th Ave. (08021)

Redbank The Niche
90 Broad St.

Ridgewood LaPatte
23 North Broad

Scotch Plains Ceramic Leagues, Inc.
P.O. Box 224 (07076)

Stone Harbor Sandpiper Galerie
10829 Ocean Dr.

Succasunna Morris County Fair
Cinema Bldg. (07876)

Trenton New Jersey State Fair
P.O. Box 669 (08604)

Union Associated Handweavers
2366 Steuben St. (07083)

Upper Montclair Holiday House
Bellevue Theater Bldg.

New Jersey Designer-Craftsmen
27 Duryea Rd. (07043)

West Orange First Mountain
Crafters
49 Lawrence Ave. (07052)

NEW MEXICO

Albuquerque New Mexico Designer
Craftsmen
4105 Hannett, N.E. (87110)

New Mexico State Fair
P.O. Box 8546 (87108)

Studio Gallery
400 D San Felipe

Ten Craftsmen
326 San Felipe

Workshop Originals
306 San Felipe

Las Vegas La Galeria de Los
Artesanos On the Plaza

Santa Fe Centerline
207 Lincoln Ave.

Leather & Sterling
652 Canyon Rd.

The Market
111 E. Palace

Taos Casa de Artes
N. Pueblo Rd.

NEW YORK

Alfred Glidden Galleries
43 N. Main St.

Altamont Altamont Fair
P.O. Box 495 (12009)

Auburn Muggleton Art Gallery
7 William St.

Batavia Genesee County Fair
Basom, New York (14013)

Bedford Hills The Handweavers
Guild of Westchester
3 Babbitt Rd. (10507)

Binghamton The Red Hedgehog
25 Main St.

Buffalo Todorf Galleries
476 Elmwood Ave.

Canandaigua Ontario County Fair
Rte. 2 (14424)

Cedarhurst Five Towns Woman's
Exchange, Inc.
111 Cedarhurst Ave. (11516)

Chatham Columbia County Fair
(12037)

Cobleskill Cobleskill Fair
N. Grand St. (12043)

Dunkirk Chautauqua County Fair
P.O. Box 191 (14048)

Elmira Chemung County Fair
P.O. Box 191, Horseheads (14945)

Falconer Chautauqua County
Weavers' Guild
308 Central Ave. (14733)

Florida Craft Barn
Wheeler Rd.

Pot-Pourri
85 N. Main St.

Garrison Garrison Art Center
Avery Rd. (10524)

Gouverneur Gouverneur & St.
Lawrence County Fair
95 E. Main St. (13642)

Great Neck Adult Program, Great
Neck Public Schools
345 Lakeville Rd. (11020)

Hamburg Erie County Fair &
Exposition
P.O. Box 526 (14075)

Henrietta Monroe County Fair
P.O. Box 83 (14467)

Huntington Long Island
Craftsmen's Guild, Inc.
155 Crooked Hill Rd. (11743)

Irvington Galeria Del Sol
Railroad Station

Ithaca Bosworth Handcrafts
132 Indian Creek Rd.

York State Craftsmen
2 Hillcrest Drive (14850)

Kew Gardens Glass Guild, Inc.
P.O. Box 157

Malone Franklin County Fair
7 Harding St. (12953)

Mamaroneck Topkapi Gifts &
Crafts, Inc.
910 E. Post Rd.

Manhasset The Grapevine Boutique
1673 Northern Blvd.

Middletown Orange County Fair
Wisner Ave. (10940)

New York City American Indian
Arts Ctr., 1051 Third Ave.

Art Enamels Ltd.
33 Christopher St.

The Art Image
232 E. 63rd St.

Artist-Craftsmen of New York, Inc.
180 Riverside Dr. (10024)

Arts & Crafts Ctr.
27 W. 55th St.

Bonniers, Inc.
605 Madison Ave.

Brooklyn Museum Gallery Shop
200 Eastern Parkway (Brooklyn)

Design Research
53 E. 57th St.

The Elder Craftsman Shop
850 Lexington Ave.

Georg Jensen
667 Madison Ave.

Greenwich House Potters &
Sculptors
16 Jones St. (10014)

Impressions in Wood
872 Lexington Ave.

Lee Nordness Galleries, Inc.
236 E. 75th St.

Lore Contemporary Concepts
1415 Lexington Ave.

Meuniers
140 Montague St., Brooklyn

New York Exchange for Woman's
Work
541 Madison Ave. (10022)

Norsk, Inc.
114 E. 57th St.

The Phoenix
793 Lexington Ave.

Piñata Party
129 Macdougal St.

Woman's Exchange of Brooklyn,
Inc.
76 Montague St. (11201)

Northport Artists & Craftsmen's
Showcase, 91 Main St.

Orchard Park Buffalo Craftsmen,
Inc., 7975 Jewett-Holmwood
Rd. (14127)

Ossining The Pottery Market
1 Nelson Ave.

Pittsford The Three Crowns
3850 Monroe Ave.

Rhinebeck Dutchess County Fair
P.O. Box 389 (12572)

Roslyn Hand Crafters Gallery
1365 Old Northern Blvd.

Saratoga Springs Farmers'
Hardware, 492 Broadway

Scarsdale The Scarsdale Woman's
Exchange
33 Harwood Ct. (10583)

Setauket Gallery North
North County Rd.

Shagticoke Rensselaer County Fair

Syracuse Bernard W. Potter
New York State Fair (13209)

Syracuse Ceramic Guild
131 Brooklea Pl. (13207)

Tappan The Fat Cat Gallery
92 Main St.

Troy Birchkill Arts & Crafts Guild,
Inc., 189 Second St. (12180)

Victor Mrs. John M. Freund
Weavers Guild of Rochester
321 Valentown Rd. (14564)

Watertown Jefferson County Fair
565 Mill St. (13601)

White Plains Conasons, Inc.
137 E. Post Rd.

Williamsville Studio 67
67 Fenwick Rd.

Woodstock The Freewheel Pottery
5 Larson Lane

Woodstock Guild of Craftsmen,
Inc., 34 Tinker St. (12498)

Yorktown Heights Vantage Point
265 Underhill Ave.

NORTH CAROLINA

Asheville A 'n L's Hobbicraft, Inc.
50 Broadway

The Spinning Wheel
1096 Hendersonville Rd.

Southern Highland Handicraft
Guild, P.O. Box 9145 (28005)

Charlotte Le Masters Design Ctr.
115 Cherokee Rd.

McDonald Art Gallery
753 Providence Rd.

Metrolina Fair & Exposition
(36226)

Plants & Things
6001 E. Independence Blvd.
(28212)

Cherokee Indian Arts & Crafts Bd.
P.O. Box 292

Concord Cabarrus County Fair
P.O. Box 321 (28025)

Durham Design Gallery at Straw
Valley, Rte. 7

Greensboro Folk Festival Arts &
Crafts, 121 S. Greene St.

Hickory Catawba Fair (28601)

Lexington Davidson County Fair
P.O. Box 339 (27292)

Mt. Airy Surry County Fair
1526 Park Dr. (27030)

Ocracoke The House of Crafts

Pinehurst Midland Crafters
Midland Rd.
Sandhills Woman's Exch. (28734)

Raleigh The Garden Gallery
Pottery Shop, Rte. 8
Little Art Gallery
North Hill Shopping Ctr.
North Carolina State Fair
P.O. Box 5565 (27607)

Salisbury Rowan County Fair
P.O. Box 66 (28144)

Winston-Salem Dixie Classic Fair
P.O. Box 7525 Reynolds Station
(27109)
Piedmont Craftsmen, Inc.
610 Coliseum Dr. (27106)

NORTH DAKOTA

Jamestown Stustman County Fair
P.O. Box 757 (58401)

Minot North Dakota State Fair
P.O. Box 1796 (58701)

West Fargo Red River Valley Fair
P.O. Box 645 (68078)

OHIO

Akron Akron Art Institute
69 E. Market St.
Ghent Art Gallery
3461 Granger Rd.
The Keeping Room Gallery
831 N. Cleveland Massilon Rd.
John Mazzola Interiors
143 W. Market St.

Bay Village Potpourri
585 Dover Center Rd.

Berea Cuyahoga County Fair
P.O. Box 135 (44017)

Bowling Green Wood County Fair
636 Wallace Ave. (43402)

Canfield Canfield Fair
P.O. Box 27 (44406)

Cincinnati Carthage Fair
77th & Vine (45216)
The Eye Opener
1041 St. Gregory St.
Good Design Shop
158 W. McMillan Ave.

Ohio Designer Craftsmen
208 Riddle Rd. (45215)
The Woman's Exchange
113-115 W. 4th St. (45202)

Cleveland The Homecrafters Shop
13017 Woodland Ave.
Ross Widen Gallery
11308 Euclid Ave.

Cleveland Heights Design Corner
2482 Fairmount Blvd.

Cleves Ceramic & Craft Guild of
Cincinnati
159 Zion Hill Rd. (45002)

Coshocton Coshocton County Fair
707 Kenilworth Ave. (43812)

Columbus Columbus Gallery of
Fine Arts, 480 E. Broad St.
Ohio State Fair
632 E. 11th Ave. (43211)

Dayton Montgomery County Fair
1043 S. Main St. (45409)

Delaware Delaware County Fair
60 N. Franklin St. (43014)

Fremont Sandusky County Fair
1010 Linden Blvd. (43420)

Kenton Hardin County Fair
P.O. Box 270 (43326)

Lancaster Fairfield County Fair
131 W. Main St. (43131)

Lebanon Warren County Fair
P.O. Box 58 (45036)

Lima Allen County Fair
P.O. Box 1015 (45802)

Lucasville Scioto County Fair
2825 Willow Way, Portsmouth
(45662)

Maumes Lucas County Fair
1406 Key St. (43537)

Medina Medina County Fair
P.O. Box 551 (44256)

Montpelier Williams County Fair
311 N. Platt St. (43543)

Norwalk Huron County Fair
Rte. 3, Willard (44890)

Shaker Heights Textile Arts Club
22300 Parnell Rd. (44122)

South Marion Artisan's Guild
1141 Prospect-Upper Sandusky
Rd. (43302)

Springfield Clark County Fair (45501)

Troy Miami County Fair
625 N. Dixie P.O. Box 399 (45373)

Urbana Champaign County Fair
934 Amherst Dr. (43078)

Wapakoneta Auglaize County Fair
P.O. Box 431 (45895)

Wauseon Fulton County Fair
336 E. Chestnut St. (43567)

Wellington Lorain County Fair
P.O. Box 15 (44090)

Wooster Wayne County Fair
P.O. Box 3 (44691)

Worthington Design Center
2287 W. Granville Rd.

OKLAHOMA

Enid Garfield County Fair
P.O. Box 586 (73701)

Bartlesville Talisman Gallery
307 Delaware St.

Muskogee Muskogee State Fair
P.O. Box 1099 (74401)

Oklahoma City State Fair of
Oklahoma
500 N. Land Rush St. (73107)

Stillwater The Orange Crate
113½ E. 8th St.
Oklahoma Designer Craftsmen
Oklahoma State U. (74075)

Tulsa Tulsa Designer-Craftsmen
3411 S. Birmingham (74105)
Tulsa State Fair
P.O. Box 4531 (74104)

OREGON

Corvallis Corvallis Arts Ctr.
309 S. 7th St. (97330)

Eugene Art Ctr. Gallery Shop
1910 E. 15th Ave.
The Eugene Weavers Guild
3085 University St. (97405)
The House of Crafts
288 River Rd.

Salem Oregon State Fair
2060 Silverton Rd., N.E. (97310)

Portland Arts & Crafts Society
Hoffman Gallery
616 N. W. 18th Ave.
Contemporary Crafts Gallery
3934 S. W. Corbett
The Fountain Gallery of Art
115 S. W. 4th Ave.
The Red Balloon, Inc.
1023 S. W. Front Ave.

PENNSYLVANIA

Allentown Great Allentown Fair
17th & Chew Sts. (18104)

Bethlehem Penn. Guild of Crafts
223 E. Union Blvd. (18018)
The Pottery
734 N. New St.

Bryn Mawr The Peasant Shop
845 Lancaster Ave.

Bucks County Pennsylvania Guild
of Craftsmen
George School (18940)

Clearfield Clearfield County Fair
P.O. Box 712 (16830)

Dallas Cocaluschu Craftsmen
Rte. 1, P.O. Box 54 (18612)

Ebensburg Cambria County Fair
P.O. Box 147 (15931)

Gladwyne Philadelphia Guild of
Hand Weavers
436 Williamson Rd. (19035)

Harrisburg Pennsylvania Guild of
Craftsmen
2731 N. Second St. (11710)
Pennsylvania Guild of Craftsmen
Harrisburg Craftsmen
904 Lakewood Dr. (17109)

Hughesville Lycoming County Fair
P.O. Box 116 (17737)

Kingston Shirley Troy Gallery
660 Gibson Ave.

Kutztown Kutztown Fair
P.O. Box 177 (19530)

Lahaska Creative Hands Shop

Lancaster The Gallery
248 W. Orange St.

Meadville Crawford County Fair
Courthouse (16335)

New Hope Pennsylvania Guild of
  Craftsmen
Bucks County Chapter
R. D. 1 (18938)

Philadelphia The Circle
2014 Sansome St.

Gallery 252
252 S. 16th St.

Ladies Depository Assn.
109 S. 17th St. (19103)

The Peasant Shop
17th & Spruce Sts.

Philadelphia Council of
  Professional Craftsmen
2220 Rittenhouse Sq. (19103)

Scraffitto
120 Lombard St.

The Works
2017 Locust St.

Pittsburgh G. R. Benedict,
  Silversmith
5500 Walnut St.

Embroiderer's Guild
6633 Woodwell St. (15217)

The Mart
5th & Shady Ave.

Woman's Industrial Exchange
214 Oliver St. (15222)

Port Royal Juniata County Fair
P.O. Box 295 (17082)

Reading Reading Fair
2924 N. 5th St. (19605)

Scranton Galerie des Beaux Arts
252 Adams Ave.

Sewickley Bird in the Hand
427 Broad St.

State College The Loft
212 E. College Ave.

Penn State Artists at Work Fair

Stoneboro Great Stoneboro Fair
P.O. Box 248 (16153)

Swarthmore The Circle
21½ S. Chester Rd.

Upper Darby Sage Imports
6460 Market St.

Wallingford Potters Guild of
  Community Arts Ctr.
408 Roger Lane (19086)

Wayne Woman's Exchange of the
  Neighborhood League
185 E. Lancaster Ave. (19087)

Wilkes-Barre Potpourri Arts &
  Crafts, 93 S. Main St.

York York Interstate Fair
334 Carlisle Ave. (17404)

RHODE ISLAND

Kingstown Fayerweather Craft Ctr.
Mooresfield Rd., Rte. 138

Providence Ceramic Department
Rhode Island School of Design
(02903)

The Weavers Guild of Rhode
  Island, 21 Sheldon St. (02906)

Wickford Paradigm
18 Main St.

SOUTH CAROLINA

Anderson Anderson Fair
P.O. Box 274 (29621)

Charleston Coastal Carolina Fair
P.O. Box 505 (29402)

Columbia Columbia Museum of Art
Senate & Bull Sts. (29205)

South Carolina Craftsmen
6564 Eastshore Dr. (29206)

South Carolina State Fair
P.O. Box 393 (29202)

The Studio
7124 Monticello Rd.

Greenville Upper South Carolina
  State Fair
229 Augusta St. (29606)

Greenwood Greenwood Fair
P.O. Box 834 (29646)

Newberry Newberry-Saluda County
  Fair, P.O. Box 181 (29108)

Orangeburg Orangeburg County
  Fair, P.O. Box 283 (29115)

Spartanburg Piedmont Interstate
  Fair, Montgomery Bldg. (29301)

SOUTH DAKOTA

Huron South Dakota State Fair
P.O. Box 1275 (57350)

Rapid City Central States Fair
P.O. Box 1212 (57701)

Sioux Falls Sioux Empire Fair
P.O. Box 841 (57101)

TENNESSEE

Camden Benton County Fair
P.O. Box 271 (38320)

Chattanooga Chattanooga-
Hamilton County Fair
P.O. Box 3011 (37404)

Crossville Cumberland Mountain
Craft Assn.

Fayetteville Lincoln County Fair
P.O. Box 476 (37334)

Gatlinburg Pi Beta Phi Craft
Workshop
U. of Tennessee
P.O. Box 567 (37738)

12 Designer Craftsmen
Roaring Fork Rd.

Jackson West Tennessee State Fair
P.O. Box 1404 (38301)

Jonesboro Appalachian District Fair
Rte. 5 (37659)

Knoxville Tennessee Valley Fair
P.O. Box 6066 (37914)

Lawrenceburg Middle Tennessee
Fair, P.O. Box 563 (38464)

McMinnville Warren County Fair
P.O. Box 759 (37110)

Memphis Memphis Guild of
Handloom Weavers
3235 N. Waynolka Dr. (38111)

Mid-South Fair
P.O. Box 14808 (38114)

Murfreesboro Tennessee Artists-
Craftsmen's Assn.
Middle Tennessee State U. (37130)

Nashville Tennessee State Fair
P.O. Box 9008 Melrose Sta. (37204)

Oak Ridge Foothills Craft Guild,
Inc.
115 E. Geneva Lane (37839)

Laughing Monkey
125 Broadway

Pidgeon Forge Tennessee Artists-
Craftsmen's Assn.

Union City Obion County Fair
P.O. Box 126 (38261)

TEXAS

Abilene West Texas Fair
P.O. Box 3016 (79604)

Amarillo Tri-State Fair
P.O. Box 1087 (79105)

Beaumont Beaumont Art Museum
2675 Gulf St. (77703)

South Texas State Fair
P.O. Box 3207 (77704)

Dallas Contemporary Fine Arts
Gallery
Quadrangle, 2800 Routh St.

Craft Guild of Dallas
Dallas Museum of Fine Arts
(75225)

The Museum Shop
Dallas Museum of Fine Arts
Fair Park

State Fair of Texas
P.O. Box 26010 (75226)

El Paso Two Twenty Two Gallery
222 Cincinnati

Fort Worth Southwestern
Exposition
P.O. Box 150 (76101)

Houston Contemporary
Handweavers of Texas
2105 Swift (77025)

Creative Stitchers of Texas
12419 Huntington Dr. (77024)

Handmakers, Inc.
3813 Main St.

Houston Craft Guild
7602 Fairdale (77042)

Houston Designer-Craftsmen
3511 Link Valley #50 (77025)

Lubbock The Little Shoppe
2610 Salem
1 Cactus Alley

Panhandle South Plains Fair
P.O. Box 208 (79408)

Rosenberg Fort Bend County Fair
P.O. Box 428 (77471)

San Antonio Southwest Craft Ctr.
420 Villita St. (78205)

San Marcos Texas Designer-
Craftsmen
Southwest Texas State (78666)

Texarkana Four States Fair
P.O. Box 1468 (75501)

Waco Heart o' Texas Fair
P.O. Box 7581 (76710)

Texas Art Education Assn.
Baylor U. (76703)

Wichita Falls Texas Designer-
Craftsmen
1300 Burnett (76301)

UTAH

Salt Lake City Hugh C. Bringhurst
Utah State Fair
155 N. 9th St., W. (84116)

Prof. Max Weaver
Art Dept., Brigham Young U.

VERMONT

Bennington Ed Levin Arts
Workshop
The Bennington Gallery
U.S. Rte. 7

Essex Junction Champlain Valley
Exposition
P.O. Box F (05452)

Montpelier Vermont Arts & Crafts
Service
Dept. of Education (05601)

Plainfield Community Crafts
Rte. 2

Plymouth The Plymouth
Schoolhouse

Rutland Cottage Crafts Shop
116 N. Main St.

Edward C. Congdon, Pres.
Vermont State Fair (05701)

Shelburne Shelburne Craft School
(05482)

Stowe The Stowe Pottery
Yankee Craftsmen

Waitsfield Ware's, The Craft
Workshop

VIRGINIA

Alexandria Kiln Club of
Washington
810 S. Lee St. (22314)

Woodlawn Natl. Needlework
836 Harriet Springs Rd. (22305)

Arlington Cherry Tree Textile
Designers
2731 Lorcom Lane (22207)

Danville Greater Danville Fair
2600 Riverside Dr. (24541)

Fredericksburg Fredericksburg
Fair, P.O. Box 887 (22401)

Lynchburg Virginia Handcrafts,
Inc.
20008 Langhorne Rd. (24501)

Manassas Prince William County
Fair
P.O. Box 91 (22110)

Monterey Highland County
Crafts, Inc.

Richmond Richmond Craftsmen
203 Old Oak Rd. (23229)

Richmond Craftsmen's Guild
4300 Forest Hill Ave. (23225)

State Fair of Virginia
P.O. Box 1757 (23214)

Virginia Beach Tidewater Weavers
Guild
P.O. Box 5103 (23455)

Waterford Waterford Foundation

WASHINGTON

Bainbridge Island Bainbridge Arts
& Crafts, Inc.
P.O. Box 161 (98110)

Bellingham Gallery 217, Inc.
217 E. Holly St.

Whatcom Museum Shop
121 Prospect St.

Chehalis Southwest Wash. Fair
P.O. Box 831 (98532)

Colfax Palouse Empire Fair
Courthouse (99111)

Ellensburg Ellensburg Community
Art Gallery, Inc.
111 S. Pearl St.

Kittitas County Fair
Rte. 1, P.O. Box 430 (98926)

Elma Gray's Harbor Fair
Rte. 1, P.O. Box C (98541)

Ephrata Columbia Basin Arts &
Crafts Assn.
42 G St., S.W. (98823)

Friday Harbor The Creative Eye
Roche Harbor Rd.

Gig Harbor White Whale Gallery
Rte. 5

Kennewick Benton-Franklin Fair &
Rodeo, P.O. Box 6894 (99336)

Longview Los Tres Gallery
2609 N.W. Nichols Blvd.

Monroe Evergreen State Fair
P.O. Box 129 (98272)

Moses Lake Grant County Fair
P.O. Box 927 (98837)

Port Townsend Port Townsend Art
Gallery

Richland Jaid Gallery
702 George Washington Way

Seattle Burien Arts Gallery
15619 4th Ave., S.W.

Mobilia
301 E. Pine St.

Northwest Designer Craftsmen
1441 S.W. 158th St. (98166)

Opus 204
204 Broadway East

Spokane Interstate Fair
P.O. Box 143 Parkwater Station
(99211)

Museum Shop
Cheney Cowles Memorial Museum
2316 First Ave.

Vancouver Clark County Fair
P.O. Box 1824 (98663)

Walla Walla Southeastern
Washington Fair
P.O. Box 1060 (99362)

Yakima Central Wash. Fair
P.O. Box 1381 (98901)

WEST VIRGINIA

Charleston West Virginia Artists &
Craftsmens Guild
Rm. 404, State Capital (25305)

W. Virginia Mountain Artisans
715 Kanawha Valley Bldg. (25301)

Helvetia Arts & Crafts Gift Shop

Lewisburg W. Virginia State Fair
P.O. Box 829 (24901)

Parkersburg The Parkersburg Art
Ctr., Inc.
1015 Julian St. (26101)

Wheeling Oglebay Inst. Craft Dept.
84172 National Rd. (26002)

WISCONSIN

Bayfield L'Atelier Summer Gallery

Beaver Dam Dodge County Fair
P.O. Box 96 (53916)

Chippewa Falls N. Wis. State Fair
P.O. Box 48 (54729)

Elkhorn Walworth County Fair
P.O. Box 286 (53121)

Fond du Lac Fond du Lac County
Fair, Rte. 6 (54935)

Green Bay Brown County Fair
2159 Ridge Blvd. (54304)

Lake Geneva Art Independent
Gallery & Boutique
706 Main St.

Manitowoc Manitowoc County Fair

Marshfield Central Wis. State Fair
P.O. Box 748 (54440)

Mequon Wis. Federation of
Handweavers, Inc.
9226 W. Hawthorne Rd. (53902)

Middletown The Gallery Haycock
1904 Parmenter St.

Milwaukee L'Atelier
2010 N. Farwell Ave.

Wis. Designer Craftsmen
3245 N. Oakland #205

Wis. State Fair (53214)

Monroe Green County Fair
P.O. Box 213 (53566)

Oshkosh Winnebago County Fair
P.O. 1186 (54901)

Plymouth Sheboygan County Fair
623 E. Mill St. (53073)

Seymour Outagamie County Fair
P.O. Box 67 (54165)

Shawano Shawano County Fair
(54166)

Waukesha Waukesha County Fair
Courthouse (53186)

Wausau Wisconsin Valley Fair
P.O. Box 1091 (54401)

Wilmot Kenosha County Fair
P.O. Box 96 (53192)

WYOMING

Casper Central Wyoming Fair &
Rodeo, P.O. Box 2187 (82601)

Cheyenne Wyoming Homemakers
Council, 920 Foyer Ave.

Douglas Wyoming State Fair
P.O. Box 10 (82633)

Grand Teton Natl. Park Grand
Teton Lodge Gift Shops

Jackson Hole Vende Waters

3 Trade and Industry Shows

The following is a representative list of trade and industry shows throughout the United States. The letter or number in parentheses after the name of the organization indicates the number of shows a year. (A indicates Annual show; SA indicates Semiannual show; BA indicates Biennial show.) Although the headquarters of an organization is listed, the shows themselves are not necessarily confined to the specified states or cities. Refer to the Chamber of Commerce for full information concerning trade events.

ADVERTISING

Natl. Assn. of Display Industries
(SA)
207 E. 37th St.
New York, N.Y. 10016

Natl. Premium Show (A)
407 S. Dearborn St.
Chicago, Ill. 60605

Specialty Advertising Assn. (SA)
740 N. Rush St.
Chicago, Ill. 60611

ANIMALS

Empire Cat Club (A)
309 W. 57th St.
New York(N.Y. 10019

Empress Chinchilla Breeders
Co-op (A)
101 W. 30th St.
New York, N.Y.

Independent Pet Industry
Trade Show (A)
2151 N. Hudson Ave.
Chicago, Ill. 60614

Intl. Kennel Club of Chicago
Dog Show (A)
116 Exchange Bldg.
Chicago, Ill. 60609

Pet Industry Natl. Trade Show (A)
432 Chauncey St.
Brooklyn, N.Y. 11233

Texas Kennel Club
6300 N. Central Expressway
Dallas, Tex.

Western Wholesale Pet Supply
Assn. (A)
3625 MacArthur Blvd.
Oakland, Calif. 94602

Cat Shows

Alamo City Cat Club, CFA
San Antonio, Tex. 78201

Buffalo Cat Fanciers, CFA
Buffalo, N.Y.

California Silver Fanciers
La Palma, Calif. 90620

Camellia Longhair Cat Fanciers,
    CFA, Sacramento, Calif. 95825

Cascade Cat Fanciers, CFA
Seattle, Wash. 98125

Cat Alliance of Tuscaloosa, CFA
    Tuscaloosa, Ala. 35401

Cat Fanciers' Club of Iowa
Waterloo, Iowa 50703

Cats of Charlotte, CFA
Charlotte, N.C. 28210

Cats Royale, CFA
E. Richmond, Calif. 94805

Chesapeake Cat Club, CFA
Glen Arm, Md. 21057

City Beautiful Cat Club, CFA
Orlando, Fla. 32809

Compadres de los Gatos de Santa
    Barbara Club, CFA
Ventura, Calif. 93003

Confederation Cat Fanciers, CFA
Bramalea, Ont., Canada

Cotton States Cat Club, CFA
Atlanta, Ga. 30340

El Paso Texas Cat Club, CFA
El Paso, Tex.

Everglades Cat Club, CFA
Miami, Fla. 33165

Feline Fanciers of Oregon, ACFA
Eugene, Oreg. 97402

Greater St. Louis Cat Club, CFA
Florissant, Mo. 63033

Hacienda Cat Club, CFA
Pasadena, Calif.

Hollywood Cat Club
Pasadena, Calif.

Houston Cat Club, CFA
Houston, Tex. 77024

Indianapolis Feline Assn., CFA
Indianapolis, Ind. 46227

Jewel City Cat Club, ACA
Glendale, Calif. 91207

Johnny Appleseed Feline Fanciers,
    CFA, Wadsworth, Ohio

Kentuckiana Cat Club, ACFA
Jeffersontown, Ky. 40299

Lincoln State Cat Club, CFA
Blue Island, Ill. 60406

Lone Star Cat Club, CFA
Dallas, Tex. 75211

Long Island Cat Club, CFA
Baldwin, N.Y. 11510

Madison Cat Club, ACFA
Madison, Wis. 53711

Magic City Cat Club, CFA
Miami, Fla. 33143

Memphis Dixieland Cat Club
Memphis, Tenn. 38117

Miami Florida Cat Fanciers, CFA
Miami, Fla.

Mo-Kan Cat Club, CFA
Kansas City, Mo. 64138

Neptune Cat Club, CCA
Wedgewood Pk., Halifax, N.S., Can.

Oil Capital Cat Club
Tulsa, Okla. 74129

Old Dominion Cat Club
Richmond, Va. 23222

Platinum Coast Cat Club, ACFA
Merritt Island, Fla. 32952

Salt Lake Cat Club
Salt Lake City, Utah 84108

San Diego Cat Fanciers, CFA
Chula Vista, Calif. 92011

Seattle Cat Club, CFA
Seattle, Wash. 98125

Shorthair Cats & Other Things, CFA
Shorthair Specialty Show,
1461 N.E. 133 Rd.
North Miami, Fla. 33161

The Siamese Fanciers, CFA
Hawaiian Gardens, Calif.

Tropical Trail Cat Club, ACFA
Harlingen, Tex. 78550

United Persian Society, CFA
Racine, Wis.

Western Reserve Cat Club, CFA
Youngstown, Ohio 44512

Westshore Shorthair Cat Club
La Palma, Calif. 90621

William Penn Cat Club, CFA
Civic Ctr., Trenton, N.J.

Windy City Cat Fanciers, CFA
Chicago, Ill. 60052

Dog Shows

Agathon Kennel Club
Amherst Park Civic Ctr.
 (Unbenched)
Massillon, Ohio

Antelope Valley Kennel Club
Antelope Valley Fairgrounds
 (Unbenched)
Lancaster, Calif.

Berrien Kennel Club
Berrien Co. Youth Fairgrounds
 (Unbenched)
Berrien Springs, Mich.

Birmingham Kennel Club
Alabama State Fairgrounds,
 Exposition Bldg. (Unbenched)
Birmingham, Ala.

Boardwalk Kennel Club
Convention Hall (Unbenched)
Atlantic City, N.J.

Bryn Mawr Kennel Club
Polo Grounds (Unbenched)
Bryn Mawr, Pa.

Burlington County Kennel Club
Dough Boy Field (Unbenched)
Fort Dix, N.J.

Cabrillo Kennel Club
Grape Day Park, Escondido Blvd.
 (Unbenched)
Escondido, Calif.

Camden County Kennel Club
Ivystone Inn (Unbenched)
Pennsauken, N.J.

Cedar Rapids Kennel Assn.
Memorial Stadium S.W.
 (Unbenched)
Cedar Rapids, Iowa

Central Wyoming Kennel Club
Central Wyoming Fairgrounds
 (Unbenched)
Casper, Wyo.

Chain O' Lakes Kennel Club
Lake County Fairgrounds
 (Unbenched)
Grayslake, Ill.

The Cincinnati Kennel Club
Cincinnati Gardens (Unbenched)
Cincinnati, Ohio

Columbia Kennel Club
Carolina Coliseum (Unbenched)
Columbia, S.C.

Cornhusker Kennel Club, Inc.
Neb. State Fairgrounds Coliseum
 (Unbenched)
Lincoln, Neb.

Danville Kennel Club, Inc.
Eastern Illinois Fairgrounds
 (Unbenched)
Danville, Ill.

Del Monte Kennel Club
Collins Polo Field (Unbenched)
Pebble Beach, Calif.

Del Sur Kennel Club
Wells Park (Unbenched)
El Cajon, Calif.

Eastern Dog Club
War Memorial Auditorium (Benched)
Boston, Mass.

Electric City Kennel Club
4-H Bldg., N. Mont. State
 Fairgrounds (Unbenched)
Great Falls, Mont.

Erie Kennel Club, Inc.
Fairview Elementary School
 Grounds (Unbenched)
Fairview, Pa.

Five Valley Kennel Club
U. of Montana Fieldhouse
 (Unbenched)
Missoula, Mont.

Framingham Dist. Kennel Club
Marlboro High School Grounds
 (Unbenched)
Marlboro, Mass.

Gallatin Dog Club
Montana State U. Fieldhouse
 (Unbenched)
Bozeman, Mont.

Greater Miami Dog Club
Dinner Key Auditorium
 (Unbenched)
Miami, Fla.

Greater Muskegon Kennel Club
L. C. Walker Sports Arena
 (Unbenched)
Muskegon, Mich.

Greenwich Kennel Club
Richard Cahoum Estate, Davenport
  Ridge Rd. (Unbenched)
Stanford, Conn.

Harrisburg Kennel Club
State Farm Show Bldg. (Benched)
Harrisburg, Pa.

Hawkeye Kennel Club
University of Iowa Fieldhouse
  (Unbenched)
Iowa City, Iowa

Hockamock Kennel Club
Norton Elem. School (Unbenched)
Norton, Mass.

Illinois Capital Kennel Club
Illinois State Fairgrounds
  (Unbenched)
Springfield, Ill.

Illinois Valley Kennel Club of
  Peoria
Exposition Gardens (Unbenched)
Peoria, Ill.

Kennel Club of Pasadena
Brookside Park (Unbenched)
Pasadena, Calif.

Kennel Club of Philadelphia
Phila. Civic Center (Benched)
Philadelphia, Pa.

Ladies' Dog Club
900 Washington St. (Unbenched)
Wellesley, Mass.

Ladies Kennel Assn. of America
Hofstra University (Unbenched)
Hempstead, N.Y.

Lake Minnetonka Kennel Club
Wayzata Jr. High School Athletic
  Grounds (Unbenched)
Wayzata, Minn.

Lima Kennel Club
Allen County Fairgrounds
  (Unbenched)
Lima, Ohio

Long Island Kennel Club
Piping Rock Horse Show Grounds
  (Benched)
Locust Valley, N.Y.

Longshore-Southport Kennel Club
Wilton Jr. High School Athletic
  Field (Unbenched)
Wilton, Conn.

Mad River Valley Kennel Club
Clarke County Fairgrounds
  (Unbenched)
Springfield, Ohio

Marion Kennel Club
Marion Armory (Unbenched)
Marion, Ind.

Maryland Kennel Club
5th Regiment Armory (Benched)
Baltimore, Md.

McKinley Kennel Club
Canton Memorial Auditorium
  (Unbenched)
Canton, Ohio

Memphis Kennel Club
Youth Bldg., Fairgrounds
  (Unbenched)
Memphis, Tenn.

Mensona Kennel Club
Sonoma County Fairgrounds
  (Unbenched)
Santa Rosa, Calif.

Merrimack Valley Kennel Club
Hood Memorial School
  (Unbenched)
Derry, N.H.

Mid-Continent Kennel Club of
  Tulsa
Tulsa Assembly Center
  (Unbenched)
Tulsa, Okla.

Middlesex County Kennel Club
Concord Carlisle, Regional H.S.
  (Unbenched)
Concord, Mass.

Mid-Hudson Kennel Club
Springbrook Park (Unbenched)
Rhinebeck, N.Y.

Mountaineer Kennel Club
National Guard Armory
  (Unbenched)
Fairmont, W. Va.

Muncie Kennel Club
Muncie Athletic Fieldhouse
  (Unbenched)
Muncie, Ind.

National Capitol Kennel Club
National Guard Armory (Benched)
Washington, D.C.

Oakland County Kennel Club
The Detroit Artillery Armory
  (Unbenched)
Oak Park, Mich.

Onondaga Kennel Assn., Inc.
Onondaga War Memorial
  (Unbenched)
Syracuse, N.Y.

Oshkosh Kennel Club
Winnebago County Fairgrounds
  (Unbenched)
Oshkosh, Wis.

Palm Beach County Dog Fanciers
Colonnades Beach Hotel
  (Unbenched)
Palm Beach Shores, Fla.

Plainfield Kennel Club, Inc.
St. Joseph's High School
  (Unbenched)
Metuchen, N.J.

Queensboro Kennel Club
Queen's Children's Hospital
  (Unbenched)
Queens Village, N.Y.

Quincy Kennel Club
Quincy Senior High School Gym
  (Unbenched)
Quincy, Ill.

Ramapo Kennel Club
Paterson, N.J. Armory (Unbenched)
Paterson, N.J.

Richland County Kennel Club
Commercial Exhibitors Bldg.
  (Unbenched)
Mansfield, Ohio

Rio Grande Kennel Club
Tingley Coliseum, New Mexico
  State Fairgrounds
Albuquerque, N.M.

Rockingham County Kennel Club
Grounds of Portsmouth Sr. High
  School (Unbenched)
Portsmouth, N.H.

San Mateo Kennel Club
Hall of Flowers, San Mateo
  Fairgrounds (Unbenched)
San Mateo, Calif.

Santa Clara Valley Kennel Club
Santa Clara Co. Fairgrounds
  (Unbenched)
San Jose, Calif.

Silver State Kennel Club
Cashman Field, Las Vegas Blvd.
  (Unbenched)
Las Vegas, Nev.

Southeastern Iowa Kennel Club
Ottumwa Coliseum (Unbenched)
Ottumwa, Iowa

Southern Colorado Kennel Club
Agricultural Bldg., Colorado State
  Fairgrounds (Unbenched)
Pueblo, Colo.

Staten Island Kennel Club
Fort Wadsworth (Unbenched)
Staten Island, N.Y.

Stone City Kennel Club
Fred Francis 4H-Field (Unbenched)
New Lenox, Ill.

Sussex Hills Kennel Club
National Guard Armory
  (Unbenched)
Morristown, N.J.

Tacoma Kennel Club
Heidelberg Field (Unbenched)
Tacoma, Wash.

Tallahassee Kennel Club
Northern Florida Fairgrounds,
  Bldgs. 2 & 4 (Unbenched)
Tallahassee, Fla.

Thronateeska Kennel Club
Hasan Temple (Unbenched)
Albany, Ga.

Tidewater Kennel Club of Virginia
Norfolk Municipal Arena
  (Unbenched)
Norfolk, Va.

Tucson Kennel Club, Inc.
Randolph Park (Unbenched)
Tucson, Ariz.

Vancouver Kennel Club
Exhibition Bldg., Calrk County
  Fairgrounds (Unbenched)
Vancouver, Wash.

Western Reserve Kennel Club
Cleveland Convention Ctr.
  (Unbenched)
Cleveland, Ohio

Westminster Kennel Club
Madison Square Garden (Benched)
New York, N.Y.

Whidbey Island Kennel Club, Inc.
Evergreen Fairgrounds
(Unbenched)
Monroe, Wash.

Wichita Kennel Club
Wichita Civic Ctr. (Unbenched)
Wichita, Kans.

Winnegamie Dog Club
Appleton Municipal Service Bldg.
(Unbenched)
Appleton, Wis.

Wisconsin Kennel Club
Milwaukee Auditorium (Benched)
Milwaukee, Wis.

Yellowstone Valley Kennel Club
Shrine Auditorium (Unbenched)
Billings, Mont.

Yuma Kennel Club
Yuma Co. Fairgrounds
(Unbenched)
Yuma, Ariz.

ANTIQUES

Annual Old Post Rd. Antiques Show
Mamaroneck, N.Y.

Annual Peninsula Antiques Show
Exposition Hall, Monterey
Fairgrounds
Monterey, Calif.

Antique Dealers Assn.
The Armory, Shewell Ave.
Doylestown, Pa.

Asheville Annual Antiques Fair
Municipal Auditorium
Asheville, N.C.

Atlanta Merchandise Mart
Museum Antiques Show
Atlanta, Ga.

Bayhead Annual Antiques Show
and Sale
Bridge & West Lake Ave.
Bayhead, N.J.

Bennington Antique Show and Sale
Second Congregational Church
Hillside, Vt., Bennington, Vt.

Brandeis Antique Show and Sale
5700 Oakland Ave.
St. Louis, Mo.

Burlington Antique Show and Sale
1271 North Ave.
Burlington, Vt.

California Intl. Antique Shows
6438 Benvenue Ave.
Oakland, Calif. 04618

Camden 20th Annual Show
Community Hospital Aux.
Camden, Maine

Chatham Antiques Sale
Memorial Auditorium
Chatham, Mass.

The Clubhouse-Women's Club
Chevy Chase, Md.

Columbus Antique Show
12730 E. Warren Ave.
Detroit, Mich.

Connecticut Antiques Show
State Armory, Broad St.
Hartford, Conn.

Cook's Field Tri-County Antique
Dealers Assn., Rte. 80 North
Cooperstown, N.Y.

Corning Glass Center Antique Show
72 Valencia Ave.
Staten Island, N.Y. 10301

Cortland Annual Antiques Show
and Sale, Cortland, N.Y.

County Antiques Fair
Westchester Enterprises, 29 Elm Pl.
Freeport, N.Y. 11520

Detroit Antiques Show
12730 E. Warren Ave.
Detroit, Mich. 48215

Evanston Annual Antiques Show
and Sale, Woman's Club
Evanston, Ill.

Fitzwilliam Historical Society
Antiques Show and Sale
Fitzwilliam, N.H.

Gerry's Landing Rd.
Cambridge, Mass.

Greenwich Village Antiques Show
Greenwich House
27 Barrow Street
New York, N.Y. 10014

Guernsey Antiques
Sales Pavilion, U.S. 30
E. Lancaster, Pa.

Heritage Promotion Cranston, R.I.

Ho-Ho-Kus Annual Antique Show
St. Bartholomew's
Ho-Ho-Kus, N.J.

Hollywood Fall Antique Show
1248 Point View
Los Angeles, Calif. 90035

Hornell Annual Antique Show
Beacon Inn, Hornell, N.Y.

Houston Antique Show
Albert Thomas Exhibit and
  Convention Center
Houston, Tex.

Illinois Annual Antiques Show
Emmanuel Episcopal Church
La Grange, Ill.

Indianapolis Antique Show
Exposition Bldg.
1500 E. 38th St. (U.S. 36)
Indianapolis, Ind.

Lexington Antiques Show
High School Gymnasium
Lexington, Mass.

Massapequa Annual Antiques Fair
  and Sale
Temple Judea, Jerusalem Ave.
Massapequa, N.Y.

Milford Antique Show
Milford, Pa.

Millbrook Flea Market
Hope Farm
Millbrook, N.Y.

Milwaukee Art Ctr.
Friends of Art
Milwaukee, Wis.

Mint Museum Antiques Show
Merchandise Mart
Charlotte, N.C.

Montclair Antiques Fair and Sale
Westchester Enterprises
29 Elm Place
Freeport, N.Y. 11520

Montclair Antiques Show
551 Valley Rd.
Montclair, N.J.

Moorestown Annual Antiques Show
Church and Main Sts.
Moorestown, N.J.

Morristown Annual Antiques Show
2 Whippany Road
Morristown, N.J.

Morristown Antiques Fair and Sale
Armory, Western Ave.
Morristown, N.J.

Mt. Lebanon Antiques Show
750 Hollycrest Drive
Mt. Lebanon, Pa.

Mount Vernon Antiques Show
Lloyd Hall, Mt. Vernon College
Washington, D.C.

Nathan Hale Antiques Festival
Coventry, Conn.

National Antiques Show
97 Duane Street
New York, N.Y. 10007

New England Rural Antiques Mkt.
Country Barn Meadow
Higganum, Conn.

New Haven Antiques Show
26 Grove St.
New Haven, Conn. 06511

Newton Antique Sale and Show
Newton, Conn.

New York Antiques Fair
Lexington Ave. and 26th Street
New York City, N.Y.

Okemo Mountain Base Lodge
  Annual Antique Show
Ludlow Chamber of Commerce
Ludlow, Vt.

"Old Bedford Days" Antique Show
Historical Hall, Village Green
Bedford, New York

Park Avenue Antiques Fair and Sale
Westchester Enterprises
29 Elm Place
Freeport, N.Y. 11520

Petoskey Antique Fair (A)
12730 E. Warren Ave.
Detroit, Mich. 48215

Philadelphia Antiques Show (A)
706 S. Washington Square
Philadelphia, Pa. 19106

Pilgrimage Antique Show and Sale
National Guard Armory
Eufaula, Ala.

Richmond Antique Show (A)
Manakin, Va. 23103

St. James Annual Fair & Sale
Brookhaven, N.Y.

Salisbury Annual Antique Fair
Town Hall
Salisbury, Conn.

Salisbury Antiques Show
72 Valencia Ave.
Staten Island, N.Y. 10301

Salisbury Flea Market (Benefit)
Salisbury, Conn.

South St. Seaport Flea Market
Foot of Fulton Street
New York, N.Y.

Syracuse Antiques Show
72 Valencia Ave.
Staten Island, N.Y. 10301

Tailgate Antiques Sale
Pownalborough Courthouse Rt. 128
Dresden, Maine

Texas Antique Show "Oktoberfest"
Round Top, Tex.

Texas Antiques Show
3315 Gallahad St.
Dallas, Tex.

Tulsa Antique Show (SA)
4321 S. Lewis
Tulsa, Okla.

Weston Annual Antique Show
  (Benefit)

Weston Community Club
Weston, Vt.

Whitefield Historical Society
South Union Street
Guilford, Conn.

Wilmington Talleyville Antique
  Show
Concord Pike Rte. 202
Wilmington, Del.

Winchester Antiques Show
Rte. 50 East
Winchester, Va.

APPAREL, FASHION & TEXTILE

American Apparel Mfrs. Assn. (A)
2000 K St., N.W.
Washington, D.C.

American Fashion Assn. (4)
2300 Stemmons Freeway, Rm. 3651
Dallas, Tex. 75207

Arkansas-Oklahoma Fashion
  Exhibitors (4)
1000 Washington Ave.
St. Louis, Mo. 63101

Bandwagon of Infants', Children's
  & Girls' Wear
Suite 406, 1627 N. Fort St.
Detroit, Mich. 48216

Bluefield Fashion Exhibitors (3)
P.O. Box 555
Bluefield, W. Va. 24701

Carolina-Virginia Fashion
  Exhibitors (5)
2500 N. Independence Blvd.
Charlotte, N. C.

Children's Wear Show
Wyncote House
Wyncote, Pa.

Cotton States Fashion Exhibitors (4)
Sheraton-Peabody Hotel
Memphis, Tenn.

Deep South Fashion Exhibitors (4)
P.O. Box 4100
New Orleans, La. 70118

Denver Women's & Childrens'
  Wear Markets (4)
451 E. 58th Ave.
Denver, Colo. 80216

Dixie Children's Show
Brentwood Lane, Rte. 5
Franklin, Tenn. 37064

Fashion Exhibitors of America (5)
1000 Washington St.
St. Louis, Mo. 63101

Florida Fashion Mart
777 N.W. 2nd Ave.
Miami, Fla.

Greater Kentucky & West Virginia
  Children's Apparel Market (6)
1587 Mallard Drive
Mayfield Heights, Ohio 44124

Intl. Assn. of Clothing Designers (A)
12 S. 12th St.
Philadelphia, Pa.

Iowa Fashion Market (5)
4316 New York Ave.
Des Moines, Iowa 50310

Louisiana Fashion Exhibitors (4)
P.O. Box 236, 3110 Williams Blvd.
Kenner, La.

Metropolitan Fashion Sportswear
  Exhibitors (3)
1407 Broadway
New York, N.Y. 10036

Metropolitan Juvenile Style Mart (4)
Hotel McAlpin, Rm. 1919
New York, N.Y. 10001

Mid-Atlantic Fashion Exhibitors
7703 Pickering St.
Philadelphia, Pa. 19119

Midwest Fashion Exhibitors (5)
Palmer House
Chicago, Ill.

Millinery Displayers Assn. (A)
P.O. Box 153 Midtown Station
New York, N.Y. 10018

Natl. Fabric & Home Sewing
Accessories Show
475 Fifth Ave.
New York, N.Y. 10017

New England Apparel Traveler's
Show (4), 32 West St.
Sharon, Mass.

New York State Infants' & Children's
Wear, 124 Colonial Rd.
Great Neck, L.I., N.Y.

Northwest Salesmen's Assn.
Fashion Week
Radisson Hotel
Minneapolis, Minn. 55402

Ohio Children's Apparel Market
1587 Mallard Drive
Mayfield Heights, Ohio 44124

Pacific Northwest Apparel Assn. (4)
220 Olympic Hotel
Seattle, Wash.

Pittsburgh Children's Apparel
Caravan (4)
1587 Mallard Drive
Mayfield Heights, Ohio 44124

Portland Apparel Show (3)
3155 Azalea Drive
South Salem, Oreg. 97302

San Antonio Apparel Market (4)
P.O. Box 1628
San Antonio, Tex.

San Francisco Salesmen's Fashion
Guild (5)
901 Sheraton-Palace
San Francisco, Calif. 94119

Southern Apparel Exhibitors (3)
351 N.E. 17th St.
Miami, Fla. 33132

Southern Fashion Exhibitors (4)
13th Floor, Dinkler Tutwiler
Birmingham, Ala.

Southern Mart Infants' & Children's
Wear
P.O. Box 8124, Station F
Atlanta, Ga. 30306

Style Exhibitors (5)
222 W. Adams St.
Chicago ,Ill. 60606

Tri-State Fashion Exhibitors (3)
1433 Carol Drive
Memphis, Tenn.

United Boston Children's Wear
Show (3)
115 Chauncy St.
Boston, Mass.

United Fashion Exhibitors of
Arkansas (4)
7500 N.W. 25th, P.O. Box 278
Bethany, Okla. 73008

Utah Market Assn. (4)
3551 E. Oaks Drive
Salt Lake City, Utah 84109

Washington Market Week Assn.
P.O. Box 207, 5th & Virginia
Seattle, Wash. 98101

Women's Apparel Club of N.Y. State
393 7th Ave.
New York, N.Y. 10001

Women's Apparel Trade Exhibitors
(5)
330 Candlewood Rd.
Broomall, Pa.

Women's & Children's Apparel
Club of Ohio
2499 Dysart Rd.
University Heights, Ohio 44118

Women's & Children's Fashion
Market (4)
2300 Stemmons Freeway
Dallas, Tex.

ARTS & GRAPHIC ARTS

Graphic Arts Congress Florida (B)
P.O. Box 6683
Orlando, Fla. 32803

Graphic Arts Fair (B)
P.O. Box 4487
Charlotte, N.C. 28204

Natl. Art Materials Trade Assn. (A)
252 Harrison Ave.
Hasbrouck Heights, N.J. 07604

Screen Printing Assn. (A)
1145 19th St., N.W.
Washington, D.C. 20036

BARBER, BEAUTICIAN & COSMETICS

All Texas Beauty Show (A)
1500 Jackson St. Rm. 711
Dallas, Tex. 75201

Beauty & Barber Supply Institute (A)
18 W. 46th St.
New York, N.Y. 10036

Beauty & Barber Supply Institute,
Western Buying Conf. (A)
18 W. 46th St. New York, N.Y. 10036

Natl. Hair Fashion Show (A)
16 W. 46th St.
New York, N.Y. 10036

Calif. Beauty & Trade Show (SA)
278 Post St.
San Francisco, Calif. 94108

California Toiletries Show (A)
1680 N. Vine St.
Los Angeles, Calif. 90028

Calif. Beauty & Harvest Festival (A)
320 E. 11th St., P.O. Box 1868
Charlotte, N.C. 28201

Hairdressers & Cosmetologists
Assn. (A), 6900 Ralston St.
Arvada, Colo. 80002

Dallas Cosmetics & Gift Show (A)
332 Oakcrest Drive
Richardson, Tex. 75080

Greater Southwest Hair Fashion
Show (A)
10935 Ferguson Rd.
Dallas, Tex. 75228

Indiana Hairdressers &
Cosmetologists Assn. (A)
6249 N. College
Indianapolis, Ind.

Intl. Beauty Show (A)
16 W. 46th St.
New York, N.Y. 10036

Los Angeles Coiffure Guild Beauty
& Trade Show (A)
P.O. Box 3174 Terminal Annex
Los Angeles, Calif. 90054

Mid-America Beauty Trade Show
P.O. Box 308
Big Rock, Ill.

Midwest Beauty Trade Show (A)
407 S. Dearborn St.
Chicago, Ill. 60605

Natl. Bath Products Show (A)
220 Fifth Ave.
New York, N.Y. 10001

Natl. Beauty Culturists League (A)
25 Logan Circle, N.W.
Washington, D.C. 20005

Natl. Hairdressers & Cosmetologists
Assn. (A), 175 Fifth Ave.
New York, N.Y. 10010

Natl. Hairdressers & Cosmetologists
of Iowa (A)
305 22nd St.
Ames, Iowa 50010

New Jersey Master Hairdressers &
Cosmetologists (SA)
47 Woodland Ave.
East Orange, N.J. 07017

New Mexico Hairdressers &
Cosmetologists Trade Show (A)
428 Val Verde, S.E.
Albuquerque, N.M.

North American Beauty & Fashion
Show (A)
720 West Eleven Mile Rd.
Royal Oak, Mich. 48067

Northwest Beauty & Trade Show (A)
3033 Excelsior Blvd.
Minneapolis, Minn. 55416

Ohio Assn. of Beauticians
OAB-6059 Kennedy Ave.
Cincinnati, Ohio 45213

Oklahoma Beauty & Trade Show
3020 Pase
Oklahoma City, Okla.

Pacific Coast Beauty & Trade
Show (A), 1772 Grove St.
Eugene, Oreg.

Pennsylvania Hairdressers &
Cosmetologists Assn.
1631 Chestnut St.
Philadelphia, Pa.

Philadelphia Cosmetic Assn. (A)
P.O. Box 426
West Chester, Pa. 19380

Tennessee State Beauticians
1940 Dandridge Ave., S.E.
Knoxville, Tenn.

Virginia State Hairdressers &
Cosmetologists Assn.
3459 W. Cary St.
Richmond, Va.

Wisconsin Hairdressers &
Cosmetologists (A)
637 N. Washington Ave.
Cedarburg, Wis.

BUILDING & BUILDING MATERIALS

Home Builders of Indiana
1456 N. Delaware St.
Indianapolis, Ind. 46202

Home Manufacturers Assn. (A)
1701 18th St., N.W.
Washington, D.C. 20009

Natl. Assn. of Women in Constr. (A)
2238 Loop Expressway, N.W.
San Antonio, Tex. 78213

Natl. Home Improv. & Remod. Exp.
50 E. 42nd St.
New York, N.Y. 10017

BUSINESS & MANAGEMENT

Amer. Business Women's Assn. (A)
9100 Ward Parkway
Kansas City, Mo. 64114

Boston Franchise Exp. (A)
Boston College
Chestnut Hill, Mass.

Chicago Franchise & Bus.
Opportunity Show
188 W. Randolph St.
Chicago, Ill. 60601

Cleveland Own-Your-Own Business
Show, 1411 K St., N.W.
Washington, D.C. 20005

Orlando Own-Your-Own Business
Show
1411 K St., N.W.
Washington, D.C. 20005

Conference for Secretaries of
Louisiana (A)
P.O. Box 48, U. of S. W. Louisiana
Lafayette, La. 70501

Connecticut Business Show (A)
26 Grove St.
New Haven, Conn.

Florida Industries Exp. (A)
Exp. Park
Orlando, Fla. 32801

Franchise & Business Opportunities
Show (4)
892 W. 16th St.
Newport Beach, Calif. 92660

Mass Merchandising Research
Foundation
570 7th Ave.
New York, N.Y. 10018

Natl. Career Exp.
110 W. 57th St.
New York, N.Y. 10019

Natl. Merchandise Show (A)
161 Great Neck **Rd.**
Great Neck, L.I., N.Y.

Philadelphia Franchise & Business
Opportunity Show (A)
188 W. Randolph St.
Chicago, Ill. 60601

Start Your Own Business Exp. Show
541 Lexington Ave.
New York, N.Y. 10022

Variety Merchandise Fair
161 Great Neck Rd.
Great Neck, L.I., N.Y.

CANDY (*see* FOOD)
CATERING (*see* HOTELS & RESTAURANTS)
CERAMIC & GLASS (*see also* DECORATING & DECORATING SUPPLIES)

American Ceramic Show (A)
37 W. 39th St.
New York, N.Y. 10018

Ceramic Tile Institute (A)
3415 W. 8th St.
Los Angeles, Calif. 90014

Greater Tulsa Ceramic Show (A)
423 S. 37th Ave.
Tulsa, Okla.

Intl. China Painting Teachers
Assn. (A)
4055 N.W. 29th St.
Oklahoma City, Okla. 73107

New England Ceramic Show (A)
80 Boylston St.
Boston, Mass.

Society of Glass Decorators (A)
60 Greenway Dr.
Pittsburgh, Pa. 15204

Southwest Ceramic Show
4826 W. Hanover
Dallas, Tex.

Stained Glass Assn. of America
3600 University Dr.
Fairfax, Va. 22030

CLUBS

Natl. Federation of Business &
  Professional Women's Clubs
475 Fifth Ave.
New York, N.Y. 10017

Chicago Doll Collectors Club
c/o Mrs. Edna Kilburn
2300 Linden Ave.
Waukegan, Ill. 60085

DAIRY (see FOOD & FOOD PROCESSING)

DECORATING & DECORATING SUPPLIES

China Decorators of Oklahoma (A)
3111 N.W. 19th St.
Oklahoma City, Okla. 73107

Natl. Decorating Products Show (A)
2101 S. Brentwood Blvd.
Brentwood, Mo.

Ohio Council of Painting &
  Decorator Contrs. of America (A)
1737 Euclid Ave.
Cleveland, Ohio 44115

Paint & Wallpaper Dealers Assn.
  Greater New York (A)
161-9 Jamaica Ave.
Jamaica, N.Y. 11432

Painting & Decorating Contrs. of
  America (A)
2625 W. Peterson Ave.
Chicago, Ill. 60645

Painting & Decorating Contrs. of
  America (A)
57 Hughes Ave.
Pawtucket, R.I. 02861

Painting & Decorating Contrs.
  S. E. Council
P.O. Box 9067
Knoxville, Tenn.

EDUCATION

Amer. Black Culture &
  Opportunities Exp.
501 Madison Ave.
New York, N.Y. 10022

American Industrial Arts Assn. (A)
State College
Millersville, Pa. 17551

American Vocational Assn. (A)
1510 H St., N.W.
Washington, D.C. 20005

Natl. Art Education Assn., Eastern
  Region (B)
1201 16th St., N.W.
Washington, D.C. 20036

Natl. Education Assn., Pacific Arts
  Assn. (B)
1201 16th St., N.W.
Washington, D.C. 20036

Natl. Educational Assn., South-
  eastern Arts Assn. (B)
Eastern Tennessee State University
Johnson City, Tenn.

New Jersey Vocational Arts Assn. (A)
236 Lexington Ave.
Jersey City, N.J.

New York State Art Teachers
  Assn. (A), 23 Forest Ave.
Ossining, N.Y. 10562

Southern Business Education Assn.
  (A)
Southeastern Louisiana College
Hammond, La. 70401

Vocational Assn. of Iowa (A)
4025 Towawanda Drive
Des Moines, Iowa 50312

Vocational Assn. of Minnesota (A)
Vocational Evening School
Minneapolis, Minn. 55404

Vocational Assn. of W. Va. (A)
E. 208 State Capital Building
Charleston, W. Va. 25305

Wis. Assn. for Vocational & Adult
  Education (A)
2020 University Ave.
Madison, Wis. 53705

ENGINEERING

Amer. Society for Quality Control
  Technical Conference (A)
161 W. Wisconsin Ave.
Milwaukee, Wis. 53202

Southern Industrial Exp. S. E.
  Shows (A)
2500 Independence Blvd.
Charlotte, N.C. 28205

FLOWERS & GARDENING

Amer. Orchid Society S.W. Region
  (SA)
P.O. Box 188
Whitewright, Tex. 75491

American Rose Society (SA)
4048 Roselea Place
Columbus, Ohio 43214

Arkansas Florists Assn. (A)
305 Cordell
El Dorado, Ark.

Calif. State Florists Assn. (A)
16 California St.
San Francisco, Calif.

Chicago World Flower & Gardens
  Show (A)
6 N. Michigan Ave.
Chicago, Ill. 60602

Connecticut Florists Trade Fair (A)
584 Campbell Ave.
West Haven, Conn. 06016

Dallas Garden & Flower Show (A)
Dallas, Tex. 75220

Florida Federation of Garden Clubs
  (A)
503 E. Fairfield Drive
Pensacola, Fla. 32503

Florida Nurserymen &Growers
  Assn. (SA)
180 W. Brorein St.
Tampa, Fla. 33606

Florida State Florists Assn. (A)
807 W. Adams St.
Jacksonville, Fla. 32202

Flower & Patio Show of Indiana (A)
P.O. Box 20189
Indianapolis, Ind. 46220

Greater Kansas City Flower &
  Garden Exp. (A)
P.O. Box 7007
Kansas City, Mo.

Indiana Assn. of Nurserymen (A)
Purdue University
Lafayette, Ind. 47906

Intl. Flower Show (A)
212 Essex House
New York, N.Y. 10019

Metropolitan Retail Florists
  (Display & Show)
99 Bradley Pl.
Mineola, N.Y. 11501

Michigan State Florists Assn. (SA)
217½ Ann St.
East Lansing, Mich. 48823

Midwest Design Trade Fair Assn. (A)
P.O. Box 20189
Indianapolis, Ind. 42620

Natl. Council State Garden Clubs (A)
18 Dellwood Rd.
Bronxville, N.Y. 10708

New England Spring Garden &
  Flower Show (A)
300 Massachusetts Ave.
Boston, Mass. 02115

N. Jersey Flower & Garden Show (A)
P.O. Box 128
Oakland, N.J.

N.Y. State Horticultural Society (A)
Albion, N.Y. 14411

Ohio Florists Assn. (A)
1827 Neil Ave.
Columbus, Ohio 43210

Oklahoma Florists Assn.
815 Chickasha Ave.
Chickasha, Okla.

Philadelphia Spring Flower Show (A)
325 Walnut St.
Philadelphia, Pa. 19106

Portland Rose Festival (A)
Portland Hilton, Suite 416
Portland, Ore. 97204

Southeastern Florists Assn.
Rivermont Orchids
Signal Mountain, Tenn. 37377

Texas State Florists Assn. (A)
1005 Perry Brooks, P.O. Box 39
Austin, Tex. 78767

United Floral Industries Trade
  Show of Colorado (A)
5650 E. Evans Ave.
Denver, Colo. 80222

FOOD & FOOD PROCESSING

American Bakers Assn.
20 N. Wacker Drive
Chicago, Ill. 60606

American Commercial Fish Exp. (A)
253 Northern Ave.
Boston, Mass. 02210

Confectionery Industry Exp. (A)
36 S. Wabash Ave.
Chicago, Ill. 60603

Food & Dairy Industries Exp. (B)
1145 19th St., N.W.
Washington, D.C. 20036

Food Fair of Dallas
Trade Mart
Dallas, Tex.

Great Plains Candy Club (A)
2414 Crown Point
Omaha, Nebr. 68111

Holiday Merchandise Show (A)
Supermarket Representatives
1225 Broadway
New York, N.Y. 10001

Great Western Dairy Show
P.O. Box 22108
Los Angeles, Calif. 90022

Institute of Food Technologists (A)
221 N. LaSalle St.
Chicago, Ill. 60601

Kentucky Wholesale Grocers Assn.
(A)
P.O. Box 362
Lexington, Ky. 40501

Natl. Dog 'n' Suds Convention (A)
702 W. Bloomington Rd.
Champaign, Ill. 61820

Natl. Fancy Food & Confection
Show (A)
331 Madison Ave.
New York, N.Y. 10017

Natl. Retail Candy & Allied Trades
Exh. (A)
Suite 1254, 211 N. LaSalle St.
Chicago, Ill. 60601

New England Candy & Fancy Food
Show (SA)
80 Boylston St.
Boston, Mass. 02116

New Jersey Retail Bakers
Convention (A)
48 Claremont Ave.
New Brunswick, N.J. 08902

Pennsylvania Food Merchants Assn.
(A)
1120 State Street, P.O. Box 2029
Erie, Pa. 16512

Philadelphia Candy Show (SA)
703 Grove St.
Havertown, Pa. 19083

Virginia Food Dealers Trade Exh.
(A)
5 S. 12th St.
Richmond, Va. 23219

Wash. State Food Dealers Assn. (A)
416 Lloyd Building
Seattle, Wash.

World Food Exp. (A)
736 E. Washington Ave.
Madison, Wis. 53703

GIFTS & JEWELRY

Antique Show of Indianapolis (SA)
7370 Old National Trail E.
New Carlisle, Ohio 45344

Atlanta Gift & Decorative
   Accessories Market (3)
1142 W. Peachtree St., N.W.
Atlanta, Ga. 30309

Boston Gift Show (SA)
Little Brothers
220 Fifth Ave.
New York, N.Y. 10001

Buffalo Gift Show (SA)
Drawer U
Knox, Pa. 16232

California Gift Show (SA)
Trade Show Ltd.
3510 Council St.
Los Angeles, Calif. 90004

Cleveland Gift Show (SA)
Drawer U
Knox, Pa. 16232

Corning Glass Ctr. Antiques Show
   (SA), 72 Valencia Ave.
Staten Island, N.Y. 10301

Dallas Trade Mart Gift & Jewelry
   Show (SA)
3000 Trade Mart
Dallas, Tex. 15207

Denver Gift & Jewelry Show (SA)
3510 Council St.
Los Angeles, Calif. 90004

Detroit Gift Show (SA)
First Natl. Bank Bldg.
Zanesville, Ohio 43701

Florida Assn. of Handbag, Jewelry &
   Accessories Salesmen (4)

149 N.E. 20th Terrace
Miami, Fla. 33137

Gift Show (SA)
Tremont & School Streets
Boston, Mass. 02107

July Xmas Gift & Houseware Show
(A), 3000 Trade Mart
Dallas, Tex. 75207

Kansas City Gift & Toy Show (SA)
216 W. 17th St.
Kansas City, Mo. 64108

Mfg. Jewelers & Silversmiths of
America (2 shows odd years)
575 Sheraton-Biltmore
Providence, R.I. 02902

Memphis Gift & Jewelry Show (SA)
6 E. Monroe St.
Chicago, Ill. 60603

Miami Gift & Jewelry Show (SA)
6 E. Monroe St.
Chicago, Ill. 60603

Natl. Notion & Novelty Show (SA)
350 Fifth Ave.
New York, N.Y. 10001

Ohio Retail Jewelers Assn. (A)
1900 Euclid Building
Cleveland, Ohio 44115

Ohio State Gift Show (SA)
P.O. Box 2788
Zanesville, Ohio 43701

Pacific Jewelry Show (A)
Suite 304, 215 W. 5th St.
Los Angeles, Calif. 90013

Philadelphia Gift Show (SA)
Little Brothers
220 Fifth Ave.
New York, N.Y. 10001

Pittsburgh Gift Show (SA)
Drawer U
Knox, Pa. 16232

Portland Gift Show (SA)
1355 Market St., Space 223A
San Francisco, Calif. 94103

Rocky Mountain Gift Show (SA)
Merchandise Mart
451 E. 58th Ave.
Denver, Colo. 80216

San Francisco Gift Show (SA)
1355 Market St., Space 223A
San Francisco, Calif. 94103

Seattle Gift Show (SA)
1355 Market St., Space 223A
San Francisco, Calif. 94103

Southern Christmas Show (A)
S. E. Shows Exp. Management
D-339 Merchandise Mart
Charlotte, N.C. 28205

Southern Jewelry Show (SA)
631 Candler Building
Atlanta, Ga. 30303

Spokane Gift Show (SA)
1355 Market St., Space 223A
San Francisco, Calif. 94103

HOBBIES & TOYS

American Toy Fair (A)
200 Fifth Ave.
New York, N.Y. 10010

Atlanta Toy Show (SA)
6075 Roswell Rd.
Atlanta, Ga. 30328

Hobby Industry Trade Show (A)
200 Fifth Ave., Suite 1605
New York N.Y. 10010

Indiana Hobby & Gift Show (A)
P.O. Box 20189
Indianapolis, Ind. 46220

HOME FURNISHINGS

American Furniture Mart (3)
666 Lake Shore Drive
Chicago, Ill. 60611

American Institute of Kitchen
Dealers (A)
199 Main St.
Hackettstown, N.J.

Atlanta Home Furnishings Mkt. (SA)
240 Peachtree St., N.W.
Atlanta, Ga. 30303

Calif. Curtain & Drapery Show (A)
3510 Council St.
Los Angeles, Calif. 90004

Dallas Homefurnishings Mart (SA)
2100 Stemmons Freeway
Dallas, Tex. 75202

Dallas Home Furnishings Gift &
Accessories Market Days
2100 Stemmons Freeway
Dallas, Tex. 75202

Jamestown Furniture Mart (SA)
111 W. 2nd St.
Jamestown, N.Y. 14701

The Lamp Show in New York (SA)
15 E. 26th St.
New York, N.Y. 10010

Los Angeles Home Furnishings
    Market (SA)
1933 S. Broadway
Los Angeles, Calif. 90007

Pacific Furniture Guild (SA)
2660 River St., S.
San Gabriel, Calif. 91777

Southwest Curtain Drapery &
    Upholstery Market (A)
2004 Dallas Trade Mart
Dallas, Tex. 75207

Western Home Furnishings Market
    (SA)
1355 Market St., Space 223A
San Francisco, Calif. 94103

HOME SHOWS

Annual Parade of Homes & Home
    Show (A)
2520 St. State St.
Salt Lake City, Utah 84115

Arizona Home Beautiful Show (A)
1129 N. 1st St.
Phoenix, Ariz. 85004

Cincinnati Home & Garden Show
7060 Greenfield Dr.
Cincinnati, Ohio 45224

Cleveland Home & Flower Show (A)
636 St. Clair Ave., N.E.
Cleveland, Ohio 44114

Colorado Garden & Home Show (A)
2785 N. Speer Blvd., #305
Denver, Colo. 80211

Home-A-Rama
3339 Eagle Blvd.
Orlando, Fla. 32804

Home Fashion Fair (A)
1045 James St.
Syracuse, N.Y.

Home Show of Hawaii (A)
1210 S. Queen St., Rm. 1
Honolulu, Hawaii 96814

Indianapolis Home Show (A)
1456 N. Delaware St.
Indianapolis, Ind. 46202

Merchants Home Show
231 Madison St., S.
St. Petersburg, Fla.

Milwaukee Home Show (A)
606 W. Wisconsin Ave.
Milwaukee, Wis. 53202

New England Home Show
1300 Boyleston St.
Chestnut Hill, Mass. 02167

New Jersey Home Show (A)
410 Haddon Ave.
Collingswood, N.J. 08108

New Products Show of Hawaii
1210 S. Queen St., Rm. 1
Honolulu, Hawaii 96814

Parade of Homes & Home Show (A)
313 W. Main St.
Madison, Wis. 53703

San Antonio Home & Hobby Show
    (A), 1013 Loop 410, N.W.
San Antonio, Tex. 78213

San Diego Spring Home Show (A)
233 A St., Suite 1007
San Diego, Calif. 92101

Santa Barbara Home Show (A)
P.O. Box 988, 30 W. Mission St.
Santa Barbara, Calif. 93102

Southern Living Show
S. E. Shows Exp.
Rm. D-339 Merchandise Mart
Charlotte, N.C. 28202

Southwest Builders Exp. & Home
    Show (A)
2355 Stemmons Freeway
Dallas, Tex. 75207

Toledo Flower & Home Show (A)
1 Main St.
Toledo, Ohio 43605

Total Home Showcase (A)
501 Madison Ave.
New York, N.Y. 10022

HOTELS & RESTAURANTS

Mobile Industrial Caterers Assn. (A)
2011 Eye St., N.W.
Washington, D.C.

Upper Midwest Hospitality (A)
112 N. 7th St.
Minneapolis, Minn.

MACHINERY

Intl. Woodworking Machinery &
    Furniture Supply Fair (B)
666 Lake Shore Drive
Chicago, Ill. 60611

The Bobbin Show (A)
P.O. Box 527, 1120 Shop Rd.
Columbia, S.C. 29202

MINERALS

Dallas Gem & Mineral Show
410 Collins St.
Irving, Tex.

NURSING & NURSING HOMES

Eastern Amer. Nursing Home
Smith Bucklin & Associates
333 N. Michigan Ave.
Chicago, Ill. 60601

Massachusetts Ind. Nurses Assn. (A)
134 Cambridge St.
Cambridge, Mass. 02141

Natl. Assn. for Practical Nurse
  Education & Service (A)
535 Fifth Ave.
New York, N.Y.

Natl. Federation of Licensed
  Practical Nurses (A)
250 W. 57th St.
New York, N.Y. 10019

N. Y. State League for Nursing (B)
184 Washington Ave.
Albany, N.Y. 12210

Texas Nursing Home Assn. (A)
6225 U.S. Highway 290E
Austin, Tex. 78723

Virginia Nursing Homes Assn. (A)
2820 Bisvey Drive
Falls Church, Va. 22042

PACKAGING

Food & Drug Packaging Show &
  Seminar (B)
Shea Exp. Corp.
250 Gateway Towers
Pittsburgh, Pa. 15222

Produce Packaging & Marketing
  Exp. (A)
P.O. Box 674
Newark, Del. 19711

Society of Packaging & Handling
  Engineers (A)
14 E. Jackson Blvd.
Chicago, Ill. 60604

Western Material Handling &
  Packaging Show
3951 E. Huntingon Dr.
Pasadena, Calif. 91107

Western Packaging Exp. (A)
245 Park Ave.
New York, N.Y. 10017

PHOTOGRAPHY

Master Photo Dealers & Finishers
  Assn. (A)
603 Lansing Ave.
Jackson, Mich. 49202

Professional Photographers Assn.
  of New England (A)
68 Maple St.
Danielson, Conn. 06239

Professional Photographers Assn.
  of Ohio (A)
80 E. Long St.
Columbus, Ohio 43215

Professional Photographers Assn.
  of Pennsylvania (A)
1756 Clinton Ave.
Shamokin, Pa. 17872

Professional Photographers Assn.
  of Wisconsin (A)
525 S. Memorial Dr.
Appleton, Wis. 54911

Virginia Professional Photographers
  Assn. (A)
611 E. Franklin St.
Richmond, Va. 13219

SPORTS, SPORTING GOODS AND TRAVEL

Catskills Resort Show (A)
11 W. 42nd St.
New York, N.Y. 10036

Chicago Sportsmen's Vacation &
  Trailer Show (A)
6310 N. Lincoln Ave.
Chicago, Ill. 60645

Columbus Sports Vacation & Travel
  Show (A)
7060 Greenfield Dr.
Cincinnati, Ohio 45224

Detroit Sportsmen & Vacation
  Show (A)
6310 N. Lincoln Ave.
Chicago, Ill. 60645

Intl. Ski & Winter Sports Show (6)
110 W. 57th St.
New York, N.Y. 10019

Mountain States Winter Recreation
  & Vacation Show
2785 N. Speer Blvd.
Denver, Colo. 80211

Natl. Sporting Goods Assn. (SA)
717 N. Michigan Ave.
Chicago, Ill. 60611

Philadelphia Sports Camping
  Vacation & Travel Show (A)
137 Chestnut St.
Philadelphia, Pa. 19106

The Sporting Goods Fair (A)
805 Merchandise Mart
Chicago, Ill. 60654

Sports & Recreation Show (10)
Reber-Friel
117 S. 17th St.
Philadelphia, Pa. 19103

Index